The Long Si

The Long Sixties

The Long Sixties

America, 1955–1973

Christopher B. Strain

WILEY Blackwell

This edition first published 2017
© 2017 Christopher B. Strain

Registered Office
John Wiley & Sons, Ltd, The Atrium, Southern Gate, Chichester, West Sussex, PO19 8SQ, UK

Editorial Offices
350 Main Street, Malden, MA 02148-5020, USA
9600 Garsington Road, Oxford, OX4 2DQ, UK
The Atrium, Southern Gate, Chichester, West Sussex, PO19 8SQ, UK

For details of our global editorial offices, for customer services, and for information about how to apply for permission to reuse the copyright material in this book please see our website at www.wiley.com/wiley-blackwell.

The right of Christopher B. Strain to be identified as the author of this work has been asserted in accordance with the UK Copyright, Designs and Patents Act 1988.

Library of Congress Cataloging-in-Publication Data

Names: Strain, Christopher B., 1970– author.
Title: The long sixties: America, 1955–1973 / Christopher B. Strain.
Description: Chichester, UK; Hoboken, NJ: John Wiley & Sons, 2016. | Includes index.
Identifiers: LCCN 2016000144 | ISBN 9780470673621 (cloth) | ISBN 9780470673638 (pbk.) |
    ISBN 9781119150442 (ePub) | ISBN 9781119150411 (Adobe PDF)
Subjects: LCSH: United States–History–1953–1961. | United States–History–1961–1969. |
    United States–Social conditions–20th century.
Classification: LCC E839.S83 2016 | DDC 973.92–dc23
LC record available at http://lccn.loc.gov/2016000144

A catalogue record for this book is available from the British Library.

Cover image: Bill Owens Archive

Set in 10.5/13pt Minion by SPi Global, Pondicherry, India
Printed and bound in Malaysia by Vivar Printing Sdn Bhd

1   2017

Contents

Preface: The Long Sixties

The 1960s was a turbulent decade. On this much we can agree. Beyond this simple assertion, however, what happened is still hotly contested. It was a time of great change and confusion, marked by a profound shift in values and punctuated by a profane and often ugly war, but consensus breaks down on the meanings and lessons therein. For some it was a time of great liberation and freedom, an Age of Aquarius when restrictive constraints fell away. For others it was a period when the United States lost its way, a Pandora's box that unleashed a host of social ills upon an otherwise idyllic world. For some it was heaven, others hell. For many it was both.

Attempting to explain that paradox, this book aims to provide a brief narrative history of the 1960s—a quick trip, as it were, through a momentous decade. Ironically but intentionally, *The Long Sixties* is a short book that makes no claim at being inclusive. Rather, it attempts to overlay a coherent narrative on a sometimes incoherent time—providing a feel for the decade while emphasizing some important persons, places, and events along the way.

It is important in doing so to distinguish between *the 1960s*—a discrete period of time beginning in 1960 and ending in 1970—and *the Sixties*: a collage of people, places, happenings, ideas, beliefs, impressions, feelings, perceptions, and stereotypes. Often used interchangeably, they are in fact two different things, involving different reference points that render different representations. "The 1960s," for example, connotes datelines and headlines but "the Sixties"—more of an idea than a decade—suggests peace signs, flower power, and Volkswagen Bugs. Unlike the 1960s, the beginning and end of the Sixties are marked less by dates than by symbols and turning points. The 1960s and the Sixties shape and mold one another, often blending together in contemporary understandings of this contentious moment in time.

"Tell me about the Byrds and the Beatles."

Figure 0.1   The 1960s are often misunderstood… (Source: © www.CartoonStock.com, artist: Andrew Toos).

Since the early 2000s, some civil rights scholars have identified a "long civil rights movement"—not simply the familiar set of events between the 1954 *Brown v. Board of Education* decision and the 1968 assassination of Martin Luther King, Jr., but the period *before* the *Brown* case, when NAACP attorneys battled Jim Crow in the courts and black veterans of World War II returned from fighting against totalitarianism abroad to battle segregation at home. The long civil rights movement also extends beyond King's death into the Black Power era, understood less as a break with the nonviolent civil rights movement and more as a logical outgrowth and continuation of it. In this framework, antecedents and codas become part of the story itself. This study borrows the same logic to contemplate "the long Sixties" in the hope that doing so might beneficially complicate our understanding of the decade. With scholars now tracing the origins of the civil rights movement at least back to the 1930s, the methodological question becomes: how long is long in contemplating the 1960s? For reasons that will become clear, this study begins rather biddably in 1955 with a discussion of civil rights and ends in 1973 with a discussion of what amounted to uncivil wrongs.

Chapter One, "Tranquility in Turmoil," discusses the 1950s as a tumultuous decade in its own right. Chapter Two, "From New Frontier to Great Society," deals with the so-called "good" Sixties: the early part of the decade, stereo-typically full of hope and optimism. Chapter Three, "The Cold War," treats competition with the Soviets. Chapter Four, "The Civil Rights Movement," details the struggle for black equality, while Chapter Five, "Student Rebellion," describes campus unrest and the rise of the New Left. Chapter Six, "The Vietnam Quagmire," summarizes the nation's military involvement in Southeast Asia. Chapter Seven, "Sex, Gender, and the New Feminism," covers "women's lib," as it was sometimes derogatorily called, and the politics of sexuality and gender. Chapter Eight, "Revolutions Left and Right," treats not only left-wing radicalism but also right-wing activism as a reaction to it. Against the twin backdrops of the space race and the back-to-earth movement, Chapter Nine—"Small Steps, Giant Leaps, New Concerns"—discusses science, technology, and the environment. Chapter Ten, "Minority Empowerment," deals with Black Power, the corollary movements that paralleled and spun out of the civil rights movement, and the rise of so-called identity politics. Chapter Eleven, "Sucking in the Seventies, or That '70s Chapter" (respectively the title of a 1981 Rolling Stones album and an allusion to *That '70s Show*, a popular sitcom that aired 1998–2006), describes aftershocks, culminating with the Watergate scandal and the American withdrawal from Vietnam. Chapter Twelve, "Legacies," focuses on memories and interpretations, particularly the notion of "the unfinished Sixties," which helps to explain not only *that* the decade is debated half a century later but also *why* it is debated, an absorbing question related in part to the powerful ways it continues to define American life.

The 1960s were long in another sense as well. The events that unfolded were often discordant and violent, but even more jarring was the breakneck pace at which they unfolded. In the span of just six days in October 1967, for example, seven Ku Klux Klan members were convicted of conspiracy in the 1964 murders of three civil rights workers in Mississippi; upwards of 30,000 anti-war protesters marched on the Pentagon, with more than six hundred people arrested after they attempted to storm the building; and the federal government eliminated draft deferments for those who burned draft cards or interfered with military recruitment for the war. Or consider that several hundred Vietnamese civilians were massacred at the village of My Lai on March 16, 1968—which was the same day that Robert Kennedy announced his candidacy for president of the United States. Ten weeks later on June 3, Andy Warhol was shot at his New York studio, "The Factory," and two days after that Robert Kennedy was shot to death in Los Angeles. Major occurrences were happening suddenly in rapid succession, and those who lived through them rode an emotional roller coaster of hope, euphoria, anxiety, and terror. Headlines blared: JFK ASSASSINATED! MALCOLM X ASSASSINATED! DR. KING ASSASSINATED! RFK ASSASSINATED! The tempo was punishing for those seeking comfort or familiarity and difficult even for those who thrived in the chaos. "Gimme shelter," begged Mick Jagger of The Rolling Stones, "or I'm gonna fade away." Every period has its ups and downs, but the 1960s seemed and continues to seem particularly acute in the height of its peaks and the depths of its troughs. On some level it took the nation a decade—the 1970s—to mop its brow and catch its breath. There was hardly time to process what was happening—which may explain why we find ourselves still processing today.

Indeed there was little boring about the Sixties, and investigating this decade can be not only exciting but also a little dangerous. In Francis Ford Coppola's Vietnam War epic *Apocalypse Now* (1979), the protagonist Captain Willard, played by Martin Sheen, remembers the advice he was given before going upriver to find Colonel Kurtz, played by Marlon Brando. "Never get out of the boat," he repeats. "Absolutely goddamn right… Unless

Figure 0.2   …and easily lampooned (Source: © www.CartoonStock.com, artist: Kes).

you're goin' all the way." Such advice remains salient, offering guidance for anyone who would study this helter-skelter decade.

To maintain historical accuracy, I have used the term "Negroes" to refer to African Americans before 1966, when the term "Blacks" began to gain favor.

Acknowledgments

A number of people had a hand in making *The Long Sixties* happen, beginning with Peter Coveney, executive editor in history at Wiley-Blackwell. The story of how he contacted me about writing a book on the 1960s (believe it or not) and how I coyly declined is barely plausible, but Peter coaxed, enticed, inveigled, and otherwise cajoled me to write it, eventually convincing me that the world might benefit from one more book about the 1960s. Without Peter there would be no *Long Sixties*, and I'm so glad I trusted him.

After I "completed" the manuscript, Wiley-Blackwell's senior editor in history, Andrew Davidson, took what I naively thought was a final draft and gave it a developmental edit that made it into exactly that, with changes big and small over seven months of revisions. At times Andrew felt like the world's toughest critic but mostly he felt like a co-author, and his sure guidance made the book much stronger than it would have been otherwise. I owe him a huge thank you.

Other people at Wiley-Blackwell played key roles, too. Julia Kirk, the project editor, handled all of the moving parts, while Galen Smith Young, Victoria White, and Maddie Koufogazos all provided editorial assistance and administrative help. Kitty Bocking suggested photos and tracked down permissions. Wiley also marshaled a small army of people unknown to me, including a commissioned survey of college professors teaching courses on the 1960s to assess their wants and needs in the classroom; five reviewers to offer suggestions (anonymously) on the original book proposal; and two reviewers who provided feedback (again anonymously) on the completed manuscript. You know who you are (even if I don't) and I appreciate your input.

A number of people at Florida Atlantic University deserve thanks. Two research assistants provided invaluable help early on in this project: Megan

Allore Bishop and Sandra Lazo de la Vega outlined, fact-checked, suggested topics and photos for inclusion, and more than earned their pay (which came from a generous award from FAU's Division of Sponsored Research, to whom I also owe a big thanks). My colleagues at FAU have listened to my observances and offered their own. A special thanks to Chris Ely, Michael Harrawood, Kevin Lanning, Tim Steigenga, Mark Tunick, and Dan White for their insights.

I'd like to thank the staff at the Florida Atlantic University Library in Jupiter, where Diane Arrieta, Marilee Brown, and Will Howerton, among others, helped me access the information I needed. As with other major research projects I have undertaken, they have made my job much easier. They are the best.

Much love and thanks to my parents, Dan and Jean Strain, who made it through the 1960s relatively unscathed, and to my daughter, Lily, and wife, Melanie. To complete this book I stole time from Lily and also Melanie, who more than anyone else argued and debated with me about the ideas herein, sharpening my thinking in the process. Knowing I had a lot to say about the 1960s, Melanie encouraged me to undertake the project and she was my greatest supporter throughout. She also made it fun.

As the saying goes, if you remember the 1960s, you weren't really there; but, to the friends, family, neighbors, and co-workers who shared their Sixties stories with me, I am grateful.

C.B.S.
Jupiter, FL
September 2015

1

The Fifties:
Tranquility in Turmoil

Even today Americans tend to remember the 1950s as a placid, antiseptic decade—a rather boring time of suburban puttering, backyard barbecues, and plastic smiles. Nothing could be further from the truth. In fact, most of what we associate with the 1960s—the struggle with the Soviets, war in Southeast Asia, television, youth culture, drug culture, rock and roll, the civil rights movement, space travel and exploration, even the anti-nuke movement—had its roots in the previous decade. Worthy of study in their own right, not simply as a prelude to the 1960s, the 1950s is one of the most dynamic decades in US history—a puzzling, paradoxical period of swift transformation, swathed in conformity and consensus.

How the 1950s garnered a reputation for sterility relates mainly to television, a new medium that rose to the fore of American culture and consciousness. Television expanded rapidly between the end of World War II and the end of the Korean War. Americans bought an average of 250,000 television sets per month between 1949 and 1952, and millions more saved their money to buy the magic box, a device that transformed the nation as no invention had done since the automobile. Purchasing a TV was a major event for any family, many of whom had scrimped and saved until the proud day that neighbors gathered to watch delivery and installation of the new "TV" by the local retailer. Television had instant appeal, bringing inexpensive, convenient, and passive entertainment right into the home for the enjoyment of the entire family. Critics worried that it leveled high culture and dulled taste, an opiate of the masses.

Sales of new sets averaged in excess of 5 million per year in the 1950s and in some years reached the 7.5-million mark; by the early 1960s, 90 percent

The Long Sixties: America, 1955–1973, First Edition. Christopher B. Strain.
© 2017 Christopher B. Strain. Published 2017 by John Wiley & Sons, Inc.

Figure 1.1 A family watching television in 1958 (Source: © Courtesy National Archives, photo no. 306-PS-58-9015).

of all American homes had at least one TV. The invention of coaxial cable and videotape in 1951 and 1956, respectively, further improved the device, which, by projecting the same formulaic programming into homes across the nation, encouraged homogeneity of interests, tastes, and opinions. In just over a decade, television had not only nationalized cultural expression and shared experience in new ways but also democratized news and entertainment—becoming an essential piece of electronics owned by rich and poor, urban and rural, white and black, illiterate and intellectual. Through advertisements, it also fed the growing appetite for consumer consumption. As historian J. Ronald Oakley has observed, no other invention—motion pictures, cars, or radio—brought so much change to so many people in so short a time.

The images television projected were happily reassuring. On westerns such as *Gunsmoke*, *The Rifleman*, *Wagon Train*, and *The Lone Ranger*, justice always prevailed; the good guys enforced law and order with cold steel and hammer fists; talented sleuths on *Dragnet* and *Perry Mason* always solved the crime du jour. Comic relief was furnished by shows starring famous comedians of the day, *You Bet Your Life* with Groucho Marx, the self-titled *The Jackie Gleason Show*, and shows featuring Milton Berle and Steve Allen. Dinah Shore and Donna Reed—multitalented actresses who hosted eponymous variety shows—and Lucille Ball, whose handsome Cuban-born co-star and real-life husband Desi Arnaz joined her on the #1 hit *I Love Lucy*, provided strong but non-threatening female role models. Clean-cut, white teenagers danced on *American Bandstand*, a local Philadelphia television program, which grew from its 1952 debut into a nationally broadcast show by 1957. Quiz shows like *The $64,000 Question* and *What's My Line?* tempted viewers with quick riches, and variety shows like *The Ed Sullivan Show* offered a kaleidoscopic array of entertainers and musicians. Programming was generally entertaining, soothing, and—due to careful producing and censorship—safe.

Most importantly, situation comedies (or "sitcoms") such as *Leave it to Beaver*, *The Adventures of Ozzie & Harriet*, and *Father Knows Best* idealized the new suburban life, purveying a gee-whiz world of narcotic consumerism and suburban euphoria. Dads ruled their households sternly but benevolently; moms catered to the needs of their husbands and children. Pot roasts browned in convection ovens; children played on cul-de-sacs. Whatever problems arose, usually small ones, were resolved in a 30-minute format. So closely did "Ozzie & Harriet" mirror its cast's lives—with real-life husband Ozzie, wife Harriet, and sons David and Ricky portraying themselves, with Ricky crooning his own songs and Ozzie editing them into early music videos—that the show's "adventures" were more prototype reality show than sitcom (the house shown in exterior shots on the show was the family's actual house in the Hollywood Hills). Theodore "the Beaver" Cleaver and his brother Wally got themselves into some real pickles on *Leave it to Beaver*—mostly due to the instigation of their rascal friend Eddie Haskell— but Ward and June Cleaver were always ready to guide their sons back onto the right path. By the conclusion of each episode, all was forgiven. It was the golden age of television and television projected a golden age: 1950s America, TV-style, was pleasant, saccharine, even bland, but almost always comforting.

And why not? In the wake of the biggest challenges the nation had ever faced, the Great Depression and World War II, times were good in America. Unprecedented military spending during the war—close to $300 billion— had brought a massive stimulus to industrial and agricultural production, ushering in a new era of economic expansion and prosperity. By the mid-1950s, the United States—with 6 percent of the world's population and

7 percent of its landmass—was producing almost half of the world's manufactured products. It contained within its borders most of the world's cars and telephones, and a sizable portion of its televisions and radios (and, not surprisingly, consumed almost half of the world's annual energy production). Over the course of the 1950s, the Gross National Product (GNP) rose from $285 billion to $500 billion, per capita income rose by 48 percent, the median family income rose from $3083 to $5657, real wages rose by almost 30 percent, and the number of millionaires rose from roughly 27,000 to almost 80,000. The expanding economy created jobs in record numbers; by 1960, the number of working Americans had risen to a record 66.5 million.

Young couples who had delayed marriage during wartime now got married and had children in record numbers, and at younger ages. By 1953, almost one-third of married American women had "tied the knot" by age nineteen; by 1960, almost 75 percent of all women aged 20–24 were married. And in the 1950s couples tended to stay married, as divorce remained a social stigma, a badge of personal and even moral failure. Those who were married had kids—lots of them. From 1946 to 1950, an average in excess of 3.6 million children were born each year (in 1940 the number had stood at 2.6 million), and from 1950 on there was a steady rise past 4 million in 1954 to an all-time high of 4.3 million in 1957, an average of one newborn every seven seconds. It was, as everyone recognized, a baby boom, one fed by prosperity. Naturally, the boom in babies fed the nation's increasingly growing and powerful economy, as sales of maternity clothing, baby furniture, diapers, baby food, formula, clothing, toys, trikes, bikes, washing machines, clothes dryers, and televisions spiked, so did new school construction. Dr. Benjamin Spock's bestselling *Book of Baby and Child Care*, which sold a million copies per year in the 1950s, offered an informal, commonsense approach to caring for this surge of children, one that emphasized love and positivity rather than discipline and punishment. The advice was well tolerated and much appreciated: after all, the 76.4 million children born between 1946 and 1964 became the single largest generation in the nation's history, the generation that largely came of age in the 1960s.

Much of the postwar growth occurred in previously undeveloped hinterlands, neither urban nor rural; in fact, 83 percent of the total population growth occurred in so-called "suburbs," a new feature of the American landscape. A severe housing shortage had developed after World War II and developers met the crisis with ingenious new solutions—and did so quickly.

Figure 1.2 The ideal 1950s housewife: working, smiling, and pleasing (Source: © George Marks/Retrofile/Getty Images).

Between 1947 and 1951, the construction company Levitt & Sons built the first suburban development in history at Hempstead, New York, where crews followed a precise, 27-step process using prefabricated materials to produce new single-family homes, more than 30 per day at the peak of production. As Henry Ford had done to the automobile industry, the Levitts brought assembly-line production to housing: bulldozing the land and covering it with standardized units with uniform floor plans. Cost-cutting techniques meant that the American dream of owning one's own home had suddenly become much more affordable. Other so-called "Levittowns" followed, changing the American landscape in their sprawl, as middle-class, and mostly white families moved out of the nation's cities and into the new "collar" or "bedroom" communities, with many of the men of the family commuting to their jobs in the city each morning and back home again come five o'clock. One and a half million New Yorkers moved to the city's surrounding suburbs in the 1950s; right outside Los Angeles, Orange County more than tripled in population. With the suburbs came shopping centers and supermarkets, offering a cornucopia of consumer items and foods. By mid-decade there were more than 1800 shopping centers in the United States (with hundreds more being planned and built); by 1953 there were more than 17,000 supermarkets, which constituted only 4 percent of all grocery stores but accounted for 44 percent of all food sales.

The uniform building codes, the rules and regulations of homeowner associations, and the common background of suburban residents (white, middle-class) reinforced conformity and stimulated low-grade competition for consumer fulfillment, what critics would come to describe as "keeping up with the Joneses." The people of suburbia tended to buy similar houses, similar cars, and similar toys for their kids. Constrained not only by pressures to purchase contentment but also by traditional gender roles, the experiences of women were especially constant and unvarying. Expected to shop, cook, clean, and serve their husbands, and with few opportunities for fulfillment beyond housework, women had a limited lot in life. Magazines and books carried stories of happy housewives and few women publicly complained, though many presumably suffered in quiet despair.

As the film *Pleasantville* (1998) would later remind moviegoers, it was the last monochrome decade, gray-rinsed and neutral. The Fifties were captured in black-and-white by television and still photography; the Sixties, in contrast, were caught in living color on videotape and film. On December 20, 1964, the three television networks—ABC, CBS, and NBC—simultaneously broadcast in color for the first time, and color programming became the norm. Not surprisingly, as journalist-historian David Halberstam has observed, the pace of the Fifties in retrospect "seemed slower, almost languid." On the other side of the Sixties, looking back from the Seventies, the Fifties seemed even more idyllic. The name of that iconic 1970s show, *Happy Days*, said it all: in the nation's collective memory, the 1950s were a simpler, easier, and happier time.

But television is not real life—even when it purports to be reality—and just beneath the idealized world reflected on the nation's TV sets lay a nation in ferment: a golden age of apprehension. The overwhelming sense of uneasiness, the conflicts within and beyond the borders of American society, and the splinters of dissent that sometimes worked their way to the surface all belied the era's apparent tranquility, and it proved difficult to act as if nothing were awry. Black teenagers wanting to participate on *American Bandstand*, for example, found themselves excluded from the dance crew and studio audience. By the end of the decade, even teen idol Ricky Nelson chafed against his father's authoritarianism, as Ozzie kept his son from appearing on other shows that would have boosted his stardom. Lucy and Desi Arnaz got a real-life divorce in 1960.

Much of the apprehension and conflict of the 1950s can be traced to the nation's post-World War II rivalry with the Soviet Union, which left its imprint not only on foreign affairs but also on domestic life. Perhaps it was inevitable that the two most powerful nations still standing after World War II would emerge as competitors. But the Cold War—not a "hot war" of military fighting but an undeclared conflict characterized by spying, hostile propaganda, sabotage, and economic embargo—became the longest protracted confrontation in US history, lasting four decades and coloring life in the United States more than anything else since the Civil War a century earlier. Covert espionage was the order of the day as the two nations jockeyed for power—in effect battling for world supremacy.

Each side mistrusted the other and misconstrued the other's motives; each side also assumed its own righteousness and the other's evilness. Overestimating Soviet power, the United States saw the Soviet Union as a cancer, spreading communism over the globe and threatening the American way of life; Russia, gravely wounded by the Germans in World War II, became increasingly paranoid in its dealings with the West, while obsessively pursuing its own security. Twice in the twentieth century, German troops had invaded Russia via Poland, which Soviet premier Joseph Stalin recognized as a crucial buffer between Europe and the Soviet Union; he accordingly labored to bring Eastern Europe within the Soviet sphere of influence. British Prime Minister Winston Churchill noted in a speech at Fulton, Missouri, in March 1946, "From Stettin in the Baltic to Trieste in the Adriatic, an iron curtain has descended across the continent." The metaphor of the iron curtain—used to describe the political, military, and ideological barrier erected by the Soviet Union to seal itself and its dependent eastern European allies off from open contact with the West and other noncommunist areas—stuck.

President Harry S. Truman, the nation's first post-WWII president, adopted a policy of "containment" against the Soviet Union and the potential spread of communism. The term, first articulated by leading State Department official George Kennan, emphasized the inevitability of US conflict with the Soviet Union, as different nations with different interests and different economic systems. Truman liked the toughness of Kennan's approach to contain Russian efforts to expand communism and to meet the Soviets forcefully if necessary. In April 1950, President Truman approved the implementation of a secret National Security Council document, NSC-68, which called for a massive buildup in American military power, in conventional armament as well as atomic weaponry, to guarantee superiority over the Soviets. NSC-68 mapped out the US role in the Cold War by rearticulating the nation's role as global policeman and by channeling more of the nation's gross domestic product toward military use (defense spending increased from 5 to 14.2 percent under President Truman during the Korean War). Containment and military stockpiling became the cornerstones of American foreign policy.

Whatever its causes and merits, fear of the Soviets and of communism led to a staggering American military buildup, the formation of military alliances with democratic *and* dictatorial nations across the globe, US intervention in the sovereign affairs of dozens of countries, and protracted military conflicts in Korea and Vietnam. Most immediately, when North Korean soldiers crossed the 38th Parallel into South Korea in 1950, the United States called for a United Nations sanction against the invasion; the UN declared communist North Korea the aggressor and sent troops, mostly from the United States, to aid the South Korean army. Calling for a "police action," President Truman never asked Congress to pass an official declaration of war (thereby establishing a precedent for President Lyndon Johnson, who later would commit troops to the Vietnam War without ever seeking a congressional mandate for his action). Popular WWII hero General Douglas MacArthur commanded the UN troops, sometimes disagreeing vehemently with his commander-in-chief. The tide turned against North Korea with an amphibious assault at Inchon, where the North Koreans retreated; but reinforcements from the People's Republic of China soon allowed them to regain lost territory. At the same time, and in keeping with the goal of containment, the United States began stepping up its military assistance to South Vietnam by supplying arms and instruction in their use against communist forces in North Vietnam.

Inconclusive and costly, the Korean War dragged on, lasting much longer than anyone had anticipated. In 1953, with neither side having a prospect of victory, a truce was signed. The ceasefire satisfied no one—not the United Nations, not the United States, not South Korea or North Korea— and the Korean peninsula remained tensely divided along more or less the same line. In addition to substantial losses in men and material—54,200 of 1.8 million American servicemen in Korea were killed and 103,300 wounded, with 8200 classified as missing in action—the war had significant consequences, including: desegregation of the US armed forces, initially decreed by Truman's Executive Order 9981 in 1948 but accomplished in fact in Korea as black and white units, both decimated by casualties, pragmatically combined across the color line to continue fighting; a public falling-out between Truman and MacArthur; the Democrats' loss of the White House to another popular WWII hero, Dwight D. ("Ike") Eisenhower in 1952; dangerous precedents for involvement in what was essentially a civil war in another nation, Vietnam; and heightened panic about the communist menace.

It mattered little who was in the White House when it came to communism. Democrats and Republicans alike ascribed to fervent anti-communist views, as did all "good" Americans. President Eisenhower used the metaphor of tumbling dominos (which gave rise to the phrase "the domino effect") to describe how quickly communism could spread, and Secretary of State John Foster Dulles described the necessity of "brinkmanship" to bring the United States to the edge of war with the Soviet Union. To impose national will, anti-communism took on a kind of religious zeal as large numbers of Americans became caught up in an irrational fear of communist conspiracy orchestrated from the Kremlin—a conspiracy, it was said, that was subverting the United States from within, harming the nation diplomatically, and contributing to the worldwide expansion of communism. In this respect, the early 1950s recalled other periods of hysteria in the nation's past, most notably the Salem witchcraft trials of 1692 and the Red Scare of 1919–20, but the desperate search for internal security at mid-century required a kind of wartime loyalty, enforceable through strict authoritarian measures; accordingly, the 1950s became what might have been the most politically repressive era in US history. Republican Congressman Richard M. Nixon of California resuscitated the House Un-American Activities Committee (HUAC), founded by Congress in 1938 to investigate alleged subversive activities and to hold hearings on fascist, Nazi, communist, or other "un-American" organizations. In the 1950s HUAC sought to root out communists, particularly in Hollywood, whose films presumably poisoned youth, attacked Christian values, and eroded morality. There was also a not-so-subtle anti-Semitism at work as the Jewish producers, directors, and actors who wielded considerable power in Hollywood were blacklisted, smeared, and sometimes incarcerated for supposed communist sympathies.

It was this climate that produced the meteoric rise of the thuggish Senator Joseph R. McCarthy, who became one of the most admired, hated, and feared men in Washington: a demagogic powerbroker *par excellence*. The Republican Senator from Wisconsin—born in 1908 to poor Irish-American parents, a hard-drinking US Marine and former circuit judge whose early career in the Senate was undistinguished—began a witch-hunt after producing a list of alleged "moles" within the State Department. Waving a sheet of paper before a women's auxiliary meeting in Wheeling, West Virginia, on February 9, 1950, McCarthy bellowed, "I have here in my hand a list of 205—a list of names that were made known to the Secretary of State as being members of the Communist Party and who nevertheless are still working and shaping policy in the State Department." The members of the Ohio County Women's Republican Club were stunned—and so, too, was the American public as headlines repeated the accusations. McCarthy's speech—which came just a few months after Russia detonated its own atomic bomb, just a few weeks before China was "lost" to communism, just three weeks before State Department official Alger Hiss was convicted of perjury after being accused of spying for the Soviets in the 1930s, just ten days before Truman decided to build the hydrogen bomb (the fusion-based "superbomb," as it was called, five hundred times more powerful than a fission-based atomic bomb), and just six days before British scientist and Los Alamos bomb developer Klaus Fuchs confessed to supplying atomic secrets to the Russians—landed with the force of an H-bomb.

The accusations touched off a wave of anti-communist hysteria that would become known as McCarthyism, in which the senator, an unsavory and unscrupulous alcoholic, fabricated lies and leveled accusations against anyone and everyone, making wild charges of disloyalty against military personnel, politicians, celebrities, and everyday citizens. The American public took him quite seriously; that people listened to McCarthy demonstrates how frightened they were at a time when loyalty to one's country was measured by the degree of anti-communism one displayed. It was bad enough that the "commies" wanted to conquer the world like comic-book supervillains—with the Russians and the Chinese vying for control of the globe—now double-dealing traitors threatened the United States from within, touting the virtues of communism and selling atomic secrets to enemies. It was time, many believed, to close ranks and purge the nation of the critics, nonconformists, and subversives (like Julius and Ethel Rosenberg, also arrested in 1950 for passing atomic secrets to the Russians) who threatened the United States from within. McCarthy provided one solution: identify the bad guys, sully their reputations, and clap 'em in irons. Such treatment would prove too good for the Rosenbergs, who died in the electric chair after being convicted on minimal and questionable evidence.

McCarthyism had a chilling effect on the American public, frightened into conformity through fear. Senator McCarthy's wrecking-ball tendencies caught up with him when he began to accuse men such as General George C. Marshall and even President Eisenhower of being tools and dupes of the Soviets. He overreached in early 1954 when he began an investigation of the US Army—a reckless act that led to a series of televised hearings in which, at one point, Army attorney Joseph Welch looked up at the power-crazed McCarthy and asked, "Have you no sense of decency, sir?" as the senator tried to impugn the character of a young lawyer present. The trials, which television brought into the living rooms of Americans across the nation, revealed McCarthy as a bully and a brute. The Senate censured him in 1954; he died in obscurity less than three years later.

McCarthyism was a direct and obvious expression of anti-Communism and Cold-War fear, but living under what people perceived at the time as the very real threat of nuclear annihilation was a different matter, casting a pall over the era that affected life in ways both subtle and profound. Living with the fear of "the Bomb," as nuclear weapons were generically called, was no easy task. The Russians developed their own nuclear weapons, successfully testing an atomic bomb and a hydrogen bomb in 1949 and 1953, respectively, after which point Americans, too, were daily haunted by the specter of death and the kinds of suffering they had seen in magazine photographs and newsreels of the Hiroshima victims. As those nations in the "nuclear club" rushed to test bigger and better hydrogen bombs (the United States conducted 122 atomic bomb tests in the 1950s, the Soviet Union at least 50, and the UK 21), concern about nuclear warfare continued to grow. Little was known in the 1940s about the dangers of nuclear fallout, but evidence mounted in the 1950s that strontium-90 and other radioactive isotopes that caused leukemia, cancer, birth defects, and genetic mutations in humans and animals could travel far from test sites. It would be wrong to suggest that everyone in the 1950s actively worried about thermonuclear war all the time: they did not. The knowledge, however, that life as they knew it could be snuffed out in one blinding instant was ever-present, nibbling at the foundations of constancy and security like a hungry termite.

As the press unrolled story after story about atomic-bomb tests and radioactive fallout, Cold War worries and nuclear jitters crept into pop culture in weird and interesting ways. Millions of Americans went to theaters to see films dealing with animal and human monsters created by nuclear war or radiation accidents; these films included B-movie classics such as *The Beast from 20,000 Fathoms* (1953), *The Creature from the Black Lagoon* (1954), *Them!* (1954), *Godzilla* (1956), and *The Blob* (1958). A symbol of the age, the monster movies of the 1950s revealed that Americans were beginning to fear the heralded technological breakthroughs of the modern age. There was also a boom in science fiction literature and sci-fi movies. Many of the sci-fi flicks involved monsters and space battles; some were more thoughtful. In *The Day the Earth Stood Still* (1951), Earth is invaded by aliens of superior intellect who warn humans of the dangers of the atomic bomb and threaten to destroy the planet if war itself is not abolished (a common theme in 1950s sci-fi works). In novels and short stories, an endless variation of basic themes revolved around space exploration, intergalactic adventure, time travel, fear of science gone wrong, monsters and other mutations caused by nuclear radiation, atomic wars, and speculations about humankind's future in an age contemplating no future at all. Authors such as Ray Bradbury, Isaac Asimov, and Arthur C. Clarke raised science fiction to new heights of imagination and popularity. Not unpredictably, there was a rash of reports of "flying saucers" or unidentified flying objects (UFOs)—a number of which coincided with the successful launch into Earth's orbit of Sputnik 1, the first artificial satellite, by the Soviets in October 1957 (an event that spurred a "space race" between the USSR and the United States, which rapidly expanded funding for missile research at home and led swiftly to the creation of NASA, the National Aeronautics and Space Administration, in July 1958).

Scientists themselves shuddered at the destructive power they had unleashed. At the instant of the Trinity explosion—the first atomic detonation at White Sands Proving Ground in New Mexico on July 16, 1945—Manhattan Project leader J. Robert Oppenheimer quoted the Hindu scripture *Bhagavad-Gita* (having learned Sanskrit to read it in its original form): "If the radiance of a thousand suns were to burst in the sky, that would be like the splendor of the Mighty One... I am become Death, destroyer of worlds." A growing number of Americans began to argue that the key to national survival was not a civilian defense program or a deterrent nuclear force but, as science fiction suggested, a worldwide ban on nuclear tests, on the manufacture of nuclear weapons, and ultimately on war itself. Dissenters were small in number at first, dismissed by the government and the press as communists, socialists, dupes, and crazies; however, they attracted more and more supporters and attention as bombs grew bigger and the adverse effects of so much nuclear testing became clearer. They attracted even more attention as the nation's (and the world's) greatest leaders and thinkers gravitated toward a burgeoning peace movement, including: Nobel Prize-winning chemist Linus Pauling, who wrote *No More War!* (1958); philosopher Bertrand Russell, who published anti-war tracts and participated publicly in peace demonstrations; and Nobel Prize-winning physicist Albert Schweitzer, who in a 1957 radio appeal asked 50 nations to terminate all nuclear tests.

In June 1957, Pauling led 11,000 scientists in signing a petition calling for the end of nuclear testing, an act that led the US Senate Internal Security Subcommittee to investigate his patriotism. Peace activists formed the National Committee for a Sane Nuclear Policy (SANE), which grew rapidly after its founding in 1957 to 130 chapters and 25,000 members by the summer of 1958; SANE—which included intellectuals, celebrities, Old Left activists, and Quakers—was joined by other groups such as the Student Peace Union, which claimed 5000 members by the end of the decade, and the Committee for Nonviolent Action (CNVA), which, beginning in 1958, engaged in peaceful acts of civil disobedience like trespassing in restricted areas in which tests were being conducted. Protestors were arrested, jailed, and given prison sentences for sailing a ship into the area of the Bikini Atoll in the Pacific, where nuclear tests were scheduled to be held. This movement reached its height in 1960, when a large crowd jammed Madison Square Garden for a SANE rally and 3000 pacifists demonstrated in San Francisco. Pacifists across the nation walked for disarmament, and some public school students refused to participate in civil defense drills; students at Berkeley, Harvard, and other universities formed peace societies, circulated petitions, and demonstrated for peace. The 1950s peace movement failed to alter governmental policies or change public opinion on nuclear tests, but it did reveal the existence of dissent from prevailing Cold War ideology, and showed that not all intellectuals and college students were part of the so-called "Silent Generation," born between the mid-1920s and early 1940s. Importantly, it also paved the way for antiwar protests of the next decade.

As the decade progressed, adults ingested pharmaceuticals—especially tranquilizers—in record numbers to quiet the mind, numb the dread, silence the protests, and cope with the multitude of children they had birthed. Young people themselves grew increasingly restless. To their parents' horror, many young white kids were buying black rhythm-and-blues records; parental disapproval only added to the records' appeal. Bill Haley, Chuck Berry, Little Richard, and especially Elvis Presley pioneered a new kind of music and a new form of youth rebellion. Whether youth culture drove rock music or vice versa is debatable, but rock and roll—African-American blues blended with country music into what some called rockabilly—spoke to young people like nothing else before or since. Leonard Bernstein, the distinguished American composer and conductor, called Elvis Presley "the greatest cultural force in the twentieth century." Elvis, he maintained, "changed everything—music, language, clothes, it's a whole new social revolution—the Sixties comes from it." As John Lennon of the Beatles, one of Elvis's many admirers, put it, "Before Elvis there was nothing."

Young people began to form a new kind of community, one whose authority figures were disc jockeys and rock musicians. Enjoying new spending power, they flexed their economic muscle: a 1956 *Scholastic* magazine article claimed that the average teenager earned $10.55 a week, a bit less than the post-bill-paying, disposable income of the average American family fifteen years earlier. Becoming a separate, distinct part of the culture for the first time, teenagers broke away from the habits of their parents and defined themselves through the music to which they bopped.

The young people of the time particularly gravitated to nonconformists, those who deliberately flouted the status quo. Brooding, handsome actors like Marlon Brando and James Dean exuded a sense of personal freedom and projected an aura of being misunderstood. Brando's muscular sexuality and Dean's hangdog introspection both created an undeniable magnetism: alienated and ruminating, yet attractive and heroic. Wearing blue jeans, T-shirts, and leather jackets, they were silver-screen iconoclasts: flaunting convention, chafing against the oppressive constriction of societal expectations, and protesting nothing in particular. When asked what he was rebelling against in *The Wild One* (1953), Brando (as outlaw biker Johnny Strabler) famously growled, "Whaddya got?"

Other cracks in the consensus and conformity of the Fifties began to appear as well, many of them visible along the intersections of avant-garde literature, visual art, and less popular forms of music, namely jazz. Meeting as students at Columbia University, the original clutch of Beat writers—Jack Kerouac, Allen Ginsberg, Lucien Carr, John Clellon Holmes—met hanger-abouts, Greenwich Village bohemians, and con artists such as Neal Cassady, William Burroughs, and Herbert Huncke, to create a mix of seekers who explored the New York City underground via its bars and nightclubs. They listened to jazz greats Charlie "Bird" Parker and Miles Davis in the same clubs haunted by abstract expressionist painters Willem de Kooning and Jackson Pollock, both of whom experimented with new forms of gesture or "action" painting. Like the Beat writers and poets, ab-ex painters tried to capture the rhythms of jazz in their art; pieces like Pollock's *Summertime: Number 9A* (1948), featured in the August 1949 issue of *Life* magazine, moved the viewer through syncopated drips and slashes of color. In his fiction Kerouac would immortalize Cassady as Dean Moriarty, the lightly fictionalized hero of *On the Road* (1957), the Beat bible of road trips and freewheeling excess. Of course, what allowed the Beats to ricochet from one coast to the other—foregoing straight jobs, disdaining mainstream culture, and freebasing experience along the way—was the sheer affluence of the United States, so prosperous that it sheltered even those who flaunted its rules and expectations; in this sense, the Beats needed consumer-oriented America as much as—perhaps more than—it needed them. But all of these artists offered arresting counterpoints to the orthodoxy of the day. It was a difficult world for those who could not or did not fit in, and some flamed out prematurely, failing to outlive the decade. Charlie Parker, for example, died in 1955 at the age of 34 after much heroin and alcohol abuse; the following year, Jackson Pollock died in a drunken, single-car accident near his New York home.

The most visible fault line—the greatest crack in the conformity and consensus of the Fifties—came not from artists but from Negroes (the preferred term through the late 1960s for dark-skinned people of African descent in the United States), more than ever dissatisfied with Jim Crow segregation, discrimination, racist intimidation, and second-class citizenship. In 1955— the same year that Bird died; the same year that Ray Kroc opened the first, golden-arched McDonald's restaurant in Des Plaines, Iowa; the same year that Walt Disney opened Disneyland in Anaheim, California; the same year that the Food and Drug Administration approved Jonas Salk's polio vaccine for widespread use; the same year that Vladimir Nabokov published *Lolita* and Sloan Wilson published *The Man in the Grey Flannel Suit*; and the same year that James Dean finished shooting *Rebel Without a Cause*, his third and final film before his death in a car crash on a California desert highway— a brutal killing in a small town in the Mississippi Delta captured national attention. Fourteen-year-old Emmett Till, visiting family from Chicago, was kidnapped and murdered by a band of white men near Money, Mississippi, after allegedly whistling at a white woman while in a convenience store. The local men tortured and shot young Emmett before tying his mutilated body to a broken cotton-gin fan and dumping it in the Tallahatchie River. The woman's husband and his accomplice, who brazenly admitted killing the boy in an interview with *Look* magazine, were arrested, tried, and acquitted of murder. The boy's mother, Mamie, insisted on an open-casket funeral; ghastly postmortem images of the badly mutilated teenager, beaten beyond recognition, haunted a nation. Many civil rights activists would later cite these images—viewed pan optically as photographs published in *Jet*, the *Crisis*, the *Chicago Defender*, the *Pittsburgh Courier*, and the *New York Amsterdam News*, among other black publications—as the reason they became involved in the struggle for black equality.

One hundred days after Till's murder and one-and-half years after the landmark *Brown v. Board of Education* (1954) ruling in which the US Supreme Court declared racial segregation in schools illegal, a black seamstress in Montgomery, Alabama, boarded a city bus on December 1, 1955, to return home from her job. Tired from her day's work, Rosa Parks sat in the forward section of the bus, the section traditionally reserved for white passengers. When she refused to give up her seat to a white person, she was arrested and jailed. Calling for Negroes to boycott Montgomery's buses, local activists responded to Parks' arrest by organizing carpools to take boycotters to work; others walked where they needed to go. The boycott lasted more than a year, during which the 26-year-old Reverend Dr. Martin Luther King, Jr., emerged as a leader. Through his inspiring rhetoric, King helped to elevate the local challenge of citywide segregation ordinances to a transcendent struggle for human dignity. Parks' defiance and King's nonviolent leadership defined a new kind of activism in the struggle for black equality, one organized not around legal challenges in the courtroom but rather around direct action in the streets and public spaces of Southern cities and towns. This mass movement of black Southerners and their supporters against the twin evils of segregation and voter disfranchisement—what is commonly referred to now as the civil rights movement—would become the epicenter for change in the 1960s.

Mamie Till often commented on the irony that one of the last pictures of her son Emmett was taken as he leaned against a TV set: it was television, after all, that would play such a crucial role in the successes of the civil rights movement. No less ironic was the fact that television itself helped to mask the dynamism of the decade, as the iconic family sitcoms that outlasted the 1950s tended to whitewash (or black-and-whitewash) the complexity of this misunderstood moment in US history. Adjusted for hue and contrast, however, the Fifties were quite colorful indeed, bland only in comparison to the positively psychedelic decade that followed.

Further Reading

David Halberstam, *The Fifties*, reprint ed. (New York: Ballantine, 1994)

Charles C. Alexander, *Holding the Line: The Eisenhower Era, 1952–1961*, 5th ed. (Bloomington, In.: Indiana University Press, 1976)

J. Ronald Oakley, *God's Country: America in the Fifties* (New York: Norton, 1986)

Robert A. Divine, *The Sputnik Challenge* (New York: Oxford, 1993)

Elaine Tyler May, *Homeward Bound: American Families in the Cold War Era*, rev. ed. (New York: Basic, 2008)

Lizabeth Cohen, *A Consumer's Republic: The Politics of Mass Consumption in Postwar America* (New York: Vintage, 2003)

Taylor Branch, *Parting the Waters: America in the King Years, 1954–1963* (New York: Simon & Schuster, 1988)

2

From New Frontier to Great Society

The 1960s in North America began with a great burst of joy, optimism, and hope for a better tomorrow. No one embodied this positivity like the new first couple, the young and handsome John Fitzgerald Kennedy and his beautiful wife Jacqueline, who brought a new vigor and style to Washington, DC, after his upset election to the presidency in 1960. The economy was buoyant, the public mood was sanguine, and expectations ran high. It was what one historian has termed "an era of consensus." Accordingly, the early 1960s are remembered by many as the unspoiled Sixties, a time when the aura of the Kennedys shone bright and clear. As with the Fifties, however, all was not as it seemed. Not all Americans shared in the abundance and prosperity, and while some of that early optimism, even idealism, carried forward as the Sixties continued, much of it died with JFK in November of 1963.

Economically speaking, the first several years of the 1960s were indeed the best of times. The economy was in extraordinarily good shape: during the 15 years between the end of World War II and 1960, every indicator of national wealth and prosperity had surged. The Gross National Product (GNP) had increased about 250 percent, and the median family income (adjusted for inflation) had almost doubled. Bullish, the stock market began the decade more than 20 times higher than it had been when Franklin Delano Roosevelt took office in 1932. Materially, Americans were well off: the United States was, in 1960, the wealthiest nation on the planet—perhaps the richest nation ever—and that prosperity brought a sense of security and peace to those who shared in it. As historian David Farber has written, "Economic wealth—coupled with the faith that economic growth would

The Long Sixties: America, 1955–1973, First Edition. Christopher B. Strain.
© 2017 Christopher B. Strain. Published 2017 by John Wiley & Sons, Inc.

continue and the fact that for many years it did—shaped the 1960s like no other single factor."

For many, the nation's economic prosperity translated directly into material well-being. By 1960, most Americans could relax in their living rooms and watch television, listen to a record on high-fidelity ("hi-fi," soon to be replaced by "stereo") equipment, and clean clothes at home in efficient washers and dryers. Theirs was becoming a push-button world of modern conveniences. Dishwashers and refrigerators, however, were not the bench-mark of material achievement, as Vice President Richard M. Nixon had claimed in July 1959 in the so-called "Kitchen Debate" with Soviet Premier Nikita Khrushchev at the United States Exhibition in Moscow; instead, the gleaming, chromed, US-made automobile, parked in the driveway and fueled by cheap gasoline, came to symbolize the American way of life.

The economy hummed along in part because science and technology created systems that, in their complexity, simplified modern life and increased productivity. For the average American, scientific breakthroughs meant less about the advancement of knowledge than about time-saving technological innovations at home and the workplace, thanks to mechanization and automation. A shared faith in science—what the DuPont chemical company championed in its advertising as "Better Living Through Chemistry"—extolled easing the toils of everyday life through accessibility and expedience. But science also held the promise of the fantastic and the wonderful: true marvels of the modern age. In 1960, Theodore Maiman demonstrated the first "Light Amplification by Stimulated Emission of Radiation," or laser, at Hughes Research Laboratories (where scientists were also tinkering with ion propulsion and atomic clocks) in Malibu, California. Using a synthetically grown crystal, the ruby-powered device pulsed red laser light in short bursts. A 1960 *LIFE* magazine story featuring a photograph of a hand holding 16 solid-state microchips explained, "This glittering handful of gemlike electronic parts could equal the performance of a whole closetful of conventional vacuum tubes." Such parts were destined to become the inner workings of another new wonder: the computer.

There was of course a darker side to automation, as new technologies in agriculture such as the mechanical cotton picker displaced poor farmers, many of them African American, who moved out of rural communities and into urban settings. A historically rural problem in American life, poverty itself had changed by 1960, when about 55 percent of the poor lived in cities and another 30 percent lived in small towns. More whites than blacks were poor, including those on some form of public assistance; however, a majority of poor whites still lived in rural areas, out of sight and out of public consciousness. Poor African Americans, on the other hand, were becoming concentrated and highly visible in America's inner cities, the same urban areas whites were vacating in favor of the new suburbs.

Technological marvels and time-saving gadgets may have meant little to those living below the middle class, but there was still a sense that progress would help *all* Americans. About 20 percent of all Americans were poor, but even they were well off compared to the poor of other nations. For example, in the hollows of Harlan County, Kentucky—one of the most impoverished areas of Appalachia, the nation's poorest region—67 percent of households had a television and 59 percent owned a car. No other country on Earth could make such claims, and for now the majority of the American people seemed content to see where such promise might lead, without proactively addressing the poverty and inequality tucked away in invisible pockets of American society. The few worries that did exist tended to focus not on America's poor but rather on the global poor, subject as they were, to the lures of communism; but, most Americans seemed to agree that the American way was the best way, and the best model for future global development. Why, they wondered, wouldn't *everyone* want to live as Americans did?

Figure 2.1 Sprawling housing tracts such as Lakewood Park, a suburb of Los Angeles, symbolized American prosperity (Source: © Bettmann/CORBIS).

Suburbs remained the locus of growth and prosperity, and a conformity born of innate sameness remained the norm. Immigration restrictions in the 1920s had slowed the flow of immigrants to the United States to a trickle for nearly 40 years, and since then older-stock Euro-Americans—of British, German, Polish, or Scandinavian stock—had more or less blended into a generic kind of white folk at the center of American life. Mid-century suburbia *was* the melting pot of early twentieth-century lore, and while big changes wrought by the Hart-Cellar Act (1965) would challenge this ideal at mid-decade by increasing foreign-born immigrants from Asia and Latin America, for now, whiteness reigned. Black Americans were not welcomed in suburbia: in 1960, not one of the 82,000 inhabitants of Long Island's Levittown was African-American. When it came to how and where people lived, segregation governed the North and West as well as the South.

The rapid rise of suburban affluence came through the new rise of credit cards and installment-buying. Unaccustomed to buying things on credit, many Americans had to learn to be indebted, telling themselves that debt itself was, as the siren song of financiers intoned, good. Such thinking was not foreign to Americans: Thomas Paine had argued as much in his revolutionary-era pamphlet *Common Sense* (1776). Paine, however, was describing *national* debt, not individual debt, and buying on credit was novel to the average consumer. Still, the lure of shiny cars in the latest model and newly manufactured homes quickly outweighed the fiscal concern of owing money to a creditor. The United States was transforming into a consumption-based society, and the cornucopia of new products, new opportunities, and new possibilities were not only intoxicating but also, most agreed, well deserved for having endured the sacrifices necessitated by the Great Depression and World War II. Credit cards notwithstanding, Americans had worked for their success and now they were enjoying it.

Those who prospered the most were not individuals but corporations, which came to shape and define not only the economy but also American culture in new ways. Corporations such as DuPont, General Electric, General Motors, and IBM flourished in the postwar period, during which they carefully groomed their public images. In an improvement-based culture, the product itself mattered less than the image being sold, as General Electric's slogan tidily expressed. "Progress is our most important product," repeated actor Ronald Reagan, the voice of GE and keynote speaker at the company's 1961 national sales meeting in Apache Junction, Arizona. Corporate slogans were lofty and abstract; ads themselves more specific and banal. Still relatively immature, corporate advertising assumed a passive consumer, one to be manipulated by repetitive imagery and jingles, but even with less sophisticated ads, the new medium of television proved to be a highly effective selling tool. A 2005 survey of marketing, branding, and advertising, where professionals were asked to rank the best taglines since 1948, found that about half of the catchiest came from the 1960s, as big ad agencies churned out zingers such as Avis's "We try harder" and Oscar Mayer's "My bologna has a first name: it's O-S-C-A-R." Spending millions of dollars, the corporate giants used their influence to shape policy, mold public opinion, and create a favorable business environment for their own gargantuan expansions.

Big business had run big government under Eisenhower, who attached great importance to business acumen (his first cabinet was composed of "eight millionaires and a plumber," according to one running joke), and at the dawn of the 1960s, experts concurred that US mega-corporations should serve as the cornerstones of economic sustainability and national prosperity. At the time, corporate success did not necessarily come at the expense of the working class. Corporate moguls did not grossly exploit those whom they employed; rather, the abundance of riches was growing for all to enjoy, and it was in the best interest of those at the top to spread the wealth. Accordingly, factory workers in Detroit, many without high-school diplomas, brought home good wages, good enough to see them drive new cars and buy middle-class homes; many even came to enjoy generous pensions, pay rises, and bonuses. Some of these benefits were the result of pressure from one of the nation's most powerful labor unions, the United Auto Workers (UAW), but some simply flowed through the channels of corporate largesse; as auto executive Lee Iacocca would explain, "In those days we could afford to be generous." As long as profits were growing, everyone could have a helping.

Few fretted that corporations themselves—extended constitutional protection by the US Supreme Court in *Santa Clara County v. Southern Pacific Railroad* (1886), a decision that equated corporations with persons in terms of the Fourteenth Amendment—were ballooning in size and influence, or that the number of Americans gaining control of the nation's capital assets—the number of Americans at the "very top"—was steadily decreasing. And few worried that the federal government tended to favor big business over labor unions—as evidenced by the Taft-Hartley Act of 1947, which placed draconian restrictions on union activities and allowed state right-to-work laws that barred union shops—or that racial and sexual discrimination seemed a part of doing business in corporate America. If noticed, these trends would have been considered wayside casualties along the upward march of progress—but most Americans did not pause to consider them. At the beginning of the 1960s, they were too busy looking forward to continued success.

They found someone to lead them in that quest in the form of John Fitzgerald Kennedy, a young Senator and decorated war hero from a powerful Massachusetts family. "Jack" Kennedy had enjoyed a privileged upbringing that involved much yachting, travelling, and girl-chasing, before settling in as a serious student at Harvard. He joined the Navy in September 1941, a few months before the Japanese bombed Pearl Harbor. The patrol boat he commanded in World War II, PT-109, was rammed and sunk by a Japanese destroyer; Kennedy responded intrepidly by gathering the survivors and towing an injured sailor to safety—an action commended for its selfless bravery. When older brother Joseph, politically groomed by their father, was killed in action, John Kennedy continued the family's commitment to politics after the war ended: first serving in the US House of Representatives and then the US Senate, during which time he married Jacqueline Bouvier, a young debutante who had studied at the Sorbonne before becoming a Washington socialite. While convalescing from a series of surgeries on his back, injured in the PT-109 sinking, JFK wrote *Profiles*

Figure 2.2 JFK and his wife Jacqueline, pictured here in 1961, invigorated American politics (Source: © John Rous/AP/Press Association Images).

in Courage (1956) about US Senators who risked career advancement for conviction; the book won the 1957 Pulitzer Prize for Biography. Active, intelligent, and capable, with movie-star good looks, a beautiful wife, deep pockets, and the Kennedy name, JFK had what it took. Here was someone who had parlayed the obvious privileges and advantages life had given him into something even greater, and now he threw his hat into the ring for his party's nomination in the upcoming 1960 presidential election.

To the world of catchy corporate slogans, the presidential hopeful added one of his own. In his acceptance speech at the Democratic National Convention in Los Angeles, Kennedy first addressed what he knew was foremost in everyone's mind: his Catholicism. When JFK sought the presidency in 1960, anti-Catholic prejudice was still rampant in mainstream American life. Only one Catholic, Governor Alfred E. Smith of New York, had ever been the presidential nominee of a major party; his 1928 campaign—in which he was soundly defeated—was hounded by worries that he would build a tunnel connecting the White House and the Vatican, and that he would amend the Constitution to make Catholicism the nation's official religion. Eliciting mistrust from Protestants who feared a "papist" in the White House, Kennedy met the issue head on. "I hope that no American, considering the really critical issues facing this country, will waste his franchise and throw away his vote by voting either for me or against me because of my religious affiliation," he said. "It is not relevant." Lightly bashing his opponent, Vice President Nixon, Kennedy noted that: "just as historians tell us that Richard the First was not fit to fill the shoes of the bold Henry the Second, and that Richard Cromwell was not fit to wear the mantle of his uncle, they might add in future years that Richard Nixon did not measure up to the footsteps of Dwight D. Eisenhower." His preliminaries concluded, Kennedy got to the heart of his message. "We are not here to curse the darkness; we are here to light a candle… Today our concern must be with that future," he said. "For the world is changing. The old era is ending. The old ways will not do." Detailing the challenges that threatened the United States, from nuclear warfare and the spread of communism to urban overcrowding and the continued second-class citizenship of African Americans, he concluded that it was time for "a new generation of leadership." He continued:

> The Republican nominee, of course, is a young man. But his approach is as old as McKinley. His party is the party of the past, the party of memory. His speeches are generalities from Poor Richard's Almanac. Their platform, made up of old, left-over Democratic planks, has the courage of our old convictions. Their pledge is to the status quo; and today there is no status quo.

Kennedy reminded his audience of the pioneers and their hardships. "Some would say that those struggles are all over, that all the horizons have been explored, that all the battles have been won, that there is no longer an American frontier," he observed. "But I trust that no one in this assemblage would agree with that sentiment; for the problems are not all solved and the battles are not all won." He continued:

> [W]e stand today on the edge of a New Frontier—the frontier of the 1960s, the frontier of unknown opportunities and perils, the frontier of unfilled hopes and unfilled threats. Woodrow Wilson's New Freedom promised our nation a new political and economic framework. Franklin Roosevelt's New Deal promised security and succor to those in need. But the New Frontier of which I speak is not a set of promises. It is a set of challenges. It sums up not what I intend to offer to the American people, but what I intend to ask of them. It appeals to their pride—it appeals to our pride, not our security. It holds out the promise of more sacrifice instead of more security.

He asked for imagination, perseverance, courage, and leadership from "the young in heart" and "the stout in spirit," explaining: "For courage, not complacency, is our need today; leadership, not salesmanship." The address concluded with a need to choose, "between the public interest and private comfort, between national greatness and national decline, between the fresh air of progress and the stale, dank atmosphere of 'normalcy.'"

The genius of the New Frontier speech lay in how it summoned a national purpose, and did so, remarkably, by offering difficulty and strife at a time when the status quo was quite acceptable. Life was fine for most Americans in 1960. Yes, communism and nuclear weapons were scary, but for a majority of the American people the 1950s had been pretty, well, swell. Poised to inherit Ike's legacy, Nixon promised more of the same. Kennedy, with his abstract ideals, promised nothing other than hard work and a need for sacrifice; yet, his words offered a proactive approach to the difficulties of the day. The speech not only did much to assuage fears about Kennedy's background and abilities: it defined a national ideal of betterment.

Frank Sinatra voiced this yearning for betterment in the campaign theme song "High Hopes," in which he crooned, "Jack is on the right track." Kennedy locked up the election with a famous performance during a televised debate against Nixon. It was the first ever televised presidential debate. Nixon, nursing a sore knee and sporting a five-o'clock shadow, appeared haggard and uncomfortable; Kennedy, telegenic and confident, easily fielded questions and conveyed his positions. With 112,881 more votes, Kennedy edged Nixon in the closest election in the twentieth century.

In his inaugural address, Kennedy again climbed rhetorical heights. Though the Democratic Party platform in 1960 was the most extensive ever, Kennedy spoke not of taxes or jobs or intraparty politics. He spoke instead in soaring terms of humankind's highest aspirations, proclaiming "that the torch has been passed to a new generation of Americans." He spoke of an unwillingness to cave on principle and a willingness to achieve, to aspire. "Ask not what your country can do for you," he implored. "Ask what you can do for your country." Americans began to idolize the man they saw on their television screens like a matinee star.

At age 43, Kennedy—the youngest president elected to office (Vice President Theodore Roosevelt was 42 years old when President William McKinley was assassinated) and the first born in the twentieth century—had much to prove. He was not loved by all. If some Protestants still feared the prospect of a Catholic president, then as a Yankee he drew similar ire from unreconstructed white Southerners. He entered the White House without a popular mandate, having won by the skinniest of margins. But in those first few months in office, Kennedy entranced the national media and converted more than a few who had harbored suspicions. He created a brain trust not of the most loyal persons in Washington but of the most brilliant ones; with the exception of his brother Robert, whom he made Attorney General, his political appointments were un-spoils-like and atypical by DC standards. The staid businessmen of Eisenhower's regime were replaced with Ivy-League intellectuals. His advisors included not only economists and military men but also culture warriors such as historian Arthur Schlesinger, Jr., and poet Robert Frost, who recited "The Gift Outright" (1941) from memory at the inaugural. With their balls and galas and black-tie affairs, Kennedy and his wife Jacqueline transformed the capital into something more like Paris than Washington, the latter always having been characteristically "unstoried, artless, unenhanced" like the young America in Frost's poem.

JFK's rhetoric sometimes outpaced his achievement and his domestic agenda sometimes flagged. Federal aid to education and health care for the elderly, both key planks in the Democratic Platform, went unaddressed. Remembered as a friend of African Americans, his civil rights record was checkered at best. The tax cut he proposed, which failed to get through Congress in 1963, provided $10 billion in cuts over two years when it was finally passed in February 1964; but skeptics argued whether or not ensuing the economic boom, in which unemployment dropped to 4.1 percent and the GNP increased by 7–9 percent annually between 1964 and 1966, resulted directly from the tax cut or from a surge already under way when the law went into effect.

JFK's focus was clearly in the distance—on events overseas, on foreign policy and diplomacy—not in the foreground on issues at home; yet, he could claim certain victories. His domestic accomplishments included the appointment of a President's Commission on the Status of Women (chaired by former First Lady Eleanor Roosevelt), whose work culminated in the Equal Pay Act of 1963, which made gender-based wage disparities illegal; a two-billion-dollar slum clearance and urban renewal program; the Area Redevelopment Act of 1961, which incentivized companies to relocate to economically depressed areas; and the Manpower Development and Training Act of 1962, which provided training for the unemployed. He had become increasingly aware of the problem of poverty in 1960, when he visited the rural poor of Appalachia during his election campaign in West Virginia. Along with millions of other Americans, Kennedy read Michael Harrington's *The Other America* (1962), an eye-opening analysis of the hopelessness and abject living conditions of more than one in every five Americans. The summer of 1963 seemed to mark a turning point in Kennedy's attitude toward domestic reform; in addition to asking aides to plan an attack on poverty, he called for passage of a comprehensive civil rights bill. Whether he could have achieved these breakthroughs was left unanswered by his violent and tragic death: on November 22, 1963, President Kennedy was assassinated while riding in a motorcade through downtown Dallas.

Kennedy's political accomplishments as president are open to debate. At two years and ten months, the Kennedy administration was brief. JFK has since been praised by some for accomplishing much in that short period, as well as criticized by others for doing too little. Whatever can be said of Kennedy, he was true to his inaugural promise of meeting any hardship, opposing any foe—and paying any price. Perhaps most important was his ability to inspire: to encourage people to improve themselves and the world around them. It was an outright gift, and the nation mourned the loss of what he had come to represent as much as they mourned the man himself.

The Broadway musical *Camelot* had opened at the Majestic Theater on December 3, 1960—less than a month after Kennedy's election. Based on T.H. White's *The Once and Future King* (1958), the production retold the story of King Arthur and his court, who acted courageously with might and wisdom. "Don't let it be forgot / That once there was a spot," sings Arthur, as he knights a young boy in the final number. "For one brief, shining moment that was known as Camelot." Dropping the final curtain on January 5, 1963, after 873 performances, *Camelot's* production run perfectly paralleled Kennedy's run in the Oval Office, and for those swept up by the romance of medieval nobility, the Arthurian legend provided a fitting metaphor for the Kennedy administration, whose young king had jousted with his challengers, slain evil dragons, and squired the ladies, including his fair queen—only to be felled by an assassin's blade. After JFK's death, the notion of an American Camelot—of a happy, idyllic moment in US history, full of possibility— gained traction in the chaos that followed. Encouraged by Jacqueline, and by historians and biographers, the association with Camelot endures.

Perhaps no one was inspired more by Kennedy than his Vice President, Lyndon Baines Johnson, who as JFK's successor in the White House not only picked up Kennedy's standard to continue the quest for a better America but also, almost inconceivably, *expanded it* into something truly ambitious: an effort to erase racism and eradicate poverty itself. Johnson was no less visionary then Kennedy. Indeed LBJ was a man who excelled in lofty ideals; he also brought to bear a lifetime of experience—forged in tough Texas politicking—in drafting and passing legislation. If Kennedy's New Frontier was unspecific, what Johnson called his "Great Society" was explicit and detailed; if Kennedy promised, Johnson delivered.

It would be a disservice to Johnson to see his vision of a Great Society as simply an extension of Kennedy's New Frontier. It was much, much more, and in many ways it was superior to Kennedy's plan: not only more concrete but also more complete. Conversely, it would be a mistake to view the Great Society as the political vision of a single person. As bold as LBJ was and as politically ambitious his plans, the Great Society was in many ways an out-growth of the early civil rights movement. While seeing himself as continuing Kennedy's legacy, Johnson also took his cues from the activists and visionaries who saw an opportunity for profound reform, a chance to change the world. The Great Society, like JFK's abbreviated life, shone brightly for a brief period as a moment of possibility. And while some of it came to pass and some of it—like Medicare, Medicaid, and Head Start— lives on, much of it never came to be and much of it was dismantled by later politicians who lacked Johnson's commitment to social justice initiatives.

In retrospect the early part of the decade seemed a time of innocence, a high point of idealism. Irony and skepticism—the latter much warranted in light of events to come—would soon displace the optimism of these years. For the moment, however, there was a sense that *anything* was possible.

Kennedy was proud of the Peace Corps he created and equally proud of the Green Berets (both of which are described in the next chapter) and saw no inconsistency in valuing both. For him, they were part of the same battle, the same quest to challenge communism and keep it from propagating. This fervent anti-communism would lead the United States deeper and deeper into the Cold War.

Further Reading

Kenneth A. Jackson, *Crabgrass Frontier: The Suburbanization of the United States* (New York: Oxford, 1987)

Richard Reeves, *President Kennedy: Profile of Power* (New York: Simon & Schuster, 1994)

David Burner, *John F. Kennedy and a New Generation*, 3rd ed. (New York: Pearson, 2008)

Irwin and Debi Unger, *LBJ: A Life* (New York: Wiley, 1999)

Robert Dallek, *Flawed Giant: Lyndon B. Johnson and His Times, 1961–1973* (New York: Oxford, 1998)

John F. Kennedy, *Profiles in Courage* (New York: Harper, 1956)

3

The Cold War

On May 5, 1960, on the eve of a historic summit in Paris between Soviet premier Nikita Khrushchev and President Dwight D. Eisenhower, Khrushchev announced that the Soviets had shot down an American spy plane over Soviet airspace. The United States initially denied that a U-2 high-altitude reconnaissance plane had been spying when brought down, but Khrushchev produced not only film of Soviet military bases taken from the plane wreckage but also the captured pilot himself, Francis Gary Powers, who had parachuted to safety. Caught in a lie, Eisenhower hesitatingly accepted full responsibility for the incident and announced that there would be no future flyovers. Unfortunately, the damage had already been done: coupled with increasingly shrill arguments over the imminent partitioning of Berlin (divided in 1961 by a concrete wall, guard towers, machine-gun posts, and barbed wire to prevent East Germans from leaving Soviet-controlled East Berlin for the democratic western section of the city), the U-2 incident ruined chances for success at the Paris summit. Nor would it be the last time that a downed U-2 would end up jeopardizing diplomatic negotiations at a key moment in US-Soviet relations. Indeed, such would be the pattern of events throughout the nearly 45-year-long period of tense US-Soviet relations known collectively as the Cold War, with all of its brazen lies, calculated bluffs, embarrassed retractions, and bold posturing by each side. During the long but never officially "hot" conflict, chance after chance for reconciliation seemed almost preordained to derail through diplomatic blunder or military gambit.

The Cold War began as World War II was ending, even as the atomic blasts in Hiroshima and Nagasaki mushroomed into the atmosphere.

The Long Sixties: America, 1955–1973, First Edition. Christopher B. Strain.
© 2017 Christopher B. Strain. Published 2017 by John Wiley & Sons, Inc.

The United States now squared off against its recent ally in the epic struggle against the Axis powers, the Soviet Union. Having two seemingly contradictory ideologies, these two "Superpowers" found themselves pitted in an ideological struggle that reflected the perceived needs of the Americans and the Soviets to ensure national security, increase global influence, and consolidate power. A decade after the end of World War II, the Cold War showed no signs of abating.

In the name of securing its own borders, the Soviet Union maintained an expansionist policy into the 1960s—indeed, throughout the duration of the Cold War. Having invaded several Eastern European neighbors weakened by World War II, the USSR had used aggressive military action in the late 1940s and 1950s to create a buffer zone of communist countries—often referred to as Soviet "satellite" states—along its western border. When the Soviets pushed into these other nations in the wake of World War II, the United States and its allies in the North Atlantic Treaty Organization (NATO), fearing the outbreak of another world war, responded, but did so cautiously, applying political pressure rather than military force. Emboldened by the lack of direct military intervention from the United States and Europe, Khrushchev contemplated expanding the Soviet military presence into the Western Hemisphere.

For many Americans the Cold War came home, so to speak, in 1959 when guerrilla leader Fidel Castro ousted the US-supported dictator in Cuba, an island nation only 90 miles from the tip of Florida. Castro, a young revolutionary and a lawyer, alarmed his neighbors to the north when he announced he was communist and commandeered American-owned businesses on the island. It seemed to Americans, in Washington as well as on Main Street, that communism, a Soviet phenomenon a world away, had cropped up in the United States' own backyard. President Eisenhower publicly protested Castro's agrarian reforms throughout 1960 and eventually broke diplomatic relations with Cuba. No longer a faraway, even ephemeral concept, the Cold War—heretofore largely a propaganda battle with the Soviets—had suddenly become much more concrete as the USSR moved to support Castro's regime economically. An initial agreement to buy Cuban sugar led to beefed-up trade between the Caribbean nation and the Soviet Union.

Propping up Castro seemed to fit into the larger strategy of Soviet dealings with the West. Russian history provided ample evidence to mistrust outsiders and sustain the impression of a hostile world aligned against Moscow; therefore, supporting Cuba could be understood as a logical defensive measure by the Russians. As far as the Americans were concerned, however, the move constituted a dangerous kind of Soviet expansionism. Whether through an obsession with national security, or a genuine ideological commitment to creating an international classless society, the Soviets seemed to be advancing communism by spreading it to other nations far and wide. Alliances with other nations also played a central part of each superpower's overall strategy, as did covert operations and the practice of brinkmanship. "The ability to get to the verge without getting into the war is the necessary art," Secretary of State Dulles openly told *LIFE* magazine in 1956.

In many ways Eisenhower's response to Castro's takeover and Soviet support of the new regime in Cuba seemed to mirror the Soviet's strategy, especially in the conviction that making bold announcements and striking aggressive poses would increase difficulties for the other side. Together, President Eisenhower and Secretary of State John Foster Dulles articulated an uncompromising vision of US hegemony at mid-century. The United States, like the Soviet Union, felt that it had to appear willing to resort to the use of nuclear weapons whenever and wherever its interests were at stake. And it was this sort of drastic, even apocalyptic mindset, that gave birth to what became known as the nuclear arms race, as the Soviet Union continually tried to achieve "parity" with the United States in terms of numbers of nuclear warheads, even as the United States continually tried to increase its nuclear stockpile to "stay ahead" of the Soviets. It was understood by American strategists that, whatever their differences, communists worldwide shared common interests hostile to those of the "free world," and that eventually they would act on that basis. Under President Eisenhower, Secretary of State Dulles advanced a theory of what one scholar has termed "asymmetrical strategic deterrence," a bold response sometimes mis-characterized as "massive retaliation." The idea was not to resort to nuclear weapons, "nukes" for short, upon minimal provocation; rather, it was to make the cost of aggression so great that aggression itself became cost-prohibitive; with his conceptualizations of first-strike and second-strike capabilities, Robert McNamara, the Secretary of Defense under Presidents Kennedy and Johnson, would later hone this idea into what came to be called "mutually assured destruction."

If the situation should escalate, the United States should not sway from its duty to use all of the weapons at its disposal—up to and including nukes. As far as Dulles and other US leaders were concerned, nuclear weapons, the massive use of which could, of course, end human life on Earth, were simply bigger and better weapons—another step in the progression of warfare, akin to the technological advancement of gunpowder over the crossbow. Dulles felt it was morally irresponsible to watch communism spread, threatening democratic ideals, and he seemingly convinced Eisenhower that the nuclear option should always be available to thwart the Russians or the Chinese. The general idea, the President told Congressional leaders in late 1954, was "to blow hell out of them in a hurry if they start anything."

This hardline approach carried the United States through the 1950s, but the policy had reached its limits by the end of Eisenhower's tenure in office. In his "Farewell Address" in January 1961, Ike warned the American people against the "conjunction of an immense military establishment and a large arms industry" that was "new in American experience" and whose influence was felt in every city, state house, and federal building. "In the councils of government, we must guard against the acquisition of unwarranted influence, whether sought or unsought, by the military-industrial complex," declared the President, now a lame duck. "The potential for the disastrous rise of misplaced power exists and will persist." It was a strong warning from Eisenhower, one which the Kennedy administration promptly ignored.

Indeed, upon taking office Kennedy took steps to grow the very "military-industrial complex" that his predecessor had just cautioned against, establishing a special post in the Defense Department in 1961 to sell American arms through private corporations to foreign nations. By 1965, American companies had exported $1.9 billion worth of arms to Europe, Japan, Iran, Venezuela, and Saudi Arabia, and other nations, whether democratic or dictatorial, deemed to be sufficiently anti-communist. The General Dynamics Corporation alone sold more than $1 billion worth of military goods, mainly sophisticated and expensive electronic equipment, overseas between 1962 and 1965. These sorts of collusions between private companies and the US government would feed the impression that American corporations were directing foreign policy as much as US foreign policymakers were.

Military spending was, in fact, a vital engine that drove the American economy during the early 1960s and well beyond. Seeing military expenditures in peacetime as a creeping problem, President Eisenhower had reined in spending on defense as best he could, mindful that unrestrained growth of the military might imperil American idealism. "We must not destroy," he told reporters, "what we are attempting to defend." In 1961, however, Kennedy and his advisors feared the outbreak of nuclear war far less than

Figure 3.1 Employees at the General Dynamic Astronautics Plant in San Diego check a row of Atlas missiles in 1962 (Source: © Ralph Crane/Time & Life Pictures/ Getty Images).

conventional war with the Soviets and the Chinese, and accordingly increased the nation's defense budget by 15 percent, doubled the number of ready-combat divisions in the army's strategic reserve, expanded the Marine Corps, added 70 vessels to the military's active fleet, and augmented the tactical air forces. The rationale behind this showy military buildup was to contain communism and minimize revolutionary instability that might lead to communism. The struggle against the spread of communism had seemingly shifted from Europe to Asia, Africa, and Latin America (where many former European colonies had been destabilized by World War II); from nuclear and conventional combat to irregular warfare and insurrection; and from regular armies to "special forces" such as Kennedy's pet Green Berets, modeled after England's elite commandos. Such tactical shifts insured quick and flexible response in meeting communist threats. "Flexibility," in fact, became a new byword in Kennedy-era diplomatic circles: with nuclear weapons involved in the calculus of strategic decision-making, rigidity could be dangerous indeed.

In an internal security document, one of Kennedy's advisors noted that the United States did not require conformity by developing countries to American-style democracy, instead noting that it was vital to US interests for so-called Third-World nations (those unaligned with either NATO or the Soviet bloc) to develop "along lines broadly consistent with our own concepts of individual liberty and government based on consent." Foremost, the US needed to be surrounded by "friendlies"—nations that if not actual democracies, at least had democratic aspirations and seemed disinclined to turn communist. Toward that end, less than two months after his inauguration, President Kennedy established the Alliance for Progress, a plan to provide Latin American nations with $20 billion in aid, contingent upon proportional commitments from regional governments, promises of political reform, and pledges to spurn communism. He also established the Food for Peace program, which distributed US agricultural surpluses abroad, and the Agency for International Development, which shifted the thrust of foreign aid to Latin America from military to economic assistance. Perhaps most famously, Kennedy also established the Peace Corps, which sent thousands of young Americans overseas to organize community-level health, educational, and agricultural improvement projects. Earnest and idealistic, many of the nation's young adults answered the president's call to "ask what you can do for your country." Those who volunteered for the Peace Corps served as ambassadors on the ground, bringing knowledge of foreign lands back to the United States after they seeded the people with whom they had worked shoulder-to-shoulder with notions of political freedom and ideas for economic development. If the Green Berets were military commandos, then the Peace Corps volunteers were cultural commandos, armed with goodwill. In a postcolonial world, the soldiers of the Green Berets and the Peace Corps volunteers could be seen as two sides of the same coin, two different kinds of shock troops serving as counter-insurgents behind the front lines of US imperialism.

In other ways, however, the Kennedy years were much like the Eisenhower years in terms of the fight against the spread of communism. The collapse of German and Japanese power following World War II, coupled with the war's taxing drain on Europe, created a vacuum that sucked the United States intractably into international affairs. As long as neither the Soviet Union nor China could gain a broader foothold in Europe and Asia, the common line of reasoning went, then US security was assured. As Kennedy himself put it, there was thus "one simple central theme of American foreign policy… and that is to support the independence of nations so that one bloc cannot gain sufficient power to finally overcome us." Kennedy (and later Lyndon Baines Johnson) ascribed to the same zero-sum-game mentality that characterized the Eisenhower administration: that is, victories for communism (meaning the toppling of another nation to communism) equaled losses for the United States. "I know full well," said JFK two months before his death, "that every time a country, regardless of how far away it may be from our own borders… passes behind the Iron Curtain, the security of the United States is thereby endangered." A year later, Johnson reiterated that "surrender anywhere threatens defeat everywhere."

Kennedy's advisors—including Secretary of State Dean Rusk; Secretary of Defense Robert S. McNamara; General Maxwell D. Taylor, chairman of the Joint Chiefs of Staff; McGeorge Bundy, Assistant to the President for National Security Affairs; Dean Acheson, a consultant and one of the key architects of NSC-68 under Truman; and Walt Whitman Rostow, Chairman of the Policy Planning Council in the State Department—convinced themselves that the United States was, on some level, its own worst enemy, endangering itself by appearing weak and irresolute to the outside world. As historian John Lewis Gaddis has written, what the Kennedy and Johnson administrations came to fear most "was not communism, which was too fragmented, or the Soviet Union, which was too committed to détente, or even China, which was too impotent, but rather the threat of embarrassment, of humiliation, of appearing too weak." This fear of embarrassment would have dire consequences—in Southeast Asia, for example, but initially in the United States' own backyard, in nearby Cuba.

In April 1961, only three months after Kennedy took office, a force of 1500 Cuban exiles invaded Cuba from the United States. Trained by the CIA, the exiles hoped to oust Castro and de-communize Cuba. The operation, initially planned during the Eisenhower years, was endorsed by Kennedy, who hoped to gain credit for pushing communism out of the Western Hemisphere.

The operation was a disaster—what historian Theodore Draper termed "one of those rare events in history—a perfect failure." Poorly prepared, the invaders landed at Bahía de Cochinos (or "Bay of Pigs"), an inlet of the Gulf of Cazones on the southern coast of the island, without the expected air support from US warplanes. Brandishing a rifle, Castro rushed to the scene, where he rallied his troops and his people, who later credited him with foiling the attack and defending the nation. Some exiles escaped by sea while the rest were killed or rounded up and imprisoned by Castro's forces. President Kennedy took full responsibility for the debacle, which confirmed the American imperialists as true enemies of Castro *and* the Soviets, as both had already claimed.

It was an ugly way to begin a reign of self-described idealism and optimism, though it did fit JFK's description of a New Frontier "of unknown opportunities and perils… of unfulfilled hopes and threats." Reaction to the Bay of Pigs blunder was swift and sharp. The *New York Times* commented, "We looked like fools to our friends, rascals to our enemies, and incompetents to the rest." Cuban revolutionary Che Guevara sent a note of thanks to President Kennedy in August. "Before the invasion the revolution was weak," he wrote. "Now it's stronger than ever." Jackie Kennedy revealed in interviews taped in 1963 that in the aftermath of the incident her husband wept. Nevertheless, the American public seemed to prefer any further action against Castro to none at all: indeed, Kennedy's approval rates launched to 83 percent.

Embarrassed yet undeterred, Kennedy tried to eliminate Castro more quietly, ordering Operation Mongoose, a covert scheme overseen by the president's brother, Robert Kennedy, to assassinate the Cuban dictator. Taking its cues from the popular James Bond novels of the day by Ian Fleming, the CIA planned a number of outlandish schemes to kill Castro, including the use of poisoned fountain pens, exploding cigars—even a booby-trapped conch shell, planted at a favorite snorkeling site. CIA operatives, aware that the Mob was eager to renew the profitable gambling business it had enjoyed in Cuba under the Batista regime, even hired known Mafia hitman Johnny Rosselli to kill Castro (the hit was cancelled after the Bay of Pigs fiasco). The following month the president diverted attention from his blunders in Cuba by announcing the nation's next great challenge—the colonization of space—but the Cold War continued to spread across the globe.

That summer, as West Germany strengthened ties with the West, Khrushchev became increasingly militant about eliminating Western influence in West Berlin. On August 13, the Soviets expressed their concerns outwardly and built the Berlin Wall, partitioning the city into two sections, east and west. Lured by better opportunities than existed in East Germany but physically barred from emigrating, the outflow of skilled young technicians and other desired workers stopped cold, and the Soviets sealed off West Berlin as a free bastion within the Communist bloc. Even though the United States immediately protested, the wall remained, and hundreds of East Germans were shot to death trying to escape to the West.

The construction of the Berlin Wall was one of many factors that contributed directly to Kennedy's sense of embattlement, the perception that his first eleven months in office were a period of continual, international crisis that called for him to act.

It was in this context that the president made two fateful decisions regarding Southeast Asia. First, as communist forces in Laos—a strategically significant former French colony, encircled by China, North and South Vietnam, Cambodia, Thailand, and Burma—launched a major offensive, sweeping through the eastern part of the tiny nation, Kennedy responded by re-routing supplies from neighboring Thailand to Laos and mobilizing US troops in the area. Second, he expanded the American commitment in South Vietnam from 500 to 10,000 "advisors" (special-ops soldiers, sent officially only to train counterinsurgents but who sometimes took part in the fighting themselves), ordered US Air Force units to strike Vietcong strongholds in South Vietnam, and promised full support to the unpopular yet powerful South Vietnamese leader Ngo Dien Diem. These moves would have serious consequences for the region and for the United States. Encouraged by Vice-President Johnson, JFK had come to see Vietnam as part of the global communist threat: no longer questioning the Eisenhower-Dulles policies he had inherited, Kennedy found himself adopting ideas such as the domino theory. With these decisions, President Kennedy failed to distinguish himself from his predecessor and similarly failed to defuse Cold-War hostilities.

As Kennedy pondered what should be done in Southeast Asia, "the Cuban problem" again rudely intruded on public attention. On October 14, 1962, a U-2 spy plane photographed what seemed to be missile silos under construction in Cuba. The photos also showed what appeared to be nuclear missiles on these sites, crated but ready for quick assembly and deployment. On October 16, further recon revealed two types of missiles: medium-range ballistic missiles with a range of 1300 miles, and intermediate-range ballistic missiles capable of reaching targets as far away as 2500 miles. Such weapons would effectively give the Soviets, via their convenient new launching pad in the Caribbean, not only the ability to attack any major American city but also the quick-strike potential to negate an American counterattack. The only thing not visible to American surveillance cameras was a stamp on the crates reading "From Russia, With Love," but there was no doubt where the nukes had come from. In a nationwide survey, *Newsweek* found that "nearly all Americans are deeply concerned—but not panicked—by the presence of Soviet arms and 'technicians'" in Cuba.

President Kennedy addressed the nation on the evening of October 22, a talk in which he simultaneously tried to explain the situation to the American people and reassure them. Noting a "clear and present danger," he said that the missiles would not be allowed to remain in Cuba. "We no longer live in a world where only the actual firing of weapons represents a sufficient challenge to a nation's security to constitute maximum peril," he argued. "Nuclear weapons are so destructive and ballistic missiles are so swift, that any substantially increased possibility of their use or any sudden change in their deployment may well be regarded as a definite threat to peace." Kennedy stated that the United States would establish a naval blockade to inspect all ship traffic into Cuba for nuclear weapons, and pledged to retaliate against the Soviet Union if a nuclear missile was fired from Cuba toward *any* nation in the Western Hemisphere. The next day, US naval vessels moved into place, covering six shipping lanes between tiny islands around Cuba and Puerto Rico, with an initial line of destroyers backed by larger warships, including cruisers and aircraft carriers from bases in Norfolk, Virginia, and Mayport, Florida. It was a powerful show of force, covering thousands of square miles of blue-green ocean.

A day later, on October 24, large freighters that plied the shipping channels and tested the blockade were warned away; a few of the vessels, after seeming to ignore the directive, eventually halted their progress toward Cuba and turned around. While smaller watercraft passed through the blockade unimpeded, and only one Soviet ship was ever boarded, the blockade intercepted 25 ships that were told to return to their ports of origin. Both the Soviet and Cuban governments protested the US blockade as a violation of the UN Charter. Soviet ambassador Valerian Zorin called the action "arbitrary and piratical"; Cuban dictator Fidel Castro, readying his people for war, called it "the most temerarious and most dangerous adventure to world peace which has happened since the last world war."

Seeking a parley, Khrushchev sent a secret telegram to President Kennedy on October 26. Assuring the American leader that the Soviet missiles in Cuba were strictly defensive in nature, he admitted how the US might construe their presence there as menacing. Knowing that neither he nor Kennedy sought a nuclear showdown, the Soviet premier appealed to reason when he wrote, "we are of sound mind and understand perfectly well that if we attack you, you will respond the same way." Khrushchev feared that the situation was quickly spinning out of control and offered an olive branch. "We, for our part, will declare that our ships, bound for Cuba, will not carry any kind of armaments," he suggested. "You would declare

Figure 3.2   A US Navy destroyer and seaplane shadow a Soviet submarine during the Cuban Missile Crisis, 1962 (Contributed by Capt. Bill Rodriguez).

that the United States will not invade Cuba with its forces and will not support any sort of forces which might intend to carry out an invasion of Cuba." Seeming to sense how such a situation could quickly outstrip either Soviet or American attempts to contain it, Khrushchev finished with a masterful blend of conciliation, reproach, and threat. "Mr. President, we and you ought not now to pull on the ends of the rope in which you have tied the knot of war, because the more the two of us pull, the tighter that knot will be tied," he concluded. "And a moment may come when that knot will be tied so tight that even he who tied it will not have the strength to untie it."

On the next day, Khrushchev followed with another secret communiqué, demanding that the United States withdraw its missiles from the Turkish border, stop surveillance flights over Cuba, and promise not to invade the island nation. Kennedy responded by declaring that until the ongoing construction of missile silos ceased, and all missiles were removed, Soviet demands would go unconsidered and unanswered. That same day—October 27—yet another high-flying U-2 passed over Cuba; this time, however, Soviet radar detected it and fired two SAM-2 anti-aircraft missiles, bringing it down and killing the American pilot. The scenario that Khrushchev had predicted was unfolding: Uncle Sam and the Great Bear stood eyeball-to-eyeball, unblinking. Glued to their television sets, Americans feared the worst while also paradoxically welcoming a showdown. "Long past due," said one Iowan banker quoted in *US News & World Report*. "Long past due."

Then, as war loomed, the tense situation wound down as quickly as it had escalated. President Kennedy sent a secret telegram to Premier Khrushchev offering to end the naval quarantine in exchange for the immediate withdrawal of all Soviet missiles from Cuba; furthermore, he pledged not to invade the island. On October 28, as American officials prepared an airstrike on the Cuban missile sites, Khrushchev sent a letter to Kennedy accepting his October 27 offer. Sixteen Soviet ships steaming toward Cuba turned around in mid-ocean to return to Russian ports. The crisis was over. The world exhaled.

On October 29, acting secretary-general of the United Nations, U Thant, assembled an inspection team to oversee the dismantling of the missiles and their silos. Castro, who had not been consulted by Soviet officials, was defiantly furious, eventually capitulating to cooperate with UN inspectors. Kennedy had managed to save face and emerged as the tougher of the two negotiators. Khrushchev explained that he had saved the world from nuclear disaster, but his personal power within the Soviet bloc diminished in the wake of the crisis: removing the missiles discredited his strategy of seeking détente through intimidation. Kennedy had backed down the Soviets, and his popularity soared, though some wondered if JFK had pushed the two nations to the brink of war a bit too recklessly.

David Obst, a teenager in 1962 who would later become a war journalist in Vietnam, illustrates in his memoir how geopolitical events like the Cuban Missile Crisis reached into the lives of everyday Americans, even high-school-aged kids. Recounting the news conference in which President Kennedy announced the presence of the offending missiles in Cuba, and thinking about his own weekend plans, Obst recalls having felt a "double whammy" of concern. "My worst fears of nuclear annihilation were about to be realized," he moaned, "but worse: What about my date with Jill?" Faced with the end of the world, he could only lament that he'd "die a virgin." The story, as funny as Obst intended it to be, reveals more than how a teenaged boy's thoughts could be totally eclipsed by sex: it also provides some insight into the mentality of the 1960s generation. For these teenagers, theirs was a world which really could come to an end, one in which all life could end permanently in an instant. For many that tenuousness translated into an imperative to speak one's mind, or to challenge injustice as it arises; for others, seeing futility, it translated into an imperative to sample earthly delights widely and indiscriminately, or to find love when and where they could. For others still, it meant taking life very seriously, drinking from its metaphysical waters and imbibing its deeper meanings.

In June 1963, a hot line between Moscow and Washington opened a path of direct communication between the supreme commanders to avoid misunderstandings and avert disaster. The entire situation had become fairly absurd: with few fail-safes, a careless mistake or genuine mix-up could bring about World War III—or worse. In fact, an unhinged individual with launch codes and a slippery grasp on reality could destroy life on Earth. Such was the scenario rendered in dark humor in the film *Dr. Strangelove, or How I Came to Stop Worrying and Love the Bomb* (1964), directed by Stanley Kubrick. A black comedy, *Dr. Strangelove* carried the absurd logic of the arms race to its extreme, depicting an insane US Air Force general ("General Jack Ripper," played by Sterling Hayden) who initiates a first-strike nuclear attack against the Soviet Union, and the roomful of politicians and military men who frantically try to stop the ensuing Armageddon. Obsessed with the notion of a Communist conspiracy involving water fluoridation, leading to contamination of his "precious bodily fluids," Ripper orders US bombers to fly into Soviet airspace. The president (played by Peter Sellers), his advisors, the Joint Chiefs of Staff, and a Royal Air Force officer (also played by Sellers) try to recall the bomber as a mysterious, black-gloved, wheelchair-bound scientist (also played by Sellers), whose German accent and Nazi mannerisms bely his true allegiances, and bellicose General "Buck" Turgidson (played by George C. Scott) run interference. Questioned on the merits of a US contingency plan that allows field commanders to retaliate unilaterally, Turgidson argues, "I don't think it's quite fair to condemn a whole program because of a single slip-up." At one point, as a scuffle breaks out, the president exclaims, "Gentlemen, you can't fight in here! This is the War Room!" A parallel storyline follows the crew of a B-52 as it tries to deliver its atomic payload. "Well, boys, I reckon this is it—nuke-yular combat, toe-to-toe with the Rooskies," marvels Major T.J. "King" Kong (played by Slim Pickens), who provides a visually memorable ending. Another film released that year, *Fail-Safe* (1964) portrayed the end-game scenario in a serious manner, but *Dr. Strangelove* resonated with a younger generation already beginning to question the wisdom inherited from their elders.

The Cold War reverberated throughout American life, affecting domestic issues as much as foreign ones. The ideological war against the Soviets, for example, became an incongruous ally in the struggle for black equality. Most American politicians and government officials were not personally troubled by the moral gap between the democratic ideals that the United States trumpeted abroad and everyday racist practices at home; nevertheless, many of them were bothered by the effect that overt racial discrimination at home had upon the country's international image. Whether liberal or conservative on other issues, a wide range of politicians in both the Democratic and Republican parties came to recognize that foreign governments and peoples could be and at times were shocked and alienated by demonstrations of official American bigotry. During World War II, civil rights advocates had called for a two-front war against foreign totalitarianism and domestic racism, and these activists openly played upon the fears of international backlash in pressing for racial reform. In his book *A Rising Wind* (1945), the NAACP's Walter White had predicted that all the peoples of Asia would become communist if the United States failed to measure up to the promise of equality—and the only thing most white Americans feared more than political equality with African Americans was communism. Communism was seen as a terrible threat to the American way of life, and one's degree of anti-communism had already become a measure of allegiance to the United States among good citizens and patriots of all races. As a consequence, a degree of consensus was growing among Cold Warriors that something finally needed to be done— and soon—to address the nation's long-standing racial problems.

The Cold War also had repercussions for the American family. In a perilous world of dangerous foreign enemies, Americans tended to retreat into the security of the American way of life and the domestic shelter of the family; both offered safety from the outside world, from the Commies. Marriage was encouraged, birth rates remained high; and there seemed to exist an unspoken consensus that the "communist hordes" could only be beaten back by even larger capitalist ones. Civil defense training was encouraged with almost religious zeal. Schoolchildren learned to "duck and cover," dropping to the ground and covering their heads with their hands to protect themselves in case of nuclear attack. Once the "all-clear" bell sounded, the kids would scamper home, presumably to join their parents in backyard bomb shelters. "Grandma's Pantry Was Ready," read one Federal Civil Defense Administration brochure, depicting a well-stocked, old-fashioned larder replete with canned goods and supplies. "Is Your Pantry Ready in Event of Emergency?" If there was a certain naivety in duck-and-cover drills and full pantries in the face of the possible deployment of radioactive weapons, then there was also comfort to be found in the maintenance of normality: the only ready answer for the constant, low-level terror of life in the Atomic Age.

For thirteen days in October 1962, the nation teetered on the brink of thermonuclear war with the Soviet Union. There was a whiff of insanity about the entire episode: it was little coincidence that the acronym for "mutually assured destruction," supposedly each superpower's reason for not using nuclear weapons against the other, was MAD. After the Cuban Missile Crisis, many Americans believed that the showdown between President Kennedy and Soviet premier Khrushchev had been the closest that the United States ever came to nuclear war. In reality, the Cold War was one extended flirtation with nuclear holocaust. The false alarms and potential slipups, some of which wormed their way into public consciousness via imaginative accounts like *Dr. Strangelove*, underscored just how serious the game with the Soviets really was. Nuclear annihilation was always a button-push away, and it was against this all-or-nothing backdrop that everything else in the 1960s occurred.

Further Reading

Walter LaFeber, *America, Russia, and the Cold War, 1945–1975*, 10th ed. (New York: McGraw-Hill, 2006)

John Lewis Gaddis, *Strategies of Containment: A Critical Appraisal of Postwar American National Security Policy*, rev. exp. ed. (New York: Oxford, 2005)

Trumbull Higgins, *The Perfect Failure: Kennedy, Eisenhower, and the CIA at the Bay of Pigs* (New York: Norton, 1988)

Robert F. Kennedy, *Thirteen Days* (New York: Norton, 1969)

4

The Civil Rights Movement

Her feet hurt—or so the story goes. History remembers her as an elderly woman, tired from a long day at work, too exhausted to give up her seat to a white bus rider on December 1, 1955. In reality, Rosa Parks was neither old nor worn out, and she knew exactly what she was getting into when she refused the bus driver's request to vacate her seat that afternoon on a Montgomery city bus. A 42-year-old seamstress who worked in a department store, Parks was also the secretary of the Montgomery chapter of the National Association for the Advancement of Colored People (NAACP); she had attended the Highlander Folk School, a center for labor activism and social justice in Tennessee. Socially conscious and acutely aware of the debilitating effects of Jim Crow segregation, she quietly opted to make her stand that day not as an NAACP activist but as a private citizen. Her arrest and the boycott that followed were the beginnings of major change, not only in Montgomery, but across the South.

E. D. Nixon, a union organizer and Montgomery NAACP chapter president, had been planning a challenge of segregated seating on buses for some time before Parks' arrest, but the right opportunity had not presented itself. Working with Jo Ann Robinson, a college professor and president of the Women's Political Council, Nixon needed someone voluntarily to break the bus seating law and be arrested, but those who had already done so— including Claudette Colvin, an unwed young woman who got pregnant just as her case was going to court—were not ideal, in his eyes. After the arrest of Parks, whose character was beyond reproach, Robinson worked through the night printing, mimeographing, and circulating thousands of handbills throughout Montgomery's Negro community. These read:

The Long Sixties: America, 1955–1973, First Edition. Christopher B. Strain.
© 2017 Christopher B. Strain. Published 2017 by John Wiley & Sons, Inc.

Another woman has been arrested and thrown in jail because she refused to get up out of her seat on the bus for a white person to sit down. It is the second time since the Claudette Colvin case that a Negro woman has been arrested for the same thing. This has to be stopped. Negroes have rights too, for if Negroes did not ride the buses, they could not operate. Three-fourths of the riders are Negro, yet we are arrested, or have to stand over empty seats. If we do not do something to stop these arrests, they will continue. The next time it may be you, or your daughter, or mother. This woman's case will come up on Monday. We are, therefore, asking every Negro to stay off the buses Monday in protest of the arrest and trial. Don't ride the buses to work, to town, to school, or anywhere on Monday. You can afford to stay out of school for one day if you have no other way to go except by bus. You can also afford to stay out of town for one day. If you work, take a cab, or walk. But please, children and grown-ups, don't ride the bus at all on Monday. Please stay off all buses Monday.

The next day, the buses were empty as black Montgomerians found alternate ways to work. Some took black-owned taxis for the same fee they would have paid for the bus: ten cents. Some carpooled. And some walked.

The one-day boycott was enormously successful, and local black leaders, coming together as the Montgomery Improvement Association (MIA), opted to continue. Recognizing the inherent danger in their actions, the ministers and businessmen of the MIA elected as their president someone who was capable yet politically expendable—someone who, in their view, had less to lose. He was the new minister of Dexter Avenue Baptist Church, a 26-year-old out-of-towner who had just completed his graduate studies in theology at Boston University. His name was Martin Luther King, Jr.

The boycott lasted for more than a year, during which the boycotters congregated at frequent mass meetings held at churches, where their resolve was strengthened through speeches, sermons, songs, and strategy sessions. The boycott came at a high price, as a grand jury indicted nearly one hundred black citizens for conspiracy to boycott; they were tried and found guilty. Four Baptist churches were firebombed; insurance companies dropped coverage on those churches where mass meetings were held. King's house was firebombed too. Counseled by Bayard Rustin, an organizer for the pacifist Fellowship of Reconciliation (FOR) and advocate of Gandhian diplomacy, King persuaded the angry crowd that gathered at his demolished home not to retaliate. It was his initiation into the ways of nonviolence. The boycott finally ended when the Supreme Court affirmed a lower court decision outlawing segregation on buses. Black Montgomerians again rode the city's buses, now sitting in any available seat they wished.

The boycott followed the landmark Supreme Court ruling a year earlier, *Brown et al. v. Board of Education of Topeka, Kansas* (1954), which overturned the separate-but-equal doctrine that had governed the American South for the previous 60 years. The result of decades of legal agitation by the NAACP, *Brown v. Board* marked the end of an era. The NAACP's legal team, first under the direction of Charles Hamilton Houston and then Thurgood Marshall, had concentrated its efforts through the 1920s, 1930s, and 1940s into five areas: anti-lynching legislation, voter participation, employment, due process under the law, and education. In 1950, this last area—education—took precedent in the wake of two successfully argued Supreme Court cases: *Sweatt v. Painter* and *McLaurin v. Oklahoma State Regents*, which found that separating students by race in graduate-level university programs fell short of the legal standard of separate but equal. In *Brown v. Board*, the Court heard school desegregation cases from across the country as a single case. Petitions from black families in five different communities—Clarendon County, South Carolina; Topeka, Kansas; New Clarendon County, Delaware; Washington, DC; and Farmville, Virginia, where eleventh-grader Barbara Johns led students in a walkout and strike at Moton High School—comprised the omnibus *Brown* case. Chief Justice Earl Warren, appointed by Eisenhower in 1953, wrote the decision. "Segregation of white and colored children in public schools has a detrimental effect," he noted, whose impact is greater when it has the sanction of the law, "for the policy of separating the races is usually interpreted as denoting the inferiority of the Negro group." The nine justices therefore unanimously concluded that "in the field of public education the doctrine of 'separate but equal' has no place." Separate educational facilities were "inherently unequal."

Brown was the most important civil rights case of the twentieth century—indeed, one of the most important Supreme Court decisions ever. While often noted as the start of the modern civil rights movement, a better argument can be made for the Montgomery bus boycott, which signaled something different, a new beginning. The boycott was quickly mobilized; *Brown*, by comparison, was the culmination of decades-long efforts by the NAACP's legal defense team. The boycott involved a lot of people; *Brown*, comparatively few. The boycott was immediate; legal challenges like *Brown* took a long time to effect—if they were effective at all. Compared to the boycott, *Brown* seemed a remnant of an earlier time and an earlier mode of protest—in some ways the last hurrah of the NAACP, soon to be eclipsed by a new host of civil rights organizations touting different methods to achieve equality. Most important, Parks' arrest was the kind of gesture that would come to define civil rights protests in the 1960s: a heroically inspiring act—30 seconds of lonely, emulous courage that motivated others to agitate for reform. It was a harbinger of things to come. The NAACP was still a force through the 1960s and there were legal challenges yet to be met, but a new kind of activism, invigorated by a groundswell of popular involvement, was transforming the struggle for Negro equality into a mass movement.

In the wake of the *Brown* decision and the bus boycott in Montgomery, the white South retrenched into a period of "massive resistance": a backlash, or concerted effort to thwart "outside" (i.e. national) efforts to change Southern customs. Across the region, community after community passed new segregation ordinances. Businessmen, politicians, and other leading citizens joined new White Citizens Councils, clubs whose members used economic and political pressure to oppose racial integration; compared to the more proletarian Ku Klux Klan, these organizations were comprised mainly of middle and upper-class members who sought to oppress black Southerners socially, politically, and economically—depriving them of jobs, for example, or pressuring insurance companies to cancel policies on church-owned vans or buses. Worst of all, the era saw a resurgence of the KKK, with Southern trees once again bearing the "strange fruit" described in Billie Holliday's 1939 blues ballad (that is, black corpses swinging from nooses). In this supercharged atmosphere, Southern racists resorted to the most repressive of measures to preserve white supremacy: eight of eleven lynchings in the 1950s occurred in 1955 (including the murder of Emmett Till on August 27, 1955). As in the early twentieth century, white supremacists might feel compelled to kill an "uppity" Negro just for failing to show proper deference to a white person.

Intended to cow would-be activists into non-action, massive resistance had the opposite effect as black Southerners mobilized, forming new organizations to capitalize on the gains made between 1954 and 1956. In January 1957, Martin Luther King, Jr., and a number of other black ministers (mostly Baptist preachers) came together at a conference in Atlanta to sustain the momentum created in Montgomery. Bayard Rustin, who had coached King in Montgomery, and Stanley Levison, a white attorney and fundraiser from New York, helped to plan the conference, where Rustin presented a series of working papers on new directions for the struggle. He stressed the importance of not only the church, which he called "the most stable social institution in Negro culture," but also nonviolence as a tactic whose great effectiveness had been demonstrated in Montgomery. For Rustin, the lessons of Montgomery were clear. Bus companies were not prepared to lose money to preserve segregation, and integrated buses could be a first step toward wider equality. Such equality, however, would necessitate widespread political mobilization and social protest, namely "direct action": a shorthand phrase to describe boycotts, marches, demonstrations, protests—most everything except lawsuits (which had been the primary vehicle of protest used by the old guard civil rights leaders).

While the ministers needed no convincing about the centrality of churches, which had already become community action hubs (often to the consternation of local NAACP officials), the relationship between direct action and nonviolence was still vague. For Rustin, direct action was a political weapon, the only viable tactic for African Americans; for King, direct action had potential, when coupled with nonviolence, for positive transformation and reform, changing society for the better. King saw in nonviolence the means to bring about the "beloved community," a reconciled world governed by love—free from poverty, militarism, and racism. Direct action would become the default method of protest in the civil rights movement, but the debate over the merits of nonviolence—as both a tactic and as a way of life—would continue.

The ministers concluded the conference by forming the Negro Leaders Conference on Transportation and Nonviolent Integration, which changed its name first to Southern Leaders Conference, and then to Southern Christian Leadership Conference (SCLC). With King as the titular head, Ella Baker handled day-to-day operations as executive director. A 53-year-old North Carolinian whose grandmother had been whipped as a slave for refusing to marry the man chosen for her by her owner, Baker relocated from New York City, where she had been involved in a number of progressive causes, to Atlanta to help King's new organization. Rev. Fred Shuttlesworth of Birmingham, Rev. Joseph Lowery of Mobile, Rev. Ralph David Abernathy of Montgomery (whose house and church were bombed during the conference), and Rev. C.K. Steele of Tallahassee were instrumental in founding SCLC, which would very quickly achieve the kind of prominence and respect that it had taken the NAACP and National Urban League a half-century to attain. SCLC would become a means of linking civil rights leaders across the South, and a fundraising vehicle for King in both the South and North. SCLC's ranks would swell to include Rev. James Bevel,

Diane Nash, Rev. Jesse Jackson, Rev. C.T. Vivian, Septima Clark, Dorothy Cotton, Rev. Hosea Williams, Maya Angelou, and Rev. Andrew Young, among others.

That same year—1957—saw a dramatic showdown in Little Rock, Arkansas, between intrepid young students and hostile segregationists; between Governor Orval Faubus and President Eisenhower; between neo-Confederates and the US military; and between state and federal power. In compliance with *Brown*, the Little Rock city school board approved a desegregation plan in May 1955. In September 1957, nine black teenagers prepared to enroll at the city's Central High School, previously an all-white school. Pro-segregationists threatened to protest and physically bar the students from entering the building. The night before the students were to begin, Governor Faubus—pandering to the protestors and worried about the demonstration turning into a violent confrontation—called out the National Guard to prevent the students from entering the school. When the unsuspecting students arrived at the high school grounds, they were met by an angry mob of epithet-shouting racists along with 270 National Guardsmen who turned them away. A federal judge ordered the soldiers removed, but when the students returned the next day, a mob of angry whites again surrounded the school and effectively blocked their entrance. Over the next few weeks, a standoff occurred, finally involving a reluctant President Eisenhower, who negotiated with Governor Faubus as if he were a foreign head-of-state. Faced with continued defiance, the president eventually federalized the state Guard and dispatched one thousand paratroopers of the 101st Airborne Division to the scene, where they dispersed the crowd and escorted the students into the school.

The "Little Rock Nine"—Ernest Green, Elizabeth Eckford, Jefferson Thomas, Terrence Roberts, Carlotta Walls LaNier, Minnijean Brown, Gloria Ray Karlmark, Thelma Mothershed, and Melba Pattillo Beals—finished the school year under the watchful eye of the soldiers, who shadowed the young people everywhere on campus. Still, the students endured physical and verbal abuse. After dumping a bowl of chili on the head of one tormentor in the lunchroom, Minnijean Brown was suspended, leaving the school soon after. That spring, Ernest Green became the first Negro to graduate from the school; afterward, however, authorities closed Central High for the next two years.

Before the "Little Rock Crisis," as it was called, Govenor Faubus had been known as a racial moderate, one supported by black voters at the polls, but his actions at Central High created an international incident, one that showed the depths of Southern intransigence on the issue of integration. The image of young Elizabeth Eckford, dressed neatly for school and stoically threading her way through the ugly, screaming, spitting mob of white adults, became an iconic one, as did the image of paratroopers marching through the streets of Little Rock with fixed bayonets, a scene eerily reminiscent of the occupation of the South by federal troops during Reconstruction in the 1870s. For some white Southerners, resentful of federal intervention, it was the Civil War all over again.

By the time Central High reopened again in August 1959, the civil rights movement was burgeoning, yet still diffuse. There had been various direct-action engagements in a variety of places: Oklahoma City, Oklahoma; Wichita, Kansas; Kansas City, Kansas; Washington, DC; Richmond, Virginia; Charlotte, North Carolina; Marion, South Carolina; Durham, North Carolina; and Miami, Florida. None of these actions in 1958 and 1959 attracted national press coverage, and none spawned new, nationally known organizations or leaders; but Negroes across the nation were increasingly expectant and increasingly impatient for change. Most invidious to them were segregation laws that continued to separate blacks from whites in public accommodations—not only because the laws were insulting and inconvenient (forcing one, for example, to eat standing up at a pass-through window at the back of a restaurant with vacant seats in its front room) but also because the exclusion and differential treatment inherent in segregation gnawed at one's worth and self-esteem. Such customs, dated as they were, seemed particularly grating to young people, and it would be this age group who would lead the charge to destroy Jim Crow in the coming decade.

In some sense, then, "the Sixties" began on February 1, 1960, when four college freshmen staged a sit-in protest at the Woolworths (five-and-dime store) in downtown Greensboro, North Carolina. Ezell Blair, Jr., Franklin McCain, Joseph McNeill, and David Richmond made a few purchases, sat down at the store's lunch counter, and asked for a cup of coffee. When the four young men were refused service at the "whites-only" lunch counter, they remained seated in silent protest. Like Rosa Parks' refusal to relinquish her seat, theirs was a simple act with tremendous repercussions; and, like Parks, the four young men made history. Eleven months before President Kennedy implored young people to serve by doing, the students implored their community to do right by serving.

The next day 20 of their classmates from North Carolina Agricultural & Technical State University joined them. On February 3, the *New York Times*

Figure 4.1   From left to right: Joseph McNeil, Franklin McCain, Billy Smith, and Clarence Henderson sit in for a second day at the Woolworth's in Greensboro, 1960. In many ways their protest marked the beginning of "The Sixties" (Source: © Jack Moebes/CORBIS).

carried the story on page 22 under the single-column headline "Negroes in South in Store Sitdown," reporting that "a group of well-dressed Negro college students had staged a sitdown strike in a downtown Woolworth store that day and vowed to continue it in relays until Negroes were served at the lunch counter." On February 4, the first white student participated.

The protests spread like kudzu across North Carolina, from Winston-Salem to Durham to Raleigh; by the end of the week, different students conducted more sit-ins in Charlotte, Fayetteville, High Point, Elizabeth City, and Concord. On February 10, Hampton, Virginia, became the first community outside North Carolina where students conducted a sit-in; protests occurred soon afterward in the Virginia cities of Norfolk and Portsmouth. Twelve days after the first sit-in in Greensboro, 40 students sat in at Woolworths in Nashville. The sit-ins spread rapidly across Tennessee to Chattanooga, Knoxville, Memphis and Oak Ridge, as well as to Rock Hill,

South Carolina. By the end of February, Richmond, Baltimore, Montgomery, and Lexington were among over thirty communities in seven states where students conducted sit-ins. The following month the sit-ins spread further, becoming larger and better organized. On March 15, at exactly 11:00 a.m., two hundred students moved into ten downtown restaurants in Atlanta. The Atlanta eateries were carefully selected, all linked to city, county, or federal government buildings, and therefore subject to the 14th Amendment's requirement that public places could not discriminate. Seventy-six students were arrested across Atlanta. By mid-April, the sit-in movement had attracted about 50,000 participants.

Following a purposeful pattern, the sit-ins spread rapidly across the South because of pre-existing networks of student activists connected through church groups and NAACP youth chapters. Well-dressed and polite, the demonstrators had found a poignant way to dramatize the injustice of segregated seating at lunch counters—though some local whites, seeing only a flagrant disregard of racial custom, took exception. In those places in which violence did occur, it was provided by all-too-willing white hooligans, neither well-dressed nor polite, who harassed and menaced the students by pouring ketchup on them, extinguishing cigarettes on them, dragging them off their stools, and kicking them and beating them. More James Dean than Hillbilly Bob, the hooligans represented Southern versions of the leather-jacket-and-T-shirt-clad rebellious white male, rather than the stereotypical, gap-toothed redneck in overalls. What made the protests effective was the nonviolent, non-retaliatory way in which the protestors either ignored or absorbed abuse, refusing to respond at the level of those who mocked or threatened them. In most such incidents, police officers at the scene typically arrested the protestors for creating a disturbance instead of their tormentors, but it was the hooligans, with their uncivil behavior and demeanor, who inadvertently advanced the civil rights movement by creating an ugly spectacle for reporters and news cameras. Northern activists staged sympathy sit-ins and picketed to show solidarity.

As their elders had done after Montgomery, the students came together after the sit-ins to strategize. Across the South, 126 student delegates met at a conference facilitated by SCLC at Shaw University in Raleigh, North Carolina, April 16–18, 1960. Also in attendance were delegates from 19 Northern colleges, civil rights organizations such as the Congress of Racial Equality (described in the next paragraph), and student groups such as Students for a Democratic Society (described in the next chapter). King and his colleagues apparently hoped to create a kind of youth affiliate group for the older, male-dominated, minister-led SCLC. Ella Baker, who had carved out a space for herself in SCLC by quietly and tirelessly organizing local church affiliates, recognized the need for a more independent, student-led organization, free from the well-meaning but paternalistic influence of SCLC leadership. She spoke up in support of a new group without formal ties to SCLC. The result was the formation of the Student Nonviolent Coordinating Committee, or SNCC (pronounced "snick"), a biracial group that included students from historically black colleges and universities (HBCUs) such as South Carolina State University in Orangeburg, Howard University in Washington, DC, Fisk University in Nashville, and colleges in the Atlanta University system. Founding members included Charles McDew, Charles Jones, Julian Bond, Bernard Lafayette, Diane Nash, James Lawson, James Forman, Marion Berry, James Bevel, Stokely Carmichael, and John Lewis—all of whom became key players in the cadre of organizers who gave the next phase of the civil rights movement its youthful energy and creative drive.

By May 1961, over one hundred Southern towns and cities had desegregated soda fountains, restaurants, and other public facilities; but most of this reform had occurred in the upper South, or in the bigger cities. That month, a group known as the Congress of Racial Equality (CORE) initiated an action intended not only to bring the movement to the Deep South but also to involve the federal government in the cause. CORE had begun during World War II as a national, interracial, pacifist organization; its founder, James Farmer, organized a desegregation campaign in Chicago in 1942 after serving as a field secretary for FOR. In 1947, eight white and eight black CORE members had mounted a "Journey of Reconciliation," an interstate bus ride through the upper South; four of the riders were arrested in Chapel Hill, North Carolina and three of them, including Bayard Rustin, served time on a chain gang. In 1961, CORE planned a second journey— this one to be called a "Freedom Ride" which Farmer described as a kind of "sit-on wheels." By scheduling rides on both of the nation's major interstate bus lines, Greyhound and Trailways, the riders hoped to test the recent Supreme Court ruling in *Boynton v. Virginia* (1960), which declared that segregation in interstate bus and rail stations was unconstitutional.

Thirteen passengers of varying ages, black and white, left Washington, DC, on two buses on May 4, bound for New Orleans. After minimal resistance, the group rolled into Anniston, Alabama, where a large mob attacked the bus: slashing the tires and preventing the riders from disembarking into the bus station. Fifty carloads of white Alabamans followed the bus as it wobbled out of town, then forced it off the highway and set it on fire. When a second bus of Freedom Riders arrived in Anniston an hour later, it was "resegregated" by local whites before rolling on to Birmingham, where the riders were beaten at the local depot. Arriving ten minutes after the violence had begun, the local police did little to protect the riders, whom they viewed as "outside agitators," deserving of rough justice; in fact, a sergeant in the Birmingham police department told local Klansmen they would not intervene for a period of time. It was later revealed that the FBI, which had an informant in the local KKK chapter, also knew about the imminent violence, which they did nothing to prevent.

When the remaining freedom riders attempted to continue from Birmingham to Montgomery on a new bus, angry mobs again blocked their way, eventually forcing the riders to abandon the depot and make their way to an airport, from which they flew to New Orleans. However, a new set of riders from SNCC's Nashville contingent opted, on May 17, to pick up the bus ride where the first group had left off. This group was escorted to the Tennessee state line by Birmingham public safety commissioner Theophilus Eugene Connor, better known as "Bull" Connor. Still more riders came: the next group left for Montgomery at high speed, rocketing through the countryside at 90 mph. This group's police protection melted away when they arrived in Montgomery, where they were attacked; William Barbee, John Lewis, and Jim Zwerg were beaten unconscious. President John F. Kennedy ordered US Marshals to the scene on the following day, May 21, when supporters gathered at the First Baptist Church in Montgomery for a mass meeting. As Martin Luther King, Jr., and other SCLC ministers spoke to the assemblage, the church was besieged by a white mob, which overturned cars, set them afire, and hurled rocks through the stained-glass windows. Inside, King tried to phone Attorney General Robert F. Kennedy to request federal protection; outside, a thin line of federal marshals, state policemen, and a few local police kept the rioters at bay as tear gas wafted under the door. After hours of pressure from Robert Kennedy, Governor John Patterson begrudgingly declared martial law and used the Alabama National Guard to break the siege.

As pivotal civil rights protests, the Freedom Rides were a lot like the sit-ins—only more aggressive. They were coercive, not only forcing the involvement of federal authorities but also pressing more conservative civil rights groups, like the NAACP, to endorse direct action. They also pushed moderate whites, alarmed by the forcefulness of the Freedom Riders and the violence that followed them, to consider just how much Negro assertiveness they were willing to stomach. No less than Southern politicians like Patterson or Faubus—liberal Democrats, their civil rights records withstanding—Northern politicians like the Kennedys would have preferred to wait, to move soberly and deliberately, unrushed by activists clamoring for immediate results.

It was not to be. The sit-ins and Freedom Rides loosed a barrage of protests, and it became increasingly harder to discuss the civil rights movement as a series of discrete events. Protests were erupting all over the South, most of them unheralded and uncelebrated, without national news coverage or any news coverage at all: a housewife requesting a book at a local library, a high-school kid ordering a soda at a local drugstore, someone asking to see a menu at a roadside diner. The civil rights movement was in full swing—as were the Sixties.

SNCC workers began to refuse to post bond after being arrested while protesting and opted to stay in jail to serve out sentences. By remaining in, and filling up, local jails for petty charges like loitering or "breach of peace," for which bail could easily be posted, they dramatized their plight, garnered press attention, and clogged the system. Declining the bond option amounted to refusing to cooperate with one's oppressors, as nineteenth-century iconoclast Henry David Thoreau had done by refusing to pay his taxes in protest of the Mexican-American War. Most important, they felt, if more black activists and white sympathizers went to jail, then perhaps the fundamental fear of incarceration could be shattered, weakening the system's strongest hold on black people. Southern jails could be very dangerous places for incarcerated African Americans, subject to violent abuse away from the public gaze; however, jail would become a badge of honor for activists, not something to dread.

By the end of 1961, the young activists in SNCC and CORE were turning toward political action as the next logical step, and debating the relative values of direct action versus voter registration. One SNCC volunteer, Bob Moses, launched off to recruit help in Mississippi. A black Northerner and high school math teacher, Moses gained mythic status in the movement when he went to McComb, Mississippi, with Charles Sherrod and Marion Barry to establish clinics, or "freedom schools," to teach voter literacy to perspective registrants. With his reserved demeanor and quiet style of leadership, Moses embodied the SNCC strategy of partnering with local townspeople to effect long-term change. Culturally rich with a proud heritage, Mississippi was the most backward of the Deep South states, with its stark classism and violently enforced racial codes: if change could be had there, it could be had anywhere.

Other SNCC workers organized a voter registration project in southwest Georgia, in and around Albany, where they encountered Laurie Pritchett, the Albany police chief, in October 1961. Charles Sherrod, Cordell Reagon, and Charles Jones found Pritchett to be much different from the stereotypical, redneck sheriff they had come to expect in southern backwaters. Pritchett responded coolly to protests by whisking protestors off to jail quickly and quietly, without fanfare. Denied the dramatic, photographable moments, which made the front pages and evening news, the Albany campaign stalled. When Martin Luther King, Jr., and Ralph David Abernathy became involved and got arrested, someone paid their fines and they were released—even though they had wanted to remain in jail in solidarity with other demonstrators (it was later revealed that the mayor's law partner posted bail for King and Abernathy). At every turn, the actions of civil rights protestors were thwarted by the chief, who studied his enemies and read up on Gandhian nonviolence. If, however, Pritchett was "meeting nonviolence with nonviolence," as he claimed, then his brand was the kind that could only exist in a police state where freedom of speech, freedom of assembly, and equal protection of the law succumbed to eavesdropping, wiretapping, and massive lockups for "disorderly conduct," "tending to create a disturbance," and "parading without a permit." Gandhi he was not.

The city of Albany granted no concessions to its black citizens; but, with the understanding that the city would negotiate in good faith, civil rights leaders called off demonstrations there. As the Albany campaign lost momentum, city leaders reneged on their offer to negotiate, and the whole thing fizzled. Segregation remained in Albany—though it was weakened severely and would fall in a few short years.

Immediately after the Albany campaign, civil rights strategists began to plan a campaign to protest segregation laws in Birmingham, where they knew they could rely upon the rabid racism and violent tendencies of Bull Connor; but, in the interim, something happened that illustrated how the civil rights movement was not the product of any single organization, or group of organizations, or solitary charismatic leader. James Meredith's enrollment at the University of Mississippi in the fall of 1962 instead showed the movement to be the sum of the combined efforts of individuals who had become disgusted by unfair treatment and were brave enough to change it. Meredith's decision to attend Ole Miss was his own, and it was a brave decision at that. Though legally entitled to attend the university, he was not welcome there: Ross Barnett, the governor of Mississippi, attempted to block his enrollment. Students protested by rioting on the bucolic Oxford campus. Five hundred US Marshals were called in, along with National Guardsmen, US Army military police, and regular law enforcement personnel on the day of Meredith's enrollment; two people were killed in the ensuing melee that night. Meredith stuck it out, not only becoming the first black student at Ole Miss but also graduating with a degree in political science on August 18, 1963.

At the same time Meredith was preparing single-handedly to integrate Ole Miss, SNCC started a voter registration effort in Greenwood, Mississippi, a notoriously hardcore county seat in the Delta, early in the summer of 1962. The Voter Education Project financially supported the effort, which led to repression and violence by local whites, who burned four black-owned businesses and then arrested one of the business owners. Someone strafed a car driven by Bob Moses, Randolph Blackwell, and Jimmy Travis with machinegun fire; two other people were shot at; and someone fired a shotgun into the home of one person active in the voter drive. The office of the Council of Federated Organizations (COFO), an umbrella organization designed to coordinate the efforts of NAACP, SCLC, CORE, and SNCC workers in Mississippi, was set ablaze.

Meanwhile, King came to Birmingham in early 1963, at the behest of Rev. Fred Shuttlesworth. Demonstrations started at downtown department stores, followed by marches, sit-ins, and kneel-ins at local white churches. Protestors called the series of protests "Project C," as in "confrontation." White moderates urged a suspension of demonstrations, but local Negroes replied they had waited long enough. On April 7, Palm Sunday, protestors marched on a "prayer pilgrimage," followed by Bull Connor's officers with police dogs. As Connor declared, "We're not goin' to have white folks and nigras segregatin' together in this man's town."

King was arrested on Good Friday during a march, for parading without a permit. He was incarcerated for eight days. While in jail, a number of local white clergymen issued a statement calling his activities "unwise and untimely." King replied with a long letter, written on paper smuggled into the jail (including some toilet paper), which explained his hopes for the civil rights movement, as well as his involvement in it. He rejected the notion of being an "outside agitator," noted that critics of the movement tended to blame the victims rather than the perpetrators of racist violence, and explained the imperative to break unjust laws. "Nonviolent direct action seeks to create such a crisis and establish such a creative tension that a community that has constantly refused to negotiate is forced to confront the issue," he explained. "It seeks so to dramatize the issue that it can no longer be ignored… to create a situation so crisis-packed that it will inevitably open the door to negotiation." To those who suggested the protests were ill-timed, he suggested that freedom could not come soon enough to those suffering from segregation. "We must come to see that human progress never rolls in on wheels of inevitability." Reproached for being "extremist," King defanged the accusation by countering that Jesus Christ, Abraham Lincoln, and Thomas Jefferson were all extremists for love, justice, and equality, respectively: "So the question is not whether we will be extremist but what kind of extremist will we be. Will we be extremists for hate or will we be extremists for love? Will we be extremists for the preservation of injustice—or will we be extremists for the cause of justice?" He then soundly chastised the white, middle-class, Christian majority for preferring quiet conformity to social justice.

As was often the case after mass demonstrations had been conducted for a few days, the numbers of those who were willing to be arrested and jailed started to decline. Then, in a controversial decision at the beginning of May, SCLC sent children—some as young as six and seven years of age—into the streets to join in the protest. Connor arrested nearly a thousand of them, which provoked the outraged involvement of their parents and the undivided attention of the media. More children marched the next day, and this time Connor directed high-pressure fire hoses and police dogs at them and the other demonstrators. Photographs of these dramatic and excessive uses of force appeared in newspapers and television around the nation and the world, producing international revulsion. Still, the protests continued, the tensions heightened. On May 9, King announced an agreement that called for the commitment of downtown merchants to desegregation, progress in hiring and promotion of black employees, the release of jailed protestors, and the creation of a biracial committee to facilitate communication between blacks and whites in the city. Again, civil rights success came via mass black protest and the kneejerk reaction of bigots.

On June 11, 1963, President Kennedy announced he was sending a comprehensive civil rights bill to Congress. "The events in Birmingham and elsewhere have so increased the cries for equality that no city or state or legislative body can prudently choose to ignore them," he said. "We face, therefore, a moral crisis as a country and as a people… Next week, I shall ask Congress of the United States to act, to make a commitment it has not fully made in this century to the proposition that race has no place in American life or law." Kennedy's actions were called "the strongest ever made by a president on Negro rights." But such progress came, as was becoming alarmingly predictable, with ruthless violence by white segregationists. The day after Kennedy sent his bill down the long road to becoming a law, Medgar Evers, the NAACP field secretary in Mississippi, was murdered in Jackson. He was shot from ambush in front of his home in view of his wife and children. A white man, Byron de la Beckwith, was tried twice for the crime. Both trials ended in hung juries.

Despite such awfulness, or maybe because of it, street protests expanded throughout the South in the summer of 1963. A Justice Department study counted 758 demonstrations in 186 cities during the ten weeks after the Birmingham crisis. By the end of that year, the Southern Regional Council estimated that there had been 930 protests in 115 cities in the 11 Southern states, with more than 20,000 arrests, at least 35 bombings, and 10 deaths directly related to racial protests.

As protests spread, labor organizer A. Phillip Randolph proposed a march on Washington in early 1963 to commemorate the new national civil rights legislation. The idea met with resistance from the Kennedys; Roy Wilkins, president of the NAACP, was also skeptical, but later went along with CORE, SNCC, SCLC, the Urban League, and the Brotherhood of Sleeping Car Porters in the single greatest coalition of civil rights organizations, churches, and labor unions ever. Randolph, the most prominent black leader in the American labor movement, chose Bayard Rustin to coordinate and lead the march, officially known as the March on Washington for Jobs and Freedom. No one knew how many people would turn out for the August 28 demonstration, but more than two thousand chartered buses brought participants from all over the nation to Washington. In the end, a crowd estimated at more than a quarter million strong gathered along the Reflecting Pool at the Lincoln Memorial for a demonstration that was to become one of the major events of American history. Every logistical contingency was considered—from drinking water to toilets. The white press, along with government officials, predicted widespread violence and mobilized police accordingly, but no violence occurred. The day is remembered as a time when black and white people gathered together to celebrate democracy: a triumph of peaceful protest and free speech, and a celebration of how far black people had progressed in securing political equality. King's "I Have a Dream" speech crowned the day's activities. It was a high-water mark of the black freedom struggle.

Figure 4.2 Hundreds of thousands of demonstrators marched down Constitution Avenue during the 1963 March on Washington (Source: © Hulton Archive/Getty Images).

Despite the jubilant mood, some tensions did exist. SNCC's John Lewis, slated to speak, had prepared a speech critical of the Kennedy administration, but was pressured by other civil rights leaders to strike out faultfinding phrases. A few SNCC members expressed scorn at the lack of militancy of the march: they were beginning to move from supporting a civil rights movement that worked to secure a color-blind America to wanting a total renovation of the nation's economic and political systems. CORE's James Farmer remained in a Louisiana jail during the march as a gesture of protest, and a new voice joined King's critics, some of whom felt that he had betrayed the majority of black people by celebrating prematurely. Malcolm X, a young minister in the Nation of Islam, called the demonstration the "Farce on Washington," and wondered, "Who ever heard of angry revolutionaries swinging their bare feet together with their oppressor in lily-pad park pools, with gospels and guitars and 'I Have a Dream' speeches'?"

The good feelings left over by the success of Birmingham and the triumph of the 1963 March on Washington were short-lived, destroyed in a bomb blast just two weeks later. On September 15, dynamite rocked the 16th Street Baptist Church in Birmingham; four young black girls—two fourteen years old, one eleven, and one ten—were killed as the blast tore through their Sunday school classroom. Through the fall of 1963 (the one-hundredth anniversary of the Emancipation Proclamation), the black struggle had remained outwardly united, and an end to segregation appeared at hand; but the one-step-forward, two-steps-back headway of the movement—with every achievement now paid in blood—had become agonizing. No reform seemed to come easily, and it would take President Kennedy's assassination in November to create an outcry for peace and national harmony loud enough to spur Congress to sign his civil rights bill into law.

Segregationists were fighting against racial equality, and their resolve was every bit as powerful as that of civil rights activists. At perhaps no other time in US history did such hatred and opposition impede reform. Nor had there ever been such determination, unity, and clarity of purpose by black Americans to see that change occur: no number of bombings or beatings seemed to deter them. Still, the road between Montgomery and Birmingham was long, and equality far away.

Further Reading

Taylor Branch, *Parting the Waters: America in the King Years, 1954–1963* (New York: Simon & Schuster, 1988)

Harvard Sitkoff, *The Struggle for Black Equality*, rev. ed. (New York: Hill & Wang, 2008)

James M. Washington, ed., *A Testament of Hope: The Essential Writings and Speeches of Martin Luther King, Jr.* (New York: Harper Collins, 1991)

Clayborne Carson, *In Struggle: SNCC and the Black Awakening of the 1960s*, 2nd printing ed. (Cambridge: Harvard University Press, 1995)

Fred Powledge, *Free at Last? The Civil Rights Movement and the People Who Made It* (New York: Perennial, 1992)

David Chalmers, *And the Crooked Places Made Straight: The Struggle for Social Change in the 1960s*, 2nd ed. (Baltimore: Johns Hopkins University Press, 1996)

Barbara Ransby, *Ella Baker & the Black Freedom Movement: A Radical Democratic Vision* (Chapel Hill: University of North Carolina Press, 2005)

5

The Student Rebellion

In May 1960, The Kirby Stone Four released "Kids," a single of a production number from the musical *Bye Bye Birdie*, which had opened on Broadway a month earlier. The song became a smash hit. "Why can't they be like we were—perfect in every way?" the Four crooned. "What's the matter with kids today?" As the decade unfolded, more and more parents would come to wonder the same thing, scratching their heads as their offspring rebelled against the prosperous society they had worked so hard to create. Even today, one of the most compelling and complicated stories of the 1960s is how so many privileged, affluent, white youth began to see themselves as browbeaten and subjugated, identifying more with oppressed minorities than with their own parents and others of that generation.

The 1960s were a heady time to be young in the United States, and much has been made of Sixties-era youth. It was, after all, *their* decade—in part due to the sheer numbers of young people alive during the time. In the 1930s and early 1940s, the national birth rate had hovered between 2.3 and 2.8 million per year; in 1946—the first year after the end of World War II, when thousands of soldiers returned home to marry their sweethearts and start families—new births in the United States shot up to 3.4 million. Between 1946 and 1964, approximately 79 million American children were born in an unprecedented "baby boom." As their ranks swelled in the 1950s, this generation of young people could not be ignored. Typically neither seen nor heard in earlier times, these young people were not only acknowledged, but also valued (sometimes begrudgingly) as consumers, as citizens, and as potent new movers in American political life. Their involvement in the civil rights movement—not only as enthusiastic participants but as

The Long Sixties: America, 1955–1973, First Edition. Christopher B. Strain.
© 2017 Christopher B. Strain. Published 2017 by John Wiley & Sons, Inc.

strategists and leaders—would prove formidable, and their influence widened from there, affecting practically all aspects of American life before the decade's end. No atom bombs were dropped on the United States during this stretch of the Cold War, but the nation was nonetheless rocked by the baby boomers themselves: an explosion of unbuttoned exuberance in a buttoned-up adult world.

It is not clear whether John F. Kennedy intended to inspire young people specifically or simply intuited the potential of their latent energy when he called on his fellow Americans to ask not what they could do for themselves, but his words clearly tapped something, as young people hurled themselves into public life in a new way. Idealism and optimism carried some of them to developing nations as volunteers in the new Peace Corps, and others into political organizing and activism at home; still others, black and white alike, joined the fight against racial discrimination in the South. In 1962, representatives of the new Students for a Democratic Society (SDS) came together in Michigan to articulate a goal of creating a "New Left" in American polity. Protesting the ways in the which they saw their society as out of control—and specifically referencing the Cold War, the arms race, poverty, and racial discrimination—the homogeneous group of white college students and recent graduates helped set the mood for the decade by explaining why many students felt disaffected. Struggling for a greater voice in the decisions being made in their society, delegates from SNCC, SCLC, the National Student Association (a student-government organization founded in 1947 whose congresses mimicked political party conventions), the left-of-center Young People's Socialist League, and Young Democrats (the official youth affiliate of the Democratic Party) banded together in SDS to create a defining document of participatory democracy in the 1960s.

Drafted at a backwoods United Auto Workers (UAW) camp on the shores of Lake Huron, the SDS's Port Huron Statement was written primarily by field secretary Tom Hayden, a student editor at the University of Michigan. The statement was both a manifesto and critique of American society. Those who ratified it identified themselves as "people of this generation, bred in at least modest comfort, housed now in universities, looking uncomfortably on the world we inherit." Admitting their minority viewpoint, they accused the majority of fearing change, as most Americans lived empty and anxious lives, locked in a meaningless cycle of consumerism. In their estimation, inaction stemmed from inability, not indifference, because ordinary citizens no longer controlled their own fate; powerful elites and corporations, impersonal forces, manipulated the common man. The

students offered a corrective. "We would replace power rooted in possession, privilege, or circumstances," the statement proclaimed in a harbinger
of Flower Power, "by power and uniqueness rooted in love, reflectiveness,
reason, and creativity" to bring about "the establishment of a democracy of
individual participation." This participatory democracy would allow men
and women to join in making their own political and economic decisions;
to access knowledge to enable them to control their own lives; and to
re-enter the civic realm as empowered citizens.

The rest of the Port Huron Statement included a catalog of US failings
and further prescriptions for change: universities were isolated from the
rest of society and their student bodies were apathetic; the two major
political parties were so close on most issues of relevance as to afford the
voter no real choice; foreign policy derived from a militantly indiscriminate
anti-communism fed by the military-industrial complex; poverty and
inequality inexplicably continued to exist in a postwar nation of unprecedented wealth, even though the means to end them were well within reach.
To right all of these wrongs, the public sector should be enlarged, and the
nation should prioritize the public sector over the private one; Congress
should strengthen public housing and health insurance programs; the
United States should unilaterally disarm and refrain from foreign intervention; and the Southern wing of Democrats, the overtly segregationist
Dixiecrats, should be booted from the party. Organized labor, civil rights
volunteers, and other liberal activists would help initiate needed reform.

In hindsight, the solutions the members of SDS proposed in their call
to action were conventional and moderate. Relying on vague rhetoric to
express its aims, the statement's indictment of American life was not
particularly extreme, nor was the notion of participatory democracy
itself particularly original. Echoing not only Jeffersonian ideals but also
classic anarchism, the anti-authoritarianism and individualism in the Port
Huron Statement reflected a discomfort with institutions and bureaucracies
that would sometimes hinder SDS's effectiveness. Unlike the Old Left with
its revolutionary vanguard, the New Left recognized that the Soviet faith in
a small, disciplined party had led to an authoritarian regime marked by
brutal repression that perverted intent. So, even though many of the older
generation were quick to point to the New Left and young people in general
as "commies" or at least "pinkos," the students of SDS had no intention of
communizing the United States.

Despite its judicious approach—or perhaps because of it—the Port Huron
Statement had a significant impact. While their own role in retooling American

society was unclear, the students' notion of participatory democracy would prove refreshingly engaging, signaling a desire to reposition citizens in the political process. The document clearly identified the crucial problems in American democracy as it laid out an alternative vision of how Americans might lead more rewarding lives. Looking back, Hayden claimed that it felt "as though the Port Huron Statement wrote us, not the other way around."

Notably, the discontent of white students stemmed directly from interest and involvement in black civil rights. Having seen the power of protest in the South, they started to turn those methods of protest toward perceived injustices in their own lives. Many SDS leaders, for example, cut their political teeth in the struggle for black equality. In 1961, Tom Hayden married Casey Cason, a white YWCA project worker from Texas and active member of SNCC; the Freedom Rides later that year would serve as their honeymoon. Civil rights campaigns across the South, especially the sit-ins and Freedom Rides, invigorated not only black youth but also white youth: as black Southerners put their lives on the line for social justice, a small but committed cohort of sympathetic whites—mostly Northerners, with a few valiant Southerners salting the mix—stood shoulder to shoulder with them. It is no stretch to say that the student movement of the 1960s and the enormous changes in the ways young people thought, worked, and lived stemmed directly from the civil rights movement, which set the tone and pace of subsequent protests.

Nowhere were these changes felt more keenly than on university campuses. Acting *in loco parentis*, or "in place of the parent," college administrators had traditionally treated students like children. Through the early 1960s, undergraduates were subject to various restrictions on their private lives. Women, for example, were generally subject to curfews as early as 10:00 p.m. Single-sex dormitories were the norm. Some universities expelled female students deemed "morally undesirable" for violating strict visitation rules, including the "three feet on the floor" commandment of dorm mothers who insisted on open doors in the hopes of preventing petting from progressing too far. College administrators also restricted freedom of speech on campus by forbidding student organizations to address "off-campus" issues: organizing, demonstrating, or otherwise "causing a ruckus" on campus also were frowned upon. Students, not surprisingly, could find such restrictions stultifying, but such rules were reflective of a larger social order that encouraged conformity and consensus. The end of *in loco parentis* began in 1961, when the United States Court of Appeals for the Fifth Circuit found in *Dixon v. Alabama* that Alabama State

College could not summarily expel students without due process. It was the first tremor in a much bigger quake coming to American college campuses; in fact, much of the turmoil that embroiled American college campuses in the 1960s can be traced to the transition from authoritarianism and over-protectiveness to a new absence of paternalism in higher education.

Berkeley, California, was the epicenter of this quake. In the fall of 1964, a number of students at the University of California returned to the Berkeley campus from Freedom Summer, an intense civil rights campaign in Mississippi. Organizations like SNCC and CORE had recruited college students from across the nation to go to Mississippi to help boost the number of registered voters in the state; as of 1962, only 6.7 percent of eligible black persons in Mississippi were registered voters. Those young people who vol-unteered—predominately white, mostly Northern, many of them Jewish—came from elite colleges, including the University of California at Berkeley, the flagship university in the UC system. In Mississippi, the student volun-teers encountered vicious hostility from local whites determined to maintain segregation and dissuade black people from voting. Civil rights workers were harassed, beaten, and even killed by Klansmen and other local racists, who ran amuck, burning black churches and attacking local blacks and white volunteers with impunity. Punctuated by the murders of three civil rights workers—James Cheney, Andrew Goodman, and Michael Schwerner—at the hands of white racists, Freedom Summer ended with the formation of a new political party, the Mississippi Freedom Democratic Party, created to challenge the dominance of white Mississippians at the Democratic National Convention in Atlantic City (see Chapter 10).

Like other Freedom Summer participants, the Berkeley students returned to their studies energized by their dramatic and dangerous confrontations with hardcore Southern racists. As was customary, they distributed flyers, recruited converts, and solicited funds, along with other student activists at the corner of Telegraph Avenue and Bancroft Way, on what students believed to be city property, just outside the southern campus gate. When Katherine Towle, the dean of students, announced a new policy on September 14 that prohibited recruiting and soliciting funds for political causes on that corner (claimed by the school as campus property, hence-forth subject to all university rules and restrictions), the students protested, met with Dean Towle to petition their grievances, and continued to set up tables in violation of the ban.

Chancellor Edward Strong singled out protest leaders for sanction, indef-initely suspending them without a hearing. Not pleased by what they felt

Figure 5.1 Protestors pass beneath Sather Gate on the Berkeley campus in 1964 (Source: © The Oakland Tribune Collection, the Oakland Museum of California, Gift of the Alameda Newspaper Group).

was an arbitrary use of authority, students then scheduled a broader protest rally for October 1. At that rally, after police arrested graduate student Jack Weinberg for trespassing, students responded by surrounding the squad car. Thousands of students proceeded to sit down around the car, which could not move from the spot without running over someone. One by one, the most vocal students respectfully removed their shoes to stand on the hood of the car and describe a series of injustices that the university administration had perpetrated against them.

The speakers issued a torrent of complaints. They championed the right to assembly. They identified the alienation they felt in a gargantuan bureaucracy that robbed them of dignity and purpose. They mourned the loss of a liberal arts education in the face of increasingly professionalized curricular norms. They described being processed through the UC system by an inattentive faculty and unresponsive administration. They highlighted the break between the ideas they were taught and the expectation to disregard those ideas outside the classroom; in other words, they were being taught by their professors to think and act for themselves, but administrators, parents, and employers expected them to conform and not question. They bemoaned the attenuation of freedom of speech. Their biggest gripe was that they were tired of being treated like children. Signs, autocratic and restrictive, existed at every turn: do this, don't do that. While their problems were real and their complaints generally sound, the assembly was begrudging, abstract, and unfocused. They didn't know exactly what kind of place they wanted Berkeley to be, but they knew they didn't like what it had become. The protest lasted 33 hours, during which Weinberg languished in the back of the patrol car.

Over the next weeks and months the initial protests at Berkeley evolved into what the students termed the Free Speech Movement (FSM), a semester-long demonstration that grew to involve much more than free speech. Student organizations initially came together in a united front with no political agenda beyond that of the right to advocate. Young Democrats, Young Republicans, Youth for [Barry] Goldwater, and Students for a Democratic Society all came together with campus chapters of CORE and SNCC and other student groups to reaffirm the very right to organize. The socially engaged but apolitical nature of the protests reminded some observers of the syndicalists, anarchists, or Industrial Workers of the World (IWW) of the much earlier World War I generation; others took it less seriously, deeming the protest as little more than "a kind of socially conscious panty raid." But as the protests continued, they seemed to resonate with a student body unhappy with and resentful of how they fitted into the greater scheme of things.

On December 2, a massive sit-in was scheduled at Sproul Hall, the main campus administration building. Under an American flag, one thousand students filed up the front steps of the building with folksinger Joan Baez singing "We Shall Overcome" over a megaphone. At 4:00 a.m. the next day, the police moved in and began arresting people. More students subsequently went on strike in protest of the arrests. As national attention swiveled toward Berkeley, the larger student body began to mobilize, not just those liberal student activists who had initiated the Free Speech Movement. Even though their critics contended that none among those protesting were serious students in the first place, those who demonstrated actually represented the best at Berkeley: 47 percent of them had better than B averages; 71 of the graduate students in the crowd had averages between B and A; 20 were Phi Beta Kappa; 8 were Woodrow Wilson Fellows; 20 had published articles in scholarly journals; 53 were National Merit Scholarship winners or finalists; and 260 had received other academic awards.

Certain factors made the prestigious school ideally suited for the kind of student-rights movement that was emerging. Unlike some campuses (such as neighboring Stanford, serenely segregated from the town of Palo Alto), it was difficult to distinguish between Berkeley the town and Berkeley the university. A bohemian blend of ex-students, non-students, and part-timers invigorated a campus circumscribed by a city rich in the Bay Area's radical tradition. As one visiting professor noted, "There is no place in the world where uncomfortable people can feel so comfortable." Politically active, the campus was never quieted by the 1950s-era "Silent Generation" to the extent that other campuses were; more Peace Corps volunteers came from Berkeley than any other college or university. Furthermore, it was big (with more than 27,000 students), bureaucratic, and heavily tied to grant monies and defense contracts beyond the university. None of these traits alone made it unique, but the aggregate made Berkeley the ideal laboratory for student-driven reform.

Ironically, few college administrators were as well poised to handle such a crisis as was UC Berkeley's president, Clark Kerr, who less than two years earlier had delivered a series of lectures at Harvard in which he described a new educational system "held together by administrative rules and powered by money." Using the term "multiversity," Kerr described the transformation of the modern university into a vast techno-educational operation in the 1963 Godkin Lectures, later published as *The Uses of the University*. Kerr clearly had Berkeley in mind when defining the multiversity: with $246 million in a single year going to operate three giant atomic installations, plus $175 million in research grants and contracts, it had become an arm of the military-industrial complex of which Eisenhower had warned. Kerr also predicted that undergraduates would feel neglected and depersonalized in such an environment, with an emphasis on serving government and big business above tuition-paying students. In the great synecdoche of American higher education, students were reduced to ID numbers: human punch cards in an IBM world.

Still, Kerr misunderstood the deeper symbolism of the student groups' assembling on campus grounds. What the administration saw as a revoked privilege the students saw as a right trampled. At question was the concept of academic sanctuary and the relationship between academia and the larger world. Students sought to reclaim the university as their own. "What we have now," noted protest leader Mario Savio, a sophomore philosophy major, "is that the Pentagon, the oil and aircraft companies, the farm interests and their representatives in the Regents consider the university as a public utility, one of the resources they can look on as part of their business." Student leaders used the rhetoric of civil disobedience as they wondered aloud about the wisdom of trusting their elders. "We want a redemocratizing of the university," said Robert Starobin, a Ph.D. candidate and teaching assistant in the history department. "The seemingly inexhaustible energy which the Berkeley students had so long devoted to the struggle for Negro rights was now turned squarely on the vast, faceless University administration," Savio later recalled. "This is what gave the Free Speech Movement its initial impetus."

The movement quickly eclipsed the issue of free speech, and easy answers proved elusive for students seeking freedom from adult control. When President Kerr announced a compromise solution to 13,000 students and staff gathered in the open-air Greek Theatre on December 7, Mario Savio snatched the microphone after waiting for a chance to rebut; six policemen carried him offstage as he shouted and struggled, denied the opportunity to speak. As the semester drew to an end and students spoke of creating a nonprofit cooperative near campus—a coffeehouse for discussion and debates—it was becoming clear that Berkeley was only one dramatic manifestation of issues that stretched far beyond the main campus of the University of California. Officials eventually capitulated, allowing open political expression in certain places during certain hours.

At Berkeley it was easy, as student Margo Adler put it, "for students to feel they were being pressed out like so many pieces of sausage." The Free Speech Movement there sparked similar movements elsewhere, giving voice to pent-up feelings at universities nationwide. Again, while all of those who gathered in protest were not entirely clear about what they wanted to do, college students vociferously objected to the status quo. "I don't believe in the American ideal," said Garrett Lambrev of Stanford University. "Everything around me contradicts it." The football and dances and school spirit of early-Sixties collegiate life had begun to ring hollow for some. "These are games and lots of us don't want to play them," said Howard Romaine of the University of Virginia. "We want to deal with life and reality." Steven Block, a student at Williams College, spoke to the charge that students were acting out:

> Today most people look at students who are involved in protest as though we were still searching for an identity and not yet adjusting to our social situation. They see us as "not quite balanced." My parents, for example, still think I'm going through a phase. This common view of what we are all about is wrong—it completely misses the point. Many of us *have* found an identity. What we are trying to do now is to make our identity realizable... We believe

that there are some very fundamental problems in Western society. They have to do with our orientation toward consumption, toward materialism that doesn't account for truly human considerations.

David Smith, a student at Tufts University, noted simply that they were trying to change society. "In the 50s, the beat generation tried to run away from it [society]," he said. "My generation knows that we have to strike at the system to make it respond." If Berkeley was the first campus to erupt, best symbolizing the generalized student movement that would soon sweep the nation, then other schools were already quietly rioting, too (none *too* quietly, in actuality, as these protests came with a soundtrack—one that grew louder and more raucous as the decade progressed); likewise, the San Francisco Bay Area would become the destination of choice for those flower children interested in tasting the ripest fruits of the counterculture (see Chapter 8).

Of course, the perception that the multiversity infantilized students did occasionally relate to the fact that the students were behaving childishly. At times a protest begun in all seriousness might unfold flippantly, as when students from Berkeley and San Francisco State College "shopped-in" at a local supermarket chain that failed to hire black employees. Students filled a cart with groceries, let the cashier total the items, then left the cartful of stuff on the counter after "accidentally" coming up short on funds: a move which caused more headaches for cashiers and stock boys than it did for those doing the hiring. In some instances there existed a tension between the seriousness of a particular cause (e.g. protesting discriminatory hiring practices) and the inane ways protestors drew attention to that cause—and to themselves.

Such was the case when the Free Speech Movement of 1964 gave way to the "Filthy Speech Movement" of 1965. On March 3, John Thomson, a non-student radical attracted to Berkeley from New York by the publicity of the FSM, sat down on the steps of the Student Union and held up a piece of paper against his chest that read "Fuck." Demonstrations followed, with some shouting curse words and profanely supporting the right to say anything and others arguing that the issue badly detracted from the issue of free speech. Of nine persons arrested during the course of the disturbances only three of them were registered students. Their irreverence masked a serious intent: those involved saw their actions as a logical extension of the FSM. Others saw only a handful of vulgarians airing obscenities in public in the name of free speech. The episode convinced university administrators, state politicians, and the public at large that the Berkeley students were irresponsible and needed more discipline, not more freedom.

Some students increasingly reveled in reversions to childhood (playing, making jokes, or being irreverent, for example); if adults treated them as children, they reasoned, then they would act as children. Grown-ups saw hypocrisy in those young persons who demanded to be treated as adults even as they behaved idiotically, but to those youth enamored with their own hilarity, their goofing represented an essential ingredient missing from modern America. For them there was no hypocrisy in what they said and did, no tension between wanting to change the world and wanting to enjoy themselves. Adults had lost the ability to laugh, play, and have fun, and they themselves were not adults—not fully, not yet.

To be young (and white and middle or upper-class) in the 1960s was to be invigorated , hopeful, strong, and free. This verve often manifested itself in antipathy toward the older generation—the adults who, in the view of their progeny, had allowed America to stray off-course at best, or driven it into the weeds at worst. Accordingly, challenges to authority were often age-based and antagonistic, as reflected in the FSM motto "Don't trust anyone over thirty." By turns the older generation returned the sentiment, feeling less conflicted about shrugging away the concerns of young people as immature or childish; the counterculture's tendency toward frivolity, later exemplified by Abbie Hoffman and Jerry Rubin's antics as Yippies in the late 1960s (see Chapter 8), further justified such feelings. In this context, protest itself threatened to become a kind of youthful indulgence, as the bigger changes in youth culture, in norms and conventions, and in society itself created rifts, splitting families. In retrospect, of course, much of this generational friction was unwarranted and probably unnecessary. One of the lasting truths of the 1960s was that youth is a state of mind—a vitality, a playfulness unbounded by age. "Dr. Spock in his sixties was as much a child of that time," noted NBC journalist Tom Brokaw in 1989, "as was the barefoot girl in granny dress with daisies laced through her long blond tresses."

Regardless of the growing tensions between the older and younger generations, the transition from free speech to filthy speech symbolized a bigger shift in youth culture, from the political culture of reform to the cultural politics of revolution. A tension clearly existed between the seriousness of social reform—often youth-led in the 1960s—and the burgeoning youth rebellion, comprised of the now clichéd triumvirate of sex, drugs, and rock and roll. But few things captured this tension better than the music, which was becoming more revelatory and serious.

The predictable, three-chord, dance tunes of the 1950s gave way to newer forms of music that transcended region and especially race; whether rhythm-and-blues, folk, or rock, popular music defied the segregated norms of the day. Motown R&B, for example, provided hooks for black and white listeners alike, and in Motown young people found common ground across the racial divide. Berry Gordy, the president of Motown, rolled out chart-toppers from his Detroit-based music empire like cars off an assembly line. Smokey Robinson & the Miracles, Martha & the Vandellas, and Marvin Gaye all defined the Motown sound; Little Stevie Wonder evolved into a masterful musical savant, a keyboard wizard whose staggering repertoire of instruments included his own distinctive voice. Through all the craziness of the Sixties, one could still dance and sing along with Gordy's hit-makers: Motown remained a constant force throughout the decade, and soul singers like Aretha Franklin and Otis Redding moved both black and white feet.

In the early 1960s, singer-songwriters strummed folk music in campus taverns and in the coffeehouses of Greenwich Village, where Bob Dylan echoed the poignant questions raised by civil rights protestors; the answers, he suggested in a 1963 bestselling single, were "blowin' in the wind." Born Robert Allen Zimmerman—a middle-class Jewish kid from northern Minnesota—Dylan became a well-traveled musician, assuming the mantle of Woody Guthrie as America's lyrical poet laureate. With 100,000 copies sold a few months after its spring 1963 release, his second album, *The Freewheelin' Bob Dylan*, made him a star. Joan Baez and the folk trio Peter, Paul, & Mary appealed to the same bohemian fan base. The soft acoustic sounds of hit singles such as Barry McGuire's "Eve of Destruction" (1965) and Dylan's "Like a Rolling Stone" (1965) counterbalanced the songs' hard-edged, deeply political messages.

By mid-decade, rock supplanted folk as a portent of change, symbolizing the groundswell of youthful energy. African-American at its core, American rock music was electrified by the so-called "British invasion" of trans-Atlantic English rockers. Hordes of screaming teenage girls welcomed the Beatles on their first US tour in February 1964, as the singles "I Want to Hold Your Hand," "She Loves You," and "Please Please Me" reached number one in quick succession. Soon American teens were voicing their preference for either the Fab Four or their rougher counterparts, the Rolling Stones (most enjoyed both). Some of the greatest rock acts of the decade—including the Kinks, the Animals, the Yardbirds, and others—migrated "across the pond" from England. Influenced by earlier rock music in the States, the Brits borrowed heavily from Southern blues guitarists, whose riffs they appropriated and amplified. The rebellious tone of this music was matched only by the rebellious image of the musicians themselves.

Figure 5.2   Joan Baez performs with Bob Dylan at the Newport Folk Festival in Newport, Rhode Island, in 1963 (Source: © David Gahr/Getty Images).

Such was the cross-pollination of youthful forms and ideas that comprised the Sixties. Bohemianism and Beat culture blended with anti-establishment music into new forms of taboo-breaking in the mid-60s, when rock and roll, drugs, and protest began to swirl together into what would become the counterculture: a colorful parade of alternatives to mainstream lifestyle, fashion, and taste. Simultaneously, the civil rights movement and student-rights movement were melding with other social movements to become simply "The Movement": a disparate amalgam of dissidents, approving of youth-oriented and youth-directed change. Often indistinguishable, the counterculture and the Movement reshaped American youth, even as most did not actively join in.

This point bears emphasis. Though many dabbled in the tastes and the trends of the day, only a minority of young people participated wholeheartedly in the Sixties. Like young people of any era, the Sixties generation often shared little in common beyond their own youth. Not all who protested were "freaks," as countercultural proponents were sometimes called (a term they happily co-opted for themselves); not all who had sex advocated free love; and not all who did drugs had long hair, or vice versa. In fact, before there were hippies, there were simply young people, normal in appearance but discontent and yearning for change, trying new things, and pushing the limits of convention.

Eventually the counterculture would assume its own cultural norms—long hair (on young men), peasant blouses (on young women), and blue jeans (on both men and women) became instantly recognizable as anti-establishment badges—but those who came to the revolution of the latter decade could still pick and choose *a la carte*, sampling the counterculture like a buffet. The musical and cultural expressions of the 1960s were inescapably adolescent but the battle-lines of the cultural war they inspired were fluid. Like the Movement, the counterculture was difficult to define, identifiable more by what it stood against than by what it stood for. What ultimately unified this generation, then, was not fashion, or drug use, or free love, or even a desire for peace. It was an attitude of impatient expectation that aggressively reshaped American life along strikingly different lines.

For many young people in the 1960s, small wrongs and larger intolerables blurred together into patronizing norms that chafed and irritated. Serving subpar food in the campus dining hall, disregarding a religious holiday, suspending students for minor infractions of campus rules, continuing racial segregation, ignoring suffering in war-torn nations overseas—for the fully awake student, examples of injustice, big and little, could be found everywhere (as the Five Man Electrical Band would later sing, "Signs, signs, everywhere a sign..."). For that student, however, one issue in particular came to overshadow the rest—even as the civil rights movement made progress in the passage of the Civil Rights Act of 1964 and the Voting Rights Act of 1965. That issue was the war in Vietnam.

Further Reading

Hal Draper, *Berkeley: The New Student Revolt* (New York: Grove Press, 1965)

Seymour Martin Lipset & Sheldon S. Wolin, eds, *The Berkeley Student Revolt: Facts and Interpretations* (Garden City, N.Y.: Anchor, 1965)

Christopher G. Katope & Paul G. Zolbrod, eds, *Beyond Berkeley: A Sourcebook in Student Values* (Cleveland: World Publishing Co., 1966)

Jerry Farber, *The Student as Nigger* (New York: Pocket Books, 1969)

Robert Cohen & Reginald Zelnik, eds, *The Free Speech Movement: Reflections on Berkeley in the 1960s* (Berkeley: University of California Press, 2002)

Richie Unterberger, *Turn! Turn! Turn! The Sixties Folk-Rock Revolution* (Monclair, N.J.: Backbeat Books, 2002)

6

The Vietnam Quagmire

In May 1964, President Johnson announced the goal of a "Great Society," which "rests on abundance and liberty for all" and "demands an end to poverty and racial injustice." LBJ was serious about attacking these social ills to the point of completely eradicating them from American life. Signing a host of initiatives that Kennedy could not push through Congress—a tax cut, a civil rights bill, federal aid to education, and medical care for the aged and poor—LBJ also ramrodded through the House and Senate two landmark civil rights acts, an antipoverty program, an extensive housing program, and legislation to protect consumers, control pollution, and preserve the environment. The coarse Texan triggered a legislative avalanche to bury impoverishment and racism once and for all—to bring about a new United States, radically just in its prosperity. Yet, the America that Johnson hoped to create never came to pass, in part because LBJ's remarkable record of reform was decimated by the nation's involvement in a war in the far-away jungles of Vietnam—an involvement that Johnson himself deepened and formalized.

Picking up where his predecessor had left off, LBJ quickly eclipsed JFK in advancing his own vision of political reform. Leading the American people through the national trauma of the aftermath of Kennedy's assassination, Johnson asked Congress to act so that his predecessor "did not live or die in vain." Congress responded to Johnson's appeals with a tax cut, which Johnson signed in February 1964, and with the most sweeping civil rights legislation since Reconstruction: the Civil Rights Act of 1964, which outlawed discrimination in "public accommodations" and similarly prohibited discrimination by employers "on the basis of race, color, religion, sex, or national origin." Johnson also announced "an unconditional war on poverty"

The Long Sixties: America, 1955–1973, First Edition. Christopher B. Strain.
© 2017 Christopher B. Strain. Published 2017 by John Wiley & Sons, Inc.

in his first State of the Union address. "Unfortunately, many Americans live on the outskirts of hope—some because of their poverty, and some because of their color, and all too many because of both," said he. "Our task is to help replace their despair with opportunity."

Just two months later the White House sent a draft bill to Congress, and in August the president signed the Economic Opportunity Act of 1964, which authorized ten programs to be administered by the Office of Economic Opportunity, including: Head Start, a preschool program to prepare poor children for the 1st grade; Job Corps, to train both young people and adult heads of household in needed work skills; Volunteers in Service to America, or VISTA, which funded volunteers to work on behalf of the disadvantaged; work-study programs for college students; legal aid for those who needed lawyers; loans to businesses willing to hire the long-term unemployed and homeless; aid to small farmers and rural businesses; and the Community Action Program, or CAP, the most novel and controversial part of the law. CAP, which required "maximum feasible participation" of poor people themselves in coordinating local poverty programs, differed from other anti-poverty programs, which sought to equip the poor to succeed in the existing system. Through CAP, the urban poor began to organize to take control of their neighborhoods and to reform welfare agencies, school boards, police departments, housing authorities, and other agencies on which they relied (complaining that activists were using federal funds to attack local governments and "foster class struggle," big-city mayors would come to loathe CAP).

With Hubert Humphrey as his running mate, Johnson secured reelection in 1964 by defeating Barry Goldwater, the ultraconservative senator from Arizona who argued that "extremism in defense of liberty is no vice" ("Daisy," a controversial pro-LBJ television ad, depicted a little girl blown up in an atomic fireball, suggesting that Goldwater might endanger the United States with his reckless use of nuclear weapons). With his landslide victory at the polls and the help of Democratic majorities in the House and Senate, Johnson sought to actualize his Great Society. The White House focused on depressed regions that the general economic boom had bypassed and—in a new approach for the 1960s—promised to equip the poor with the training and skills necessary to find jobs, even as it promoted food stamps and rent supplements as direct aid. The president labored to pass numerous bills into law, and the ensuing flurry of legislation eclipsed the New Deal in scope. Reporters called the 89th Congress of 1965–1966 "unprecedented," "a political miracle"; organized labor called it "the most productive congressional session ever held," authorizing bold bills, cutting-edge programs, and entirely new government agencies. The Elementary and Secondary Education Act of 1965, Medicare and Medicaid, the Voting Rights Act of 1965 (which banned literacy tests at the polls as a requirement to vote and provided federal regis-trars to oversee registration and voting, thereby safeguarding the rights of blacks to vote in the South), the Department of Housing and Urban Development (HUD), the National Arts and Humanities Act (which created the National Endowment for the Arts and the National Endowment for the Humanities), the Water Quality Act of 1965, the Immigration and Nationality Act, the Air Quality Act, the Higher Education Act, a food stamp program—all came out of the 89th Congress.

On September 24, 1965, LBJ signed Executive Order 11246, which banned discrimination by any employers awarded government contracts and required them to "take *affirmative action* to ensure *equal opportu-nity*"—two famous phrases that symbolized the Johnson administration's commitment to racial justice—and Johnson was on his way to becoming one of the most dynamic and courageous presidents in US history. After 1966, the flood of legislation slowed to a trickle, but the Great Society would still see the passage of the National Traffic and Motor Vehicle Safety Act (1966), the Highway Safety Act (1966), the Department of Transportation, the Model Cities Act (1966), the Civil Rights Act of 1968, and the National Housing Act (1968). All told it was nothing short of astonishing.

Given all that, one might well wonder why, instead of becoming one of the most revered presidents of twentieth century, even before he left office LBJ had become one of the most reviled. The answer, in a word, was Vietnam. Indeed, it was his decisions about the level of US involvement in a Southeast Asian conflict waged in what Johnson himself once referred to as a "raggedy-ass fourth-rate country" that, like quicksand, sucked in the 36th President of the United States and never let him go, swallowing his political career. The situation in Vietnam was vast and complex and the road to American involvement long and tortured, neither beginning nor ending with Johnson; it was, however, also a logical and to some degree predictable outcome of US foreign policy in the aftermath of World War II.

French attempts at religious conversion in Indochina in the seventeenth century had devolved by 1847 into a forcible effort to colonize Vietnam; 36 years later the French colonizers could claim a tenuous success, and soon thereafter the French controlled vast rubber plantations across Vietnam. No sooner had the French guns quieted, however, than Vietnamese nationalists began to work to rid themselves of foreign domination, against which they chafed for nearly a century, until World War II. In 1940 the Japanese invaded French Indochina and would occupy it until the end of the fighting. It was also during the war that a new, militant, pro-Vietnamese independence organization emerged; called the Vietminh, it had been formed under the Communist leadership of Ho Chi Minh (an ardent admirer of American democracy) to militate against all foreign occupiers of Vietnam, French and Japanese alike, who had designs on Vietnam's rich natural resources and deep-water ports. With Japan's defeat, in the chaotic aftermath of World War II, the Vietminh announced the beginning of a free and independent Vietnam. Under pressure from the British and French, President Franklin Delano Roosevelt—initially supportive of Vietnamese liberation—tempered his enthusiasm for the anti-imperialist cause. FDR's successor, Harry Truman, under pressure to appease the French in order to secure their cooperation in the postwar security pact of Western Europe in the face of Soviet aggression, went further in supporting France's bid to reassert influence in the region and retake control of its erstwhile colony, Vietnam. Under President Truman, the United States increased anti-communist aid to the region.

In the postwar power struggle between the United States and the USSR, the fate of Indochina carried great significance for those strategists worried about the spread and possible global domination of communism. Experts in the US State Department, Department of Defense, National Security Council, Central Intelligence Agency, and Pentagon noted Vietnam's strategic importance as a stepping stone for China—and by proxy for the Soviet Union—to Japan and other Pacific-rim nations. If Vietnam fell to communism, they posited, nearby countries might be the next to fall to the red menace. When, in 1950, Communist North Korea attacked US-supported South Korea—only to be backed to the hilt by China—these designs seemed all too real. American planners saw the Vietminh not as freedom fighters in the tradition of the Minute Men at Concord and Lexington, but rather as dangerous destabilizers and levelers: enemy agents in the communist takeover of the world.

President Eisenhower used a vivid metaphor to describe the perceived threat. "You have a row of dominoes set up, you knock over the first one, and what will happen to the last one is the certainty that it will go over very quickly," he told the American people. "So you could have a beginning of a disintegration that would have the most profound influences." The dominoes teetered when General Vo Nguyen Giap's forces surrounded 11,000 French soldiers (with superior firepower) at a valley stronghold known as Dienbienphu and, after eight weeks of relentless bombardment, forced a permanent and embarrassing French withdrawal. A day later, an agreement reached at the Geneva Conference—with representatives from France, Great Britain, the Soviet Union, the United States, China, Cambodia, Laos, and Vietnam—resulted in a ceasefire between the French and the Vietminh and the geopolitical division of Vietnam roughly in half from north to south, directly along the 17th parallel. The Eisenhower administration supported the installment of Ngo Dinh Diem, a devout Catholic in a land less than 15 percent Catholic, to head the anti-Communist government of South Vietnam. Expecting an invasion of communist troops from the north, just as had happened in Korea a few years earlier, the Americans and the South Vietnamese were surprised instead by widespread guerrilla actions undertaken by the Vietminh, by the indigenous Communist insurgents with direct ties and supply lines running up to North Vietnam, and by anti-Diem forces inside South Vietnam who opposed his dictatorial regime on political and religious grounds. This coalition the government in Saigon lumped together as the "Vietcong."

President Kennedy's brain trust understood the complexity of the situation in Vietnam, although his advisors disagreed about the best course of action; accordingly, JFK chose a middle path between withdrawal and full military commitment. Kennedy sent millions of dollars of weapons and equipment, along with small numbers of military "advisors"—commandos, counterinsurgents, and black-ops experts—to fortify the South Vietnamese in what had become a civil war with North Vietnam. The number of Americans in South Vietnam—officially present only to counsel, but who often took up arms themselves—crept from fewer than a 1000 in 1961 to more than 5000 by mid-1962, as South Vietnamese peasants were forced into fortified villages, or "strategic hamlets," to segregate friendlies in areas controlled by the Vietcong.

At this point, members of JFK's brain trust, led by Secretary of State Dean Rusk, began to call for escalation. "North Vietnam will never beat us," chimed in Secretary of Defense Robert McNamara. "They can't even make ice cubes." Diem, ignoring American suasion while becoming less tractable, became widely reviled by his own people as he aggressively attacked the Buddhist majority. In one of the more horrific episodes in what was already becoming a horrifying conflict, Buddhist monks protested Diem's regime by calmly dousing themselves with gasoline and setting themselves on fire in public; cameras rolled and the world watched as the monks let themselves burn to death. Not surprisingly the American public began to wonder out loud why Diem, presumably a trustworthy US partner and ally, was so

82 The Long Sixties

loathed by his own citizens that they would resort to self-immolation in the streets of Saigon. Few mourned when, after eight years of US support, Diem was assassinated in a successful coup d'état, assisted by the CIA. Three weeks later, Kennedy himself was gone too, but not before having escalated America's commitment to and presence in Vietnam.

When Lyndon Johnson became President after Kennedy's assassination, the United States had 15,000 military advisors in Vietnam. As commander-in-chief, LBJ was determined that it would not be he who would "lose" Vietnam to communism. Like President James Polk, who seized upon an 1844 skirmish on the Rio Grande as an excuse for war with Mexico, Johnson exploited the flimsiest of pretexts to ramp up the level of US commitment to the conflict in Vietnam. In August 1964 he used sketchy reports that two American destroyers in the Gulf of Tonkin had come under fire from North Vietnamese gunboats to commit further, asking Congress to authorize him "to take all necessary measures to repel any armed attack against the forces of the United States and to prevent further aggression." Without a formal declaration of war, LBJ used the Gulf of Tonkin Resolution to intensify US

Figure 6.1 Thich Quang Duc, a Buddhist monk, burns himself to death on a Saigon street on June 11, 1963, to protest alleged persecution of Buddhists by the South Vietnamese government. This photo by Malcom Browne won a Pulitzer Prize (Source: © Malcolm Browne/AP/Press Association Images).

involvement in Vietnam, mobilizing regular troops for deployment. From that point forward the conflict became known to many as "Johnson's War," with Congress having surrendered much of its influence and oversight in the matter.

Only with the Gulf of Tonkin Resolution did the realization dawn on the American public that the United States was already deeply involved in the war in Vietnam. Many fighting men believed it was their duty to carry the battle against communism to the Far East before it crossed the Pacific and reached the West Coast. "We are primarily, basically, protecting our homeland," explained one US airman. "This [Vietnam] is a long way off, but this is our job here—to protect our people at home before the situation reaches them as it is here." By the end of the year, 23,000 US military personnel were in South Vietnam. But the escalation continued, then accelerated. Early in 1965 American B-52s commenced carpet-bombing raids over the border in North Vietnam; by the end of that year, the number of US troops in Vietnam had climbed to 184,300.

To those officials who maintained the necessity of having American combat troops fighting in Vietnam to help the South Vietnamese government and its military, the Army of the Republic of Vietnam (ARVN), a small but strident chorus of dissenters voiced their complaint. US participation in another nation's civil war was, they argued, illegal, a violation of international law and a breach of the 1954 Geneva Accords in which the United States had pledged to refrain from force. It was unconstitutional, as there had been no formal declaration of war by Congress. And it was illegitimate, meddling in a family quarrel that was none of our business. In protest of the US involvement in the war in Vietnam, scholars at the University of Michigan organized an all-night "teach-in" for professors, instructors, adjuncts, and students; by late 1965, about 120 colleges and universities had held similar teach-ins to discuss and debate the war. On November 2, another person set himself on fire—this time a 31-year-old Quaker pacifist named Norman Morrison, who poured kerosene over himself and lit a match as he stood below Secretary of Defense McNamara's third-story office window at the Pentagon. Like Thích Quảng Đức, the Buddhist monk whose death by self-immolation in 1963 was captured in a Pulitzer-Prize-winning photo, Morrison committed suicide in protest of the actions of his nation's leaders.

With anti-communism trumping all other concerns, however, President Johnson's decisions in 1964 and 1965 to heighten the US military presence in Southeast Asia raised few eyebrows. As the latest front in the global war on communism, Vietnam seemed like a necessary point of intervention, an unavoidable battleground in the Reds' spread. Those who favored American intervention argued that the fate of Vietnam had profound consequences for US national interest and the safety of the free world; that a democratic Vietnam was crucial in the East-West struggle against the Soviets and Chinese; that if Vietnam toppled, other nations in Southeast Asia would soon follow; and that failure to engage in Vietnam would invite communist insurgencies in dozens of other hotspots around the globe. The official position of the United States was that North Vietnam was aggressively threatening its peaceful, weaker neighbor to the south.

The firepower that the United States brought to bear in Vietnam was fearsome; seemingly limitless resources plus technological superiority equaled an unparalleled ability to deal death. For example, the WWII-era C-47 Skytrain, the military version of the Douglas DC-3 passenger aircraft, proved itself again in Vietnam, where it was rechristened the AC-47 Spooky and outfitted with triple M134 "Miniguns," multi-barreled Gatling guns capable of firing 18,000 rounds a minute (a rate capable of aerating a football field, one bullet in each square foot, in three seconds). Nicknamed the "Dragon Ship" by the North Vietnamese and "Puff the Magic Dragon" by US troops, the AC-47 could bank up to 60 degrees as it spewed a continuous stream of tracers, resembling nothing more than a rope of fire from the plane to the target (and sounding more like a buzz saw than a machine gun). US forces liberally used napalm, a jellified gasoline, as an anti-personnel weapon that stuck to skin and melted flesh; to expose the enemy, they defoliated the landscape with Agent Orange, a toxic chemical that not only burned away the jungle but also contaminated friend and foe alike, reappearing years later as cancer. By the end of the war, seven million tons of bombs had been dropped on Vietnam, Laos, and Cambodia—more than three times the amount of bombs dropped in World War II by US planes on Europe and Asia combined. The weaponry and tactics—including bombing itself, a morally distasteful practice as late as WWII—lent the impression of the wealthiest, most advanced nation in human history waging a campaign of annihilation against a poor peasant society.

It seemed—on paper, at least—to be a decidedly lopsided matchup, but the enemy held their own, working several non-material factors to their advantage. Because all ground fighting took place south of the 17th parallel, the resourceful Viet Cong guerillas knew the terrain well. And, whether NVA regulars or Viet Cong guerrillas, they fought with a strong, unshakable conviction, viewing themselves as freedom fighters trying to reunify their country. Such intangibles would prove crucial in wearing down and outlasting the Americans.

By day US troops would ride from secure zones into enemy territory— "Indian country," they called it—via helicopter, essentially commuting to and from combat. By night they ran sorties, "search and destroy" missions in which they sought to find the enemy and kill him; Long Range Reconnaissance Patrols, or LRRPs ("Lurps"), aimed to carry the fight into the jungle after dark (according to war correspondent Michael Herr, "night was the war's truest medium"). Progress was measured not in gaining or holding territory but in counting the enemy dead—the "body count." In late 1968, the CIA reported that US attempts to find and engage the enemy succeeded less than one in one hundred tries on average. Instead, combat patrols found booby traps and mines—which led to the impression of an invisible, wraith-like enemy. The Purple Heart, awarded to soldiers wounded in combat—"the oldest medal," noted one journalist, "no fun to win"—was ubiquitous, with more than 250,000 earned, many of them courtesy of trip wires, deadfalls, and sniper fire.

Stories trickled home about terrible things done not only by the enemy but also by US troops, maddened by what they found and exasperated by what they did not find. "Both we and the Viet Cong began to make a habit of atrocities," one officer testified. The difficulty that some servicemen had—in the heat of battle, in the fog of war—in distinguishing between enemy combatants and civilians led to an unwritten rule: if he's dead and Vietnamese, he's VC. "The men went looking for the enemy, but the enemy didn't oblige," noted a CBS war correspondent in 1965. "Frustration is now as much a part of their diet as C-rations, in a war in which they're bullies for browbeating women and cripples, and maybe dead fools if they don't."

The right and wrong of it all blurred for many soldiers as the war progressed. "Ethics seemed to be a matter of distance and technology," according to Philip Caputo, a US Marine Corps lieutenant. "You could never go wrong if you killed people at long range with sophisticated weapons." Deployed to South Vietnam in 1965, Caputo commanded a rifle platoon in the 1st Battalion of the 3d Marine Division. "There was nothing we could not do because we were Americans," he would later write, "and for the same reason, whatever we did was right." In the country for fifteen months, Caputo described a confused and confusing effort to engage and defeat the enemy:

> Without a front, flanks, or rear, we fought a formless war against a formless enemy who evaporated like the morning jungle mists, only to materialize in some unexpected place. It was a haphazard, episodic sort of combat. Most of

the time nothing happened; but when something did, it happened instanta-
neously and without warning. Rifle or machine-gun fire would erupt with
heart-stopping suddenness, as when quail or pheasant explode from cover
with a loud beating of wings. Or mortar shells would come in from nowhere,
their only preamble the cough of the tubes…

Forming a column, my platoon started toward its first objective, a knoll on
the far side of the milky-brown stream. It was an objective only in the
geographical sense of the word; it had no military significance. In the vacuum
of the jungle, we could have gone in as many directions as there were points
on the compass, and any one direction was as likely to lead us to the VC, or
away from them, as any other. The guerrillas were everywhere, which is
another way of saying they were nowhere. The knoll merely gave us a point
of reference. It was a place to go, and getting there provided us with the
illusion we were accomplishing something.

Initially gung-ho, the 24-year-old officer found himself alternating between
bloodthirstiness and cold indifference, slowly cracking under the pressure
of a kind of fighting for which he and his men were ill-prepared. The war
would continue—SNAFU if not FUBAR, to borrow two military acronyms
for a situation gone awry—for another nine years after Caputo left in 1966,
when he was acquitted of murder in the deaths of two South Vietnamese
civilian informants (while avoiding court martial, he was still found guilty
of submitting a false statement under oath), and so "learned the wide gulf
that divides the facts from the truth." He returned to Saigon in 1975 as a
correspondent for the *Chicago Tribune*; having been among the first
Americans to fight in Vietnam, he was among the last to be evacuated, a
few hours before the North Vietnamese Army entered the capital. His
personal account, *A Rumor of War* (1977), remains one of the best war
exposés ever written, "an attempt to capture something of [Vietnam's]
ambivalent realities."

For the young men under Caputo's command, the Marines offered a
guaranteed annual income, free medical care, free clothing, "and something
else, less tangible but just as valuable—self-respect," benefits that sometimes masked the conflict's classist undercurrents. Many of the young men
who had been drafted and served in Vietnam had grown up poor, "from
city slums and dirt farms and Appalachian mining towns." The US fighting
force relied on conscription. With eligibility for military service beginning
at age 18, the average age of US soldiers in Vietnam was incredibly low, 19.
About one-third of those who fought in Vietnam were drafted; but, for
every man drafted, another seven were exempted from service, often

Figure 6.2   American infantrymen crowd into a mud-filled bomb crater and look up at tall jungle trees seeking out Viet Cong snipers firing at them during a battle in Phuoc Vinh, north-northeast of Saigon in Vietnam's War Zone D, June 15, 1967 (Source: © Henri Huet/AP/Press Association Images).

excused in pursuit of higher education. All college students were automatically deferred until 1973, graduate students until 1968—but it was not simply college students who managed to get deferments from their local draft boards. Engineers, scientists, teachers, and supervisors of four or more employees were excused, as were apprentices for plumbers and electricians. Enterprising young men who proved their service at home was valuable also could be exempted; after student deferments ran out, scions of affluent families could still pull strings and call in favors to wriggle out of service. Those less well connected might head for Canada to ride out the war; but, in short, those with smarts or money or both could avoid military service if they so desired. As a result, the fighting of the war in Vietnam was primarily left to poor and working-class men. Such factors led many Americans to see Vietnam as a rich man's war and a poor man's fight.

Scared draftees and the women who loved them—worried mothers, wives, and girlfriends—increasingly spoke out. With the draft pulling more young men into the fray each year, and with more questions being raised about the justification for the US mission and how it was being executed, demonstrations against the war widened. Sometimes it was a candlelight vigil, sometimes a rally with several hundred in attendance. Some recruits burned their draft cards and some fled the country in order to evade conscription. Early on, the most visible anti-war protests were those held on college campuses, but young people were only one demographic who participated in antiwar protests. Clergymen and older women often organized and led their own anti-war protests as the anti-war movement incorporated people from all backgrounds, ages, regions—people who shared little beyond an opposition to the involvement of US forces in the war in Vietnam. Interestingly, as the war continued, many of those who protested against it were those who had once fought in it: combat veterans formed Vietnam Veterans Against the War, in June 1967, to petition for peace.

The war in Vietnam had its own language, comprised mainly of military jargon designed to whitewash the horror. Combat wounds merited their own euphemisms: "GSW" (gunshot wound), "multiple fragment lacerations" (shrapnel wound), "traumatic amputation" (losing a limb), "response-to-impact" (limbs wrenched into awkward positions by violent trauma), and "sympathetic detonation" (getting killed by your own grenade). Some of the aphorisms, like "friendly fire" (being shot by a fellow servicemen) or "acute anxiety (or depressive) reaction" (shell shock, also known as "post-traumatic stress disorder"), were easy to figure out; others, such as "harassment and interdiction" ("H&I," probing artillery fire to aggravate the enemy) and "meeting engagement" (ambush), less so. Even gunfire had its own terminology: "discrete burst," "prime selection," "constructive load." The soldiers rooted out the Vietcong, or VC—"Victor Charlie" in the NATO phonetic alphabet, soon shortened simply to "Charlie." Racist epithets for the Vietnamese included "gooks," "slopes," "slants," and "dinks." There were "soft-boiled" VC villages with tunnels and propaganda, and "hard-boiled" VC villages with booby traps and concrete fortifications. Napalmed corpses were sometimes referred to as "crispy critters."

The gallows humor that struck most listeners as callous (when asked how he could shoot women and children, a door gunner apocryphally replied, "It's easy, you just don't lead 'em as much") allowed soldiers to slog through the literal and figurative mire in order to survive. Demoralization was rampant, drug use common—so much so that the military instituted drug testing and rehab programs in the late 1960s. The high and growing incidences of mutiny, desertions, and "fraggings"—the intentional murder of officers by their own men, sometimes with a fragmentation grenade—indicated not only a breakdown in order but also a kind of ethical anarchy in which moral compasses spun like gyroscopes. "Every time there was combat you had a license to go maniac," reported Michael Herr. "Going crazy was built into the tour."

On March 16, 1968, the men of Charlie Company, 11th Brigade, Americal Division entered the village of My Lai, in VC territory 335 miles northeast of the South Vietnamese capital, Saigon. Under the command of Lieutenant William Calley, the search-and-destroy mission quickly degenerated into a massacre of more than three hundred unarmed civilians, many of them women, children, and elderly persons. According to eyewitness reports, several old men were bayoneted, women and children in the act of kneeling and praying were shot in the back of the head, and at least one girl was raped and killed; Lt. Calley himself allegedly rounded up a group of villagers, ordered them into a ditch, and mowed them down with a machine gun. The military charged Calley with murder in September 1969; word of the atrocities committed at My Lai did not reach the American public until November 1969, when journalist Seymour Hersh published a story detailing the horror (Calley was sentenced to life in prison but released in 1974, after many appeals). Americans were horror-struck, left to wonder what other outrages were being committed in Vietnam on their behalf. Anti-war protests which had once counted hundreds and thousands of demonstrators now drew tens of thousands, sometimes hundreds of thousands.

On July 31, a photographer captured LBJ rubbing his temple while listening to an audiotape sent by his son-in-law, Captain Charles Robb, who described the anguish of watching young soldiers under his command die in battle. Looking like a chronic migraine sufferer, Johnson was in fact a broken man by 1968, when the number of US military personnel serving in Vietnam crested at half a million, and when he himself faced re-election. Choosing instead not to seek his party's nomination, Johnson simply quit, passing the war on to his successor, Richard M. Nixon.

In his defense, Johnson was held responsible not only for his own mistakes but also for mistakes made by Presidents Eisenhower and Kennedy, and if LBJ had been duped, then so too were America's best strategists and military men. Like France, the United States inherited a fierce Vietnamese resistance to foreign interference and control; like the French, the Americans were out of their element. The whole affair was botched, perhaps from the very start; but, once begun Johnson could neither end it nor admit defeat, and such was his undoing. While Johnson's downfall was more complicated than any single contributing factor, the decline of his Great Society unquestionably

Figure 6.3   A candid photo of a war-weary LBJ, captured after the 1968 Tet Offensive by White House photographer Jack Kightlinger (Source: © LBJ Library photo by Jack Kightlinger).

paralleled the failure of his efforts in Vietnam: the worse things got overseas, the more the war overshadowed his legacy of reform. As Martin Luther King, Jr., lamented, "The promises of the Great Society have been shot down on the battlefields of Vietnam."

Whatever illusions about the glory of war still remained after World War II and the Korean War, evaporated in the steamy jungles of Vietnam. Never an official US war (Congress never formally declared war, instead passing a joint resolution to authorize force), the protracted conflict in Vietnam was notable insofar as the United States failed to win. In this sense it was unique, America's first lost war. And while participants and observers often commented on the particular savagery of jungle combat in Vietnam, in another sense what happened in Vietnam was not unique at all—familiar, even, in its destruction and inhumaneness. As Philip Caputo concluded, "I guess every generation is doomed to fight its war, to endure the same old experiences, suffer the loss of the same old illusions, and learn the same old lessons on its own."

What those lessons were is still open to interpretation, often depending on attitudes and opinions about the war itself. For some, the main lesson was that the United States should have shown more restraint, toning down its bellicose methods to secure its national interest. Committing US military power requires enormous judiciousness; might does not make right. For others, the primary lesson was quite the opposite. The US should have come harder and stronger into Vietnam, with more force, more ruthlessness, and more bombing, particularly in northern cities. The second guessing and lack of full commitment to all-out victory on the part of politicians handcuffed the generals, and in turn both imperiled and humiliated the men and women who had fought for their country; in this view the failure in Vietnam was a top-down failure to commit wholly to winning the war.

There are in fact a myriad of so-called "lessons of Vietnam," many of them facile attempts to reduce a complex event to glib axioms. *Don't trust the government. Never get involved in a land war in Asia.* One of these axioms—*War is hell*—was the only lesson on which Americans could find consensus; tragically and ironically, it also happens to be one of Caputo's "same old lessons," no sooner learned in war than forgotten in peacetime. There also remains another possibility, unsettling in its implications: that there were *no* lessons of Vietnam, that there was no deeper meaning in the chaos. Dug in near the DMZ in 1965, one grunt suggested as much—in unvarnished Marine-speak—while bailing a leaky, sandbagged foxhole with his helmet. "Goddamn motherfuckin' Nam," he sighed.

As friends and classmates were shipped overseas to fight an increasingly unpopular conflict, and as draft resistance became a primary tool of dissent, young women reached limits in their power to protest. With no draft cards to burn, they could only voice disapproval and demonstrate, relating to the war through the men in their lives. Frustrated by this secondary role, some found a new slogan—and a new foe as well. "Girls Say Yes to Guys Who Say No!" became a popular cry at antiwar rallies; in that maxim, women not only objected to the war but also leveraged control over men. The phrase presaged a new development, one that would explode into a movement that would directly affect more than half the population and indirectly affect everyone else.

Further Reading

Walter Cronkite, ed., *CBS News Special Report: Vietnam Perspective* (New York: Pocket Book Special, 1965)

Philip Caputo, *A Rumor of War* (New York: Holt, Rinehart, and Winston, 1977)

Michael Herr, *Dispatches* (New York: Avon, 1977)

David W. Levy, *The Debate Over Vietnam*, 2nd ed. (Baltimore: Johns Hopkins University Press, 1995)

George C. Herring, *America's Longest War: The United States and Vietnam, 1950–1975*, 3rd ed. (New York: McGraw-Hill, 1996)

Patrick J. Hearden, *The Tragedy of Vietnam*, 2nd ed. (New York: Pearson Longman, 2005)

James S. Olson & Randy Roberts, *Where the Domino Fell: America and Vietnam, 1945–1995*, rev. 5th ed. (New York: Blackwell Publishing, 2008)

Gary R. Hess, *Vietnam: Explaining America's Lost War* (New York: Wiley-Blackwell, 2009)

7

Sex, Gender, and the New Feminism

In the documentary *Makers: The Women Who Make America* (2012), Ruth Bader Ginsburg recalls being one of nine women in a class of 500 men at Harvard Law School in 1954. She remembers being shepherded with her female classmates into a room where a law professor asked why they were occupying seats that could be filled by men. Offended but undeterred, Ginsburg would later transfer to Columbia University, where she became the first woman on two major law reviews: the *Harvard Law Review* and the *Columbia Law Review*. In 1959, she finished first in her class; yet, despite a strong recommendation from the dean of Harvard Law School, she was turned down for a clerkship the following year because she was a woman (such experiences would lead her to become an advocate for women's rights as a constitutional principle). She later returned to Columbia—this time as a faculty member—before becoming Associate Justice of the Supreme Court of the United States and only the second female Supreme Court Justice (Sandra Day O'Connor preceded her on the bench).

Ginsburg's story is unique only in the heights of her accomplishments, not in the discrimination she faced along the way. Millions of women faced routine discrimination—and millions more would continue to face it at work, at school, and at home were it not for the efforts of a stalwart few in the 1960s. Women's rights did not just happen. They were earned by women who refused to accept that their gender was an obstruction, who fought and broke barriers, and who made things happen so that subsequent generations of women would be free to work in the marketplace alongside men as equals; to become doctors, scientists, lawyers, and legislators; to expect help with childcare and housework (or to define themselves as

The Long Sixties: America, 1955–1973, First Edition. Christopher B. Strain.
© 2017 Christopher B. Strain. Published 2017 by John Wiley & Sons, Inc.

something other than mothers or housewives, if they so desired); and to explore their bodies and enjoy sex. Like other social movements of the 1960s, the women's movement was a hard-fought battle, the freedoms won still relatively fresh—but it differed from other contemporaneous movements in profound ways.

Since the beginning of World War II, the number of women in the paid workforce had steadily increased, and the number of forty-something, married women with jobs rose after the war, too. More women were going to colleges and universities, acquiring new skills and expectations not easily satisfied within the domestic sphere. In 1960, however, gender roles remained traditional, with men working outside the home and women supporting those efforts, while raising families and managing the home. Stereotypes and imbalanced ideals often underpinned these traditional roles. The family breadwinner was still assumed to be a man, while a woman was assumed to be a kind of domestic goddess if married, a ready supplicant awaiting a suitor if not. Men were expected to bring home the bacon and women were expected to do virtually everything else, including caring for the children and shepherding them to and fro.

A young single woman might work, but usually only as a secretary and only until she was swept up by a male co-worker—her boss, perhaps—who would expect her to quit and cheerfully assume the duties of housewife: shopping, cooking, cleaning, laundering, hosting, entertaining and, most important, waiting on him hand and foot. Direct sexual advances by male employers and co-workers, unsolicited and unwanted physical contact, and suggestive sexual references were normative behavior in the workplace. Equal pay for equal work was wishful thinking.

Although they were no longer barred from political activities such as voting or office-holding, women were hardly integrated into the male political culture as equals. When they did participate in politics, they did so largely as sojourners in a decidedly male realm, much like the paid workplace itself. The National Women's Party had introduced a proposed Equal Rights Amendment (ERA) in 1923, not long after the Nineteenth Amendment was ratified in 1920 and women secured the right to vote; debate over whether the ERA would negate sex-specific state laws intended to protect female workers continued through the 1950s.

Victims of violence, particularly women who were raped or who suffered physical abuse at the hands of their husbands, often reacted with shame and remained silent, afraid to stigmatize themselves by reporting the crimes to the police or pressing charges; for their part, the police rarely arrested men

"*Makes you kind of proud to be an American, doesn't it?*"

Figure 7.1 The kind of sexism depicted in this 1960 New Yorker cartoon (whose caption reads "Makes you kind of proud to be an American, doesn't it?") came under increasing fire in the latter part of the decade (Source: © Peter Arno/The New Yorker Collection/The Cartoon Bank).

for domestic abuse. Rape and domestic abuse were more or less "invisible crimes" that occurred behind closed doors; as such, they were not openly discussed. And even when women managed to end an unhappy or even abusive marriage, divorce law at the time largely favored men.

The status quo regarding sex itself was neo-puritanical. A woman existed largely to support, feed, and pleasure her man—though lovemaking was a seldom mentioned, guilt-ridden subject, little more than a procreative act. For men, a double standard existed, in which they might dally and experiment sexually with many partners without being labeled as whores or sluts, as women who "put out" were often christened. Women were understandably self-conscious about doing something men had been doing all along—simply looking at their bodies, let alone exploring them or touching them.

Finally, abortion was an illegal, unregulated, quasi-medical procedure: 10,000 women—half of them poor women of color—died each year in dangerous back-alley procedures. Botched abortions were the leading cause of deaths associated with pregnancy. In this realm, as in others, the price women paid for being women was steep. In sum, they were expected to delay sex until marriage, to subordinate their own lives and wishes to the men in theirs, and to aspire to little beyond motherhood and housekeeping. Such was the lot of women in America, the "51 percent minority."

These norms and attitudes, still decidedly Victorian at the beginning of the 1960s, came under fire at mid-decade. Like the civil rights movement, the women's rights movement benefitted not only from a series of top-down governmental initiatives but also a concerted grassroots effort by dedicated activists. Unlike the civil rights movement, however, grassroots campaigns by feminists in the mid-1960s and beyond, often *followed* key federal initiatives that reenergized women's rights.

While the Civil Rights Act of 1964 and Voting Rights Act of 1965 followed civil rights campaigns in Montgomery, Greensboro, Birmingham, and elsewhere, for example, the 1961 President's Commission on the Status of Women came at a relatively quiet moment in women's rights. Proposed by Esther Peterson—a Kennedy supporter and seasoned labor activist—and chaired by Eleanor Roosevelt, the Commission was intended to combat sexual discrimination in government and private employment, and to promote measures that would enable women to "continue their role as wives and mothers while making a maximum contribution to the world around them." Esther Peterson also led the effort to push through Congress the Equal Pay Act (1963), which required employers to pay men and women the same amount when they performed the same work. A third federal initiative on behalf of employed women stemmed from an accidental alliance between women activists and conservative male Congressmen who opposed black civil rights. In an effort to kill LBJ's civil rights bill, an amendment was added by segregationists that would prohibit discrimination in employment on the basis of race, color, creed (religion), national origin, *and* sex. To them, the addendum was outlandish: what red-blooded American statesman would vote for racial equality and sexual equality—at the same time, no less? While their male counterparts joked about it, five Congresswomen, led by Martha Griffiths of Michigan, pushed earnestly for passage of the bill. The segregationists miscalculated, the bill passed, and Title VII of the Civil Rights Act of 1964 laid the basis for employment equity for women. Finally, Title IX of the Education Amendments of 1972 required an end to gender discrimination in admissions policies and mandated equal access to organized athletic activities at educational institutions that receive federal money; through Title IX, young women gained not only a new sense of their physical capabilities but also greater access to and inclusion in collegiate life.

It was the civil rights movement itself, however, and those women who helped lead it that provided instrumental models and inspiration for grassroots reform in women's rights. Women provided leadership in local civil rights struggles, and the tactics, strategies, and philosophies of the struggle for black equality provided a template for subsequent social movements in the 1960s, including the women's rights movement. Notable leaders in the civil rights movement included, among many others, Rosa Parks, Septima Clark, Jo Ann Robinson, Ella Baker, Clara Luper, Shirley Scaggins, Daisy Bates, Jane Stembridge, Diane Nash, Ruby Doris Smith, Bertha Gober, Trois J. Latimer, Mary Dora Jones, Fannie Lou Hamer, Gloria Richardson, Muriel Tillinghast, Cynthia Washington, Eleaner Holmes Norton, Casey Hayden, Mary King, Shirley Chisholm, Dollie Robinson, and Pauli Murray. Some of these same leaders experienced prejudice as women—in some cases even from male civil rights activists— that impelled them to broaden their fight for equality to include not only race but gender, too.

In 1964, Ruby Doris Smith, a young black woman and one of the founders of SNCC, wrote a paper on the position of women in that organization that was summarily dismissed by her brothers in the struggle; a year later, Casey Hayden and Mary King, two white women also active in SNCC, wrote an article on female activists for the journal *Studies on the Left*. Dollie Robinson, an African-American trade unionist from Milwaukee, suggested a "NAACP for women." Pauli Murray, who coined the phrase "Jane Crow" in the 1940s to describe the old-boy network that kept women down, noted in a 1965 speech that Title VII of the new Civil Rights Act would do nothing for women unless they organized. Hearing about the speech, writer and women's rights activist Betty Friedan sought out Murray, who introduced Friedan to the women networked through the President's Commission on the Status of Women. A year later, in 1966, this cadre formed "a new civil rights organization," the National Organization for Women (NOW), which focused on employment equity, maternity leave and child care, equal education, reproductive freedom, and passage of the Equal Rights Amendment. NOW quickly became the largest feminist organization in the United States, growing from 14 chapters with 1000 members in 1967 to more than 700 chapters with 40,000 members in 1974.

Young women—many of them recent college graduates, many of them active in the civil rights movement, the anti-war movement, and the New Left—began to come together to discuss any and all issues that affected them as women. Sharing their experiences and feelings in "consciousness raising" sessions (also called rap sessions or "bitch sessions"), they discovered that "the personal is political": that what appeared to be individual problems were often commonly shared; that these individual problems were in fact larger societal problems rooted in power relationships; and that these problems could be addressed through political solutions and collective action. Together, they identified "sexism" (a term they coined) as the main culprit in thwarting "women's liberation" (another term they coined, later corrupted by opponents and denigrated as "women's lib").

In discussing the strides made by women in the 1960s, it is important to distinguish between what may be called "the reawakening," the sexual revolution, and second-wave feminism—all related but still discrete in their different emphases and respective levels of politicization. The three overlapped and intersected in different ways, often congruently, but sometimes in opposition. All three may be discussed as part of a wider "women's rights movement" in the second half of the twentieth century. While none of the three came to full fruition until the 1970s, each had its roots in the 1960s, when a broad range of Americans—including and especially women—struggled with new meanings of identity and what society deemed admirable, desirable, or even permissible. Each phase or dimension of this struggle had its own apostle, its own spokesperson who voiced certain concerns that resonated with large numbers of women.

The reawakening, for example, was documented by Betty Friedan, who gave voice to what many women were feeling in the early 1960s. Born in 1921 to Russian Jewish immigrants, Friedan graduated summa cum laude from Smith College in 1942, trained as a psychologist at the University of California at Berkeley, and became a suburban housewife and mother in New York, where she supplemented her husband's income by writing freelance articles for women's magazines. In *The Feminine Mystique* (1963), Friedan identified what she called "the problem that has no name," based on her surveys of Smith College alumni, women of mainly upper middle-class backgrounds. The book begins:

> The problem lay buried, unspoken, for many years in the minds of American women. It was a strange stirring, a sense of dissatisfaction, a yearning that women suffered in the middle of the twentieth century in the United States. Each suburban wife struggled with it alone. As she made the beds, shopped for groceries, matched slipcover material, ate peanut butter sandwiches with her children, chauffeured Cub Scouts and Brownies, lay beside her husband at night—she was afraid to ask even of herself the silent question—"Is this all?"

Women identified with her message that their despair resulted not from personal shortcomings but rather from a "feminine mystique" that pushed women into full-time domestic roles while disregarding their other, personal needs. Widely read, the book put into words what many women were feeling but had yet to speak aloud. A great many housewives responded enthusiastically, grateful to find that they were not alone in experiencing these feelings.

The sexual revolution was likewise documented by Helen Gurley Brown, author of *Sex and the Single Girl*, a 1962 bestseller that stridently argued that women could "have it all:" a career, marriage, and a satisfying sex life. Written when Brown was married at age 40, *Sex and the Single Girl* aimed to revolutionize the attitudes of unmarried women about their existence. Her message? Women do not need to be married to enjoy sex, nor should they apologize for enjoying it. "I think marriage is insurance for the worst years of your life," she wrote. "During your best years, you don't need a husband. You do [however] need a man every step of the way, and they are often cheaper emotionally and a lot more fun by the dozen." Brown considered herself a feminist, writing for women like herself, unprivileged with beauty or a college education. To the charge that she objectified women, Brown replied, "If you're not a sex object, you're in trouble." She would go on to become the influential editor of *Cosmopolitan* magazine, which she turned from a faltering general-interest magazine into a glamour mag with a circulation of 2.5 million. Her ideal—the socially active, career-driven woman known as the "Cosmo girl"—would draw not only the admiration of millions of American women but also the ire of second-wave feminists, who found *Cosmopolitan* fluffy, overly focused on beauty and fashion. Though criticized by Betty Friedan and Gloria Steinem (see below), Brown remained adamant that her message was "for the woman who loves men but who doesn't want to live through them." *Sex and the Single Girl*, published a year before *The Feminine Mystique*, sold millions of copies, its message: that women are sexual beings—even those without wedding bands on their ring fingers (as one feminist writer later put it, "ovaries and a uterus are not wedding presents").

The third publication that shook the pillars of male entitlement was not a book like *Sex and the Single Girl* or *The Feminine Mystique* but rather a magazine founded by a writer for *New York* magazine, Gloria Steinem. A 1956 graduate of Smith College, Steinem mainly wrote potboiler pieces for *Esquire* and *New York Times Sunday Magazine* before tackling more substantive political assignments for *New York*, where an editor financed a single edition of a new magazine Steinem called *Ms.*, a properly feminist term for addressing both married and single women alike, one that did not acknowledge marital status. Aimed at consciousness raising, that first issue of *Ms.* included pieces such as "Sisterhood," "Raising Kids Without Sex Roles," "Women Tell the Truth About Abortions," "Welfare is a Woman's Issue," and "Why I Want a Wife"; this last article explained the singular benefits and support men enjoyed from their spouses. Launched as a full-time publication in July 1972, *Ms.* became the first mainstream feminist magazine, and Steinem became a highly visible spokeswoman for what became known as second-wave feminism (following the first wave of suffragettes in the 1900s and 1910s).

Often the three dimensions of the women's rights movement—the reawakening, the sexual revolution, and second-wave feminism—blurred together so as to be indistinguishable from one another. For example, many discussions of sex *and* reproductive rights *and* women's rights in the 1960s began with the development of the birth control pill, brought to market in 1960. So important was this pill that it quickly became known simply as *the* Pill. While this new form of contraception did not start the sexual revolution, it certainly played a key role in it, augmenting changes in sexual practice and behavior that dovetailed with new efforts by women to better their lives. Before the Pill, even happily married couples feared that too many births could be the difference between a comfortable middle-class life and poverty. Early contraceptives were often beyond a woman's control (condoms), risky (IUDs), or unreliable. Contraceptives were also illegal in many states.

Developed in the 1950s by Gregory Pincus and Howard Rock, the birth control pill was one of the first commercially available medicines taken by healthy individuals. Other qualities also distinguished it. It was easy to use and inexpensive. It was a legitimate medical product. It was relatively safe and highly effective. As a contraceptive, it was taken separately from the sexual act and wholly controlled by the woman. And the timing of its introduction paralleled already changing attitudes about sexuality and the roles of women. For the first time, medical science provided sexually active women with a virtual guarantee of not becoming pregnant; the Pill's failure rate was a low 2 percent. The pharmaceutical company G.D. Searle applied for approval of their new product (Enovid) in 1959 and soon thereafter announced the availability of the Pill through an advertisement in *Obstetrics & Gynecology*; the image in this first advertisement depicted the mythological Andromeda breaking free from her shackles.

The Pill was warmly received. *TIME* Magazine, called it "a miraculous little tablet." Gloria Steinem switched from a diaphragm to the Pill in the early 1960s, then wrote a rave review of the new contraceptive in *Esquire*. Within a year of its release in 1960, one million women were taking the Pill; by the middle of the decade it had become the primary means of contraception in the United States.

Many assume that the technology created a radical change in behavior—that is, that the Pill enabled sexual experimentation, in effect creating a new era of sexual liberation. Evidence suggests, however, that a sexual revolution was well underway before the advent of the Pill. Before one could take the Pill, one had to be OK with one's one sexuality and embrace the idea that sex existed for something other than simply procreation; in this case, therefore, behavior predated technology, with the latter impinging upon and accelerating the former. Oral contraceptives clearly divorced sex from procreation, but the full repercussions of what that technology meant were still in flux, and the Pill soon proved to be both a boon and a burden for women. While it did not start the sexual revolution, as some imagined—no single thing did—it undeniably contributed to a new era of family planning and sexual freedom. For better or for worse, it put the responsibility of contraception firmly in the hands of women. Expected to reduce the incidence of abortion by reducing the number of unwanted pregnancies, the rise of the use of the Pill incongruently coincided with an increase in abortion, as sexually active women may have perceived a "right not to be pregnant." On some level, female sexuality—now freer, easier, less consequential—shifted a little toward the stereotype of male sexuality as carefree and fun.

Because the women's revolution of the 1960s was in important ways a print revolution, the Pill may have revolutionized female behavior less than the written word. *Black Dwarf*, a British underground newspaper, followed 1968's "Year of the Heroic Guerrilla" with 1969's "Year of the Militant Woman." In October 1970, Germaine Greer published *The Female Eunuch*, which argued that men hate women, though women—having learned to hate themselves—do not realize this fact. Socialized from childhood to accept rules that subjugate her, a woman develops shame about her body, her libido, and her sexuality; the nuclear family, in particular, presented a toxic environment for a woman's sense of self.

Written by women for women, books about women's health and sexuality tackled taboo topics in ways similar to *The Feminine Mystique, Sex and the Single Girl, Cosmopolitan*, and *Ms.* Originally written in 1970 as a 35-cent,

136-page pamphlet for a women's health course, *Our Bodies, Ourselves* (1973) encouraged readers to straddle a mirror and actually see what was going on "down there." Still in publication 40 years later, the book revolutionized how women learned about the workings of their own bodies. Not surprisingly, nudity helped to undo the constraints that (in the eyes of young people) immobilized the older generation. The human body was something to be revealed and celebrated. It was natural to be naked—and fun. The same notions informed sex, acted out with enthusiasm as part of the larger revolution. No longer shameful, sex would be pleasurable, something to be enjoyed.

Like print media, television played a role, too, offering its own depictions of the liberated modern woman. Starring Marlo Thomas as Ann Marie, the situation comedy *That Girl* ran on ABC from 1966 to 1971. Thomas played an aspiring actress, a small-town girl who moves to New York City to make it big. *That Girl* was the first sitcom whose principal character—a single woman living in her own apartment—neither worked as a domestic nor lived with her parents. CBS followed suit with *The Mary Tyler Moore Show*, which ran from 1970 to 1977, and whose independent, career-oriented lead character also leaves home to pursue a career in a city outside her hometown, lives alone, and never marries. Neither widowed nor divorced nor seeking a man to support her, Mary Richards (played by Moore) moves to Minneapolis at age 30 after breaking off an engagement with her boyfriend of two years. Applying for a secretarial job at TV station WJM, she is instead offered a position as associate producer of the evening news. Over its seven-year run, the series' comedic plots dealt seriously with issues such as equal pay, premarital sex, infertility, adoption, marital infidelity, divorce, prostitution, and homosexuality.

Ideals of beauty and the objectification of women increasingly came under attack, often in dramatic fashion. In September 1968, activists targeted the Miss America Contest in Atlantic City, New Jersey; specifically, they protested the "Degrading Mindless-Boob-Girlie Symbol" that the winner had come to represent, comparing the pageant to a cattle auction. "The parade down the runway blares the metaphor of the 4-H Club county fair, where the nervous animals are judged for teeth, fleece, etc., and where the best 'specimen' gets the blue ribbon," their press release announced. "So are women in our society forced daily to compete for male approval, enslaved by ludicrous 'beauty' standards we ourselves are conditioned to take seriously." On the boardwalk outside the contest hall, the protestors

Figure 7.2 Activists dump beauty products into a "Freedom Trash Can" at the 1968 Miss America contest. No bras were burned (Source: © Alix Kates Shulman Papers, David M. Rubenstein Rare Book & Manuscript Library, Duke University © 1968 by Alix Kates Shulman).

threw bras, girdles, curlers, wigs, cosmetics, and false eyelashes into a "Freedom Trash Can" before crowning a sheep Miss America. Widely covered by the news media, the protest brought second-wave feminism into public view. Adopting guerrilla theater as protest, similar demonstrations came to define the more radical wing of the feminist movement. A month later, for example, on Halloween night, a group calling themselves Women's International Terrorist Conspiracy from Hell, or WITCH, hexed the New York Stock Exchange (which subsequently dropped five points). Other events intended to shock the public included a protest at a bridal fair exposition and a hairy legs exposé. No bras were burned (a common misremembrance about these protests), but those who opposed "women's lib" loudly called for women to start acting "like ladies" again, a backlash that included women as well as men. Critics painted feminists with a broad brush as bra-burning "dykes," inflexible in their hostility toward men. The stereotype stuck.

As the women's rights movement evolved, it touched on virtually every issue affecting women, reaching into parts of American life heretofore off-limits, including violence toward women. Activists opened shelters for battered women, who found not only refuge but also legal advice, childcare, and assistance in finding work and housing away from their abusers. In 1970, New York Radical Feminists held a Rape Speak Out, the first of its kind. Rape crisis centers and emergency hotlines offered support; self-defense classes offered empowerment. Feminists challenged age-old assumptions about rape: that it was a sexual act rather than an act of violence and terrorism; that women somehow bore responsibility if they were assaulted; and that rape cases warranted rules of evidence different from and more stringent than other criminal cases.

Abortion reform was slightly different, pre-dating the feminist movement and raised initially as a medical and legal issue, not a women's rights issue. In the early 1960s, concerned professionals, namely doctors and lawyers, pushed for abortion reform, seeking to allow abortions for specific reasons such as the presence of a severely damaged fetus or an imminent threat to a pregnant mother's health; they also sought to protect physicians' right to practice medicine according to their best ability and judgment. By 1969, a nationwide poll found that 64 percent of Americans believed that "the decision on abortion should be a private one"; by 1970, twelve states had reformed their abortion laws. Feminists took up the cause and redefined it as a women's issue: in demanding the repeal of all laws forbidding abortion and asserting the right of each individual to control her own body, they introduced the notion of reproductive freedom.

Feminists also revitalized the Equal Rights Amendment, which Congress approved in 1972 and sent to the states for ratification; as passed, it read simply, "Equality of rights under the law shall not be denied or abridged by the United States or by any State on account of sex." While never ratified, falling three states short of becoming part of the Constitution, the ERA neatly encapsulated the main thrust of the women's rights movement: parity between women and men. That same year, Shirley Chisholm ran for president—the first woman to seek the top spot on a major party's ticket—though her bid for the White House revealed tensions within the women's movement. Chisholm, the first black woman to win election to the House of Representatives, entered the race late with little financial backing or organizational support. Minority women in the National Women's Political Caucus supported her, as did NOW president Wilma Scott Heide; but other white feminists, such as Betty Friedan, threw their support solidly behind George McGovern. Such divisions raised questions of racial unity within the women's rights movement, and of the movement's shortcoming in addressing the concerns of women of color.

Fractures also appeared around the issue of homosexuality. The degree to which the women's rights movement should identify with lesbian rights divided feminists, most notably in 1970 when Betty Friedan warned of a "lavender menace" to NOW and to the wider movement. Some lesbians, many of whom had thrown themselves enthusiastically into women's rights, responded by accusing heterosexual feminists of "collaborating" with the enemy, meaning men. As with other social movements of the 1960s, the greatest threat sometimes came not from outside opposition but from internal divisions; still, the unique vantage point and contributions of lesbians to the movement could not be ignored. Denied some basic rights that even disadvantaged heterosexual women took for granted, and freed of dependence on men for love, sex, or money, lesbians occupied a singular social space—"an unusual minority position," as one woman put it—one with inordinate social stigma. With nothing to gain from maintaining the old hierarchy of gender relations, and untroubled by the kind of male disapproval that might silence some straight activists, lesbians spoke plainly about power relations and instructed other feminists on the social constructions of gender and sexuality. Recognizing that what made lesbians so threatening to a male-dominated society was their independence from men, NOW would later affirm lesbian rights as an integral component of sexual self-determination for *all* women.

Clearly the women's rights movement was far from simple or straightforward, and the story of the era's best-known female sports star helps to illustrate the complexities of women's issues—showing, in fact, that there were plural "feminisms" rather than a singular feminism. The top-ranked woman tennis player in the world from 1967 to 1972, Billie Jean King won almost every national and international tennis match open to women, including 71 singles titles; she still holds the record for the most total Wimbledon titles (20), male or female. Of equal significance is the way her life, both on and off the court, encapsulates the paradoxes and tribulations of the women's rights movement. Her illustrious career—cutting across the reawakening, the sexual revolution, and second-wave feminism—not only reveals much about the difficulties of being both a woman and an athlete in the 1960s (and beyond), but also dramatizes and personalizes the difficulties of being caught between worlds, between male rules and female challenges of those rules, between soft femininity and strong womanhood, between heterosexual norms and non-hetero taboos, between pre-feminist aspirations and post-feminist expectations.

During the mid-twentieth century, girls who wanted to excel in athletics were seen as strange, unseemly—weirdly ambitious. The image of the cheerleader, relegated to the sidelines and lauding male glory on the field, remained the ideal, the pinnacle of female athleticism. Labeled a tomboy by her father Bill (her namesake, a fireman), Billie Jean Moffitt honed her tennis skills on the public courts of Long Beach, California. Playing a sport controlled by conservative males—the starched stiff-necks of the country-club circuit—she faced the twin challenges of chauvinism and classism, neither of which hindered her mastery of the racquet. King aggressively dominated her opponents by playing the serve-and-volley "man's game" of her era (rushing the net and hitting opponents' shots before they bounced), rather than the baseline "woman's game" (playing behind the court's back line in extended volleys). Despite her excellence, she was an interloper—a woman in a man's world of physicality and competition. She was, in short, that most vexing of contradictions in the pre-Title IX era: the serious female athlete.

Already one of the world's greatest tennis players, she married Lawrence King on September 17, 1965. Six years later she had an abortion, which her husband revealed publicly in a 1972 *Ms.* magazine interview without consulting her in advance. Mrs. King began to realize that she was romantically interested in women in 1968, but remained married to her husband for another nineteen years. In 1971 (the same year in which she had the abortion, a consequence of the shaky foundations of her marriage), she began an intimate relationship with her secretary, Marilyn Barnett. Forced to acknowledge the relationship when it became public in a 1981 "palimony" lawsuit filed by Barnett, Billie Jean King became the first prominent professional athlete "outed" as bisexual. She later noted that she had wanted to retire from competitive tennis that year but could not afford to because of the lawsuit. "Within 24 hours [of the lawsuit being filed], I lost all my endorsements, I lost everything," she said. "I lost $2 million at least, because I had longtime contracts. I had to play just to pay for the lawyers."

King said many years later, in 1998, that fellow tennis player Martina Navratilova, who was openly gay, was not supportive when King was outed, resulting in their relationship having a "very bad five years." Furthermore,

King was often compared to her pretty blonde rival, Chris Evert, the darling of the tennis world. "It was very hard on me because I was outed and I think you have to do it in your own time," King later said, speaking about the palimony suit in 2007, 26 years after it was filed. "Fifty percent of gay people know who they are by the age of thirteen. I was in the other fifty percent." Concerning the personal cost of concealing her sexuality for so many years, King said:

> I wanted to tell the truth but my parents were homophobic and I was in the closet. As well as that, I had people tell me that if I talked about what I was going through, it would be the end of the women's tour. I couldn't get a closet deep enough. I've got a homophobic family, a tour that will die if I come out, the world is homophobic and, yeah, I was homophobic. If you speak with gays, bisexuals, lesbians and transgenders, you will find a lot of homophobia because of the way we all grew up. One of my big goals was always to be honest with my parents and I couldn't be for a long time. I tried to bring up the subject but felt I couldn't. My mother would say, "We're not talking about things like that," and I was pretty easily stopped because I was reluctant anyway. I ended up with an eating disorder that came from trying to numb myself from my feelings.

Like many other public figures, King wore the mantle of feminist uncomfortably, wrestling with her own femininity and sexual orientation as she tried to define herself as a strong-but-not-masculine woman. Uneasy about embodying an agenda that opponents painted as radically unfeminine, she did not identify with the burgeoning women's lib movement, which politicized and disrupted her personal life.

It was difficult, however, to ignore her spirit and the advances she made for women in sports and in American life. In 1971, for example, she fought for a separate women's tournament circuit, the Virginia Slims Tour. *Women's Sports*, a magazine she launched in 1974, brought greater visibility to female athletics. Exasperated by the enormous disparity between tournament payouts for men and women, she demanded that sponsors pay greater prizes to female players. She also founded the Women's Tennis Association and the Women's Sports Foundation.

This long list of accomplishments notwithstanding, it was a single match that cemented Billie Jean King's place in history. On September 20, 1973, in front of 30,472 fans at the Houston Astrodome—still the biggest crowd ever to see a tennis match in the US—King defeated Bobby Riggs, a former Wimbledon men's singles champion, in what was billed as "The Battle of the Sexes." It was this victory—trouncing the braggart Riggs, who reveled in his role as chauvinist pig during the pre-match hype—that for many confirmed her status as an icon of second-wave feminism. Riggs had boasted that no woman could beat him—indeed, that no woman could ever best a man in singles tennis—and King smashed him. Even as a kind of publicity stunt, it was not your everyday tennis match, and women all over the country relished her win.

The gay rights movement would not erupt until the 1970s, but the women's rights movement was in full swing by the end of the 1960s. So deep were the changes wrought by this movement that it affected nearly all aspects of American life: from the domestic sphere to the workplace, from the halls of government to the bedroom, from courts to hospitals, from news stands to athletic fields. Pounding like storm surge on a beach, the changes brought on by not only by the women's rights movement but also by the civil rights movement, the student rights movement, and the anti-war movement threatened to erode the foundations on which American society rested. A word used only for the most profound repudiation of the existing order came into common usage. Revolution was in the air.

Further Reading

Helen Gurley Brown, *Sex and the Single Girl* (New York: Bernard Geis, 1962)

Betty Friedan, *The Feminine Mystique* (New York: W.W. Norton, 1963)

Joanne Meyerowitz, *Not June Cleaver: Women and Gender in Postwar America, 1945–1960* (Philadelphia: Temple University Press, 1994)

Daniel Horowitz, *Betty Friedan and the Making of The Feminine Mystique: The American Left, the Cold War, and Modern Feminism* (Amherst: University of Massachusetts Press, 2000)

Avital H. Bloch and Lauri Umansky, eds., *Impossible to Hold: Women and Culture in the 1960s* (New York: NYU Press, 2005)

Stephanie Coontz, *A Strange Stirring: The Feminine Mystique and American Women at the Dawn of the 1960s* (New York: Basic Books, 2011)

8

Revolutions Left and Right

In March 1968, President Johnson's announcement that he would not run for reelection opened the field to candidates who opposed US involvement in the war in Vietnam. Senator Robert Kennedy of New York, Senator Eugene McCarthy of Wisconsin, and Senator George McGovern of South Dakota contended against Vice President Hubert Humphrey for the Democratic nomination that summer at the party's national convention in Chicago. Antiwar activists planned to hold protests outside the convention hotel in Chicago, whose powerful mayor, Richard J. Daley, promised to enforce peace (allegedly by encouraging Chicago Police Department officers to "shoot to kill" if challenged). A showdown loomed, for while the Democratic nominees made their speeches and the major networks' TV cameras rolled inside the Chicago Hilton, outside on Michigan Avenue and across the street in Grant Park camera crews were working too, as demonstrators clashed with what swelled to be a massive force of 11,900 Chicago policemen, 7500 US Army troops, 7500 Illinois National Guardsmen, and 1000 Secret Service agents, over five days. The press dubbed the worst day of rioting the "Battle of Michigan Avenue." The subsequent trial of the so-called "Chicago Eight"—a hodgepodge of radicals, academics, and pacifists charged with inciting the riots but who shared little beyond their opposition to the war—was a media circus, with one of the defendants, Black Panther Party chairman Bobby Seale, gagged and chained in the courtroom after repeated outbursts (the Chicago Eight became the Chicago Seven when Seale's trial was split from his co-defendants' trial). An official investigation of the bedlam at the convention would later place most of the blame for the violence on the police, but even before all hell broke loose in

The Long Sixties: America, 1955–1973, First Edition. Christopher B. Strain.
© 2017 Christopher B. Strain. Published 2017 by John Wiley & Sons, Inc.

Chicago, a chaotic and often violent chain of events lent the impression that a second American Revolution was underway.

Three things are worth noting about the so-called revolutionary Sixties. First, what happened on the Berkeley campus augured things to come, things that would spread eastwards. Many of the changes and challenges to the status quo that occurred in the 1960s originated in California, the birthplace not only of hippies and communes but also, by decade's end, of a new brand of American conservatism. While change occurred nationwide, in some sense California—from surf culture to the rise of Richard M. Nixon and Ronald Reagan—*drove* the Sixties. Second, changes on the right came just as hard and fast as did changes on the left. The decade that brought us flamboyant leftist Abbie Hoffman and the prank-based, anti-authoritarian Yippies also brought conservative equivalents such as presidential hopeful Barry Goldwater and the college-campus-based Young Americans for Freedom (YAF), whose manifesto—the Sharon Statement—predated the Port Huron Statement by two years. Even as campus radicals railed against the establishment, a new conservatism, in part a backlash reaction to youth seemingly gone mad, also gained traction: while the members of Students for a Democratic Society dreamed and read *Rolling Stone*—a new, pulpy magazine offering an insider's view of rock music and the anti-establishment values it engendered—the members of the arch-conservative, anti-communist John Birch Society (founded in Indianapolis in 1958) read the *National Review*, a biweekly magazine founded in 1955 by William F. Buckley, who aspired to unite right-leaning intellectuals under a common standard-bearer. In response to what they interpreted as the unraveling of American society, conservatives began to mount their own counter-revolution. Third, and finally, the "Sixties" as we now often remember them—wide-open, roaring, uninhibited—emerged stealthily, not blaringly. The early 1960s resembled the 1950s, and in certain ways the 1950s endured throughout the Sixties. Just as the civil rights movement produced the Berkeley Free Speech Movement, which in turn fomented wider student protests, so, too, did the counterculture spin out of earlier transformations. In this sense, the revolutions of the 1960s were more evolutionary than revolutionary, with even the most dramatic upheavals of the latter decade telegraphed by earlier portents and signs (sometimes quite literally, as with the 1958 debut of the peace sign, derived from the naval semaphores for "n" and "d," inscribed in a circle for total *n*uclear *d*isarmament). Some of the most profound revolutions came about rather quietly, almost peacefully, and revolutionary social change—whether political, social, or cultural—did not manifest spontaneously.

Accordingly, important developments in the rise of the counterculture of the late 1960s were born of events that transpired in the middle of the decade, when rock music, for example, charted paths in strange, new directions. When Bob Dylan appeared at the Newport Folk Festival in July 1965 with an electric guitar, diehard fans cringed, troubled by the singer's apparent defection from folk's unplugged norms, but his amped-up sound matched the spirit of the times. Folk music was yielding in popularity to rock music, the louder, harsher tones of which seemed to reflect the concerns of the day, especially racial tensions and worries over the war in Vietnam. Dylan's hit song "Like a Rolling Stone" began its steady climb up the singles charts, even as critics noted the song's vengeful, angry undertones.

And as the Beatles famously entered new musical territory with the transitional 1965 album *Rubber Soul* (a benchmark in the band's evolution from doo-wop toward something more sophisticated, both lyrically and musically), so, too, did the Beach Boys with a seminal album of their own, *Pet Sounds* (1966). Before this album, the band epitomized the LA surf scene, embodying the West Coast's intoxicating mix of cars, girls, and endless summer. Their music held special allure for white teens in places like rural Kansas or small-town Iowa, far from the warmth of the California sun. Inspired by *Rubber Soul*, Brian Wilson—the 24-year-old creative genius of the Beach Boys—aspired to create a different kind of album, sonically experimental yet thematically unified. As Wilson put it, "*Rubber Soul* was a collection of songs… that somehow went together like no album ever made before, and I was very impressed… [and it] challenged [me] to do a great album." In mixing *Pet Sounds*, Wilson layered elaborate vocal harmonies with sound effects and unconventional instruments, including electronic organs, Hawaiian string instruments, and Coca-Cola cans used as percussion. With tracks like "Wouldn't It Be Nice" and "God Only Knows," the album prompted head-scratching from some fans, but critics heard a new level of musicality in the melancholic pop masterpiece. Although it was a commercial flop, *Pet Sounds* was Wilson's masterwork. In a full-circle tribute, the Beatles sampled the sounds of barking dogs on their next album, *Sgt. Pepper's Lonely Hearts Club Band*, the following year. Rock's first concept album, *Pet Sounds*, was quickly recognized as one of the best records of the 1960s and one of the most influential of its time. (In 2003, *Pet Sounds* was ranked No. 2 by *Rolling Stone* magazine in its list of "The 500 Greatest Albums of All Time," second only to *Sgt. Pepper's*.)

In the same way the span of the Beach Boys' popularity bridged the gap between 1950s pop and 1960s psychedelia, a freewheeling road trip undertaken by a group from northern California in 1964 symbolically linked the 1950s Beat culture the 1960s counterculture, providing a coda for the former and anticipating the latter with what would become the stuff of Sixties legend. The Merry Pranksters began as a group of friends who pledged on a 1963 trip to New York to return to the next year to see the 1964 World's Fair in Queens, "to experience the American landscape, the heartscape," according to Ken Kesey, the ringleader of the group. Kesey had been a University of Oregon football player and wrestler, training for the Olympics before injuring his shoulder; later, as a straight-laced graduate student at Stanford University, he was invited to participate in LSD experiments at the university, where scientists told student test subjects they were hoping to find a cure for depression or perhaps insanity with the new drug. With no preparation, Kesey took his first trip under the watchful eyes of his professors. "And when I came out of it, I felt like it was like discovering a hole that went into the center of the earth, and you could see jewelry down there, and you wanted your people to go down there and enjoy it." An accomplished author, Kesey subsequently published two novels, including the widely acclaimed *One Flew Over the Cuckoo's Nest* (1962), before embarking on his quixotic quest to Queens.

The roadtrippers gathered at Kesey's ranch in La Honda, California, in the summer of 1964. Fresh out of the Marine Corps, Kesey's friend Ken Babbs had flown helicopters in Vietnam; he bestowed nicknames on the other group members. Paula Sundstein ("Gretchen Fetchin"), an art student at the University of Oregon, intended to get a job doing water ballet at the World's Fair. Neil Cassady, Jack Kerouac's old pal, showed up with a lug wrench to change a flat tire if needed; acting the part of Dean Moriarty, he naturally took the wheel and provided a nonstop, running commentary of the trip. The lovely "Stark Naked" (Cathy Casamo) was invited along by Mike Hagen, Kesey's old fraternity brother, who filmed the ensuing journey. Jane Burton, a professor of philosophy at Stanford University, made the trip while pregnant, which made her hungry: her nickname became "Generally Famished." She described the Merry Pranksters as "just a bunch of lunatics, running around acting idiotic, trying to get to the East Coast somehow." They traveled in a 1939 International Harvester school bus, which they named "Further." It was a pragmatic choice of vehicles, as they wanted to carry a lot of people. They added a "turret" to the bus by welding an old clothes dryer to its roof. Roy Seburn, the guy who painted the bus in psychedelic colors, didn't want to, saying, "I thought it looked really good the way it was," but was outvoted and complied. Ken's wife Faye and son Zane stayed behind at the ranch as the rest struck out on June 17, 1964, in a kind of reverse migration across the American West. The trip began inauspiciously: they ran out of gas just out of the driveway and broke down again before making it as far as San Jose.

When they got to Phoenix, where Barry Goldwater was campaigning for the presidency, they painted, "A Vote for Barry is a Vote for Fun!" on the bus and drove through the center of town in reverse. Pooling their resources (and hiding their drugs), they dumped all of their LSD into a one-quart Ball jar of lemonade—which made dosage problematic and led to difficulties down the road. Stark Naked, for example, stood nude on the rear platform of the bus on their way to author Larry McMurtry's house, in a well-to-do Houston neighborhood. Wandering off once they arrived there, she was later picked up for psychiatric surveillance by the Houston Police; the group rolled on without her. In New Orleans, they stopped on the shore of Lake Pontchartrain and rushed in for a swim, in so doing unwittingly integrating a swimming hole traditionally used by local Negroes.

Wherever they went, their bus, Further, brought smiles to the faces of those they passed "like a kid seeing an Easter egg," said Kesey. Whenever the cops pulled them over, the Pranksters whipped out their cameras and pretended they were making a feature film. People didn't think they were hippies or psychedelic drug freaks, neither of which had entered public consciousness or even really existed then. "That wouldn't have occurred to anybody," Burton said. To onlookers, they were simply eccentric weirdoes in a brightly painted bus, though the Pranksters intended something more from their journey. "The notion of us being wild crazies simply wasn't true. We weren't long-haired and we weren't irresponsible," Kesey claimed. "There was an American sense… which is why we always wore red-white-and-blue." After two weeks, the group made it to New York, where they dropped in on Jack Kerouac, who was not amused. Kerouac could not keep up with the free-wheeling Merry Pranksters (nor did he want to, having already opted for curmudgeon-hood and a slow death by drinking).

Even though the trip was more about the journey than the destination, the Fair itself proved disappointing. One among them thought it would be funny to drop acid before seeing the "The Wonderful World of Chemistry" show at the DuPont Pavilion. The return trip to California was less ebullient, somewhat anti-climactic. When they got back (by way of Yellowstone National Park) they commenced the "Acid Tests," a series of parties around the San Francisco Bay Area in 1965–1966. Advertised with poster taglines that read "Can You Pass the Acid Test?" these psychedelic extravaganzas used black lights, strobes, Glo-Paint, and spotlight gels to project light in wild arrays and patterns; music was provided by The Warlocks (Jerry Garcia's band, which became The Grateful Dead), who showed up to see what all the fuss was about. Kesey was busted in January 1965—not for LSD, but for marijuana possession. When asked if he felt that he had done something wrong, Kesey replied, "I feel like you only come to this movie once, and if you don't get something rewarding out of every minute you're sitting there, then you're blowing your ticket." As college-age students began to discover drugs, Kesey quit the Acid Tests, calling drug use a "fashion," more recreational than enlightened. The Acid Tests were notable, signaling a hippy awakening in northern California, but the road trip leading up to them, and the bus itself, also came to signify a receptiveness to experience—an open-throttled "yes" to life that young people came to embrace.

As the Acid Tests demonstrated, some drug use in the 1960s was not what would later be termed "recreational": it was (at least initially) something undertaken seriously, not simply for kicks. Some people used drugs not as ends in themselves but as means to other ends, namely altered consciousness, enlightenment, and inner peace. They took psychedelic drugs such as LSD, mescaline, and psilocybin reverentially, as a way of freeing their minds. For these psychonauts, the goal was not the good feeling but the altered state.

The 1960s in America was an era of new ideas, which manifested in new religious movements, new spiritual awakenings, and new freedoms from the conformity of the 1950s. Hippies—those who consciously participated in the new 1960s counterculture—sought peace, love, understanding, and especially freedom, rebelling against established traditions, including Judeo-Christian religious customs and the cultural norms and expectations to which their parents adhered. Some turned inward, seeking enlightenment through prayer and meditation. Others turned to new "gurus" (teachers) who spread their teachings across the United States. The counterculture encouraged the exploration of new paths, leading many hippies to embrace world religions outside the Judeo-Christian norm, including Buddhism, Hinduism, and Native American mysticism. Many hippies sought to expand the horizons of their minds, gaining fresh perspectives and new experiences, free from what they saw as the inhibitions of Western civilization.

This alternative quest for spirituality led some hippies to experiment with drugs as a form of spiritual exploration. In some cases, careful study and prescribed texts accompanied drug use. Those who smoked pot, ate mushrooms, or dropped acid might read the Vedas, the *Bhaghavad-Gita*, the *I-Ching*, the *Tibetan Book of the Dead*, and books on Buddhism by Alan

Watts and D.T. Suzuki. Other writings by Hermann Hesse, Aldous Huxley, Carlos Castaneda, Jack Kerouac, and Allen Ginsberg described not only Eastern philosophy but also drug use as paths to enlightenment. Acclaimed scientist John C. Lilly, who used LSD in a sensory-deprivation tank of his own design, and Harvard psychology professor Timothy Leary both provided some instruction. "Turn on, tune in, drop out," Leary famously recommended, meaning one should activate inner consciousness (with the help of a tab of acid), harmonize with the cosmos, and detach from all suspicion and judgment. It was an invitation to be open—an openness revealed through non-Western religious traditions. Buddhism, for example, teaches that reality is not what it seems to be, and tribal societies had long utilized natural substances to access the spirit world, the dream country where visions blurred perception and shifted minds. To those in the counterculture, drug use and Eastern philosophy seemed to go hand in hand as perfect antidotes to Western repressiveness.

Over time, though, the quest for "higher ground" fell away and drugs simply became part of the experiential ethos of the day, an "unfathomable, fascinating, magical toy," as writer Jenny Diski later put it, continuing, "there was no choice but to take whatever risk was on offer… the risk of madness was preferable to being on nothing at all." Diski opined, "We lay around and got stoned, had sex, listened to music that exalted lying around, getting stoned, and having sex, and hymned our good times." Only half-jokingly, day trippers contemplated spiking municipal water supplies with LSD. As certain horrors of the Sixties increasingly came to light, drugs also provided an escape. Drugs were prevalent in Vietnam, for example, where they were taken into the combat zone as a means of coping with a situation that could not be dealt with, and many soldiers carried their drug habits back home with them after their stints overseas. Most troublingly, drugs themselves (particularly barbiturates, heroin and opiate derivatives, and amphetamines) became part of the darker side of the Sixties as abuse, addiction, and overdose proved unavoidable for some users.

Today the 1960s are remembered as the hippy decade and as the drug decade—the heyday of illegal drug use by "long-hairs," as they were labeled—but neither of these remembrances is particularly accurate, with historical data telling a different story. Surveys in fact show that drug abuse in the 1960s was comparably rare, as was accurate information about the effects of illegal drugs. In a 1969 Gallup poll, only 4% of American adults said they had tried marijuana; 34% said they did not know the effects of marijuana, but 43% thought it was used by many or some high school kids.

In 1972, Gallup found that 60% of Americans thought that marijuana was physically addictive—even though research showed that regular users typically showed no physical symptoms of withdrawal (clear indicators of physical addiction). While college students increasingly began to experiment with marijuana—used in the 1950s only by jazz musicians, beatniks, and a handful of others on the fringe of American society—many dressed and acted in ways that would have seemed very familiar to their 1950s contemporaries.

The Sixties in popular imagination is both simple and complicated, defined as much by paradox as by collective misunderstanding and misremembering. It was a decade of amity and enmity, the best and worst of times: "years of hope, days of rage," as New Left activist Todd Gitlin would later put it. From war and assassination to civil unrest and racial strife, the reality of the 1960s belied the lava-lamp fantasies of peace and love, but of course the reality also *created* the fantasy. Without Vietnam, Bull Connor's German Shepherds, and the squares (or "straights") in their gray flannel suits there would have been no anti-war protestors, no civil rights marchers, and no hippies. Without a dominant mainstream culture there could be no counterculture. Most important, as some who earnestly embraced the counterculture learned, so, too, did living a fantasy create its own reality. A favorite quotation of Sixties reformers was labor activist Reverend A.J. Muste's didactic exhortation that there was no way to peace—peace *is* the way.

Living fantasy to create reality would in fact become a trademark of the Sixties, from heady academic theories to vapid pop songs. When influential French sociologist and theorist Jean Baudrillard described media culture as consumed by an "effect of frantic self-referentiality," a postmodern world of refractive "hyperreality" in which authenticity disappears in an infinity of self-reflected simulacra, one cannot help but wonder if he was thinking about the 1960s pop band, the Monkees. An invention of executives at Columbia Pictures who envisioned a television show about a group of young men trying to make it as a rock and roll band (in imitation of the Beatles' 1964 film *A Hard Day's Night*), the Monkees were completely manufactured. The producers of the show selected three Americans, Peter Tork, Mike Nesmith, and Mickey Dolenz, and one Englishman, Davy Jones, more for their on-screen star charisma than for their highly modest musical abilities (a popular 1960s rumor placed mass murderer Charles Manson among other disappointed hopefuls who auditioned for the band). The TV show *The Monkees* ran two seasons on NBC, during which time the group released a number of hit songs, including "Last Train to Clarksville" (1966), "I'm a

Believer" (1966), and "Daydream Believer" (1967). Several gold albums later, fans clamored for live performances—only to learn that the Monkees had not played their instruments on their records. In a vivid example of life imitating art imitating life, the band members publicly rebelled, demanding to play as well as sing on their records, and studio execs went along. Interestingly, the band's popularity did not decline as they transitioned from air guitarists to real performers, though their popularity waned at decade's end. If the Monkees—an inauthentic studio creation willed into authenticity by desirous fans willing to suspend belief—were any indication, then Baudrillard's theory of hyper-reality seemed to hold weight.

This strange admixture of fantasy and reality defined the counterculture itself, which existed within a kind of paradox. There were conservative as well as liberal hippies; there were some hippies who hated the establishment and others who were indifferent to it; there were some hippies who loved money and others who loved free love, free food, free rent—pretty much anything so long as it was free. The counterculture was, therefore, defined not so much by a uniform outlook but rather by a shared sense of a common enemy, a rejection of the taken-for-granted assumptions that underpinned mainstream American society. Attitudes about sex, pleasure, leisure, drug use, and even styles of clothes and hairdos represented a rejection of bourgeois society. Young people wore long hair, natural fibers, plenty of leather and beads; they recycled surplus Army fatigues rather than purchase new clothes off the department-store rack. Some minimized their clothing— skin was in—and, in the supreme irony of affluence, simply *being* began to replace *doing*. Having inherited the material wealth and power of the United States' post-WWII industrial economy, some of its prime beneficiaries— young, privileged, college-educated, white kids—rejected its fruits and attempted to return to small, primitive, intentional communities; to abandon suburbia and return to the land; to glorify folk culture and the attributes of rural peasants; and to adopt the cultural stylings of ethnic minorities. Terrifying for many of the older generation, the possibilities were boundless and tremendously exciting for many young people.

Such was the spirit of the Summer of Love in 1967, when 75,000 young people flooded a 25-square-block area of San Francisco to participate in the burgeoning counterculture there. Runaways and idealists poured into the city's Haight-Ashbury district ("the Haight") to partake of psychedelic rock, LSD, good dope, and freethinking communalism. They attended concerts (advertised with Day-Glo psychedelic posters) by the Charlatans, the Warlocks (soon to become the Grateful Dead), Big Brother and the Holding

Company, Jefferson Airplane, and Quicksilver Messenger Service, among others, at the Avalon Ballroom, at the Fillmore Auditorium, and (for free) in Golden Gate Park; listened to poetry readings at City Lights Bookstore, the first all-paperback bookstore in the United States; and helped each other get by. Stocked with tranquilizers and penicillin, a free medical clinic tended to bad acid trips and venereal diseases in addition to the usual bumps and sniffles. "The Aquarian Age!" exclaimed Joe McDonald, creator and lead singer of Country Joe and the Fish. It was the sunny side of revolution: serious in its earnestness, yet lighthearted and fun. "God has fingered that little block system between Baker and Stanyon Street," noted one observer-participant, "and we spend all our time, verbally and nonverbally, trying to discover why." The magic, however, had an expiration date. The freedom, openness, and love hippies cherished would prove difficult to sustain when everyone else was playing by a different set of rules: even before the summer had ended, for example, shrewd opportunists were figuring out how to take advantage—financially and otherwise—of this new and rather naive gathering of youngsters (according to Jerry Garcia's wife Carolyn, promoter Bill Graham "decided he could take everything he saw here and make a fortune"). With so many hucksters ready to take their money and their innocence, theirs was a vulnerable population.

That vulnerability, coupled with the shortcomings of paradise in San Francisco and elsewhere, made another kind of dropping out more appealing. As cities and suburbs proved untenable as long-term venues for the kind of society hippies were trying to create, some young people left the city to populate mini-utopias of their own design. Some idealists—alienated but united by a refusal to share the assumptions of bourgeois Western society—adopted a kind of voluntary primitivism and created communes, which sprang up in Mendecino, Sonoma, and the Mount Shasta area of northern California; in northern New Mexico; in southern Colorado; in Vermont and the Hudson Valley; in Oregon around Eugene and Grant's Pass; on the Northwest coast around Seattle and Vancouver, British Columbia; and in other small pockets across the country. Like nineteenth-century utopias at Brook Farm, New Harmony, and Oneida, these 1960s communes encouraged common purpose, shared work, and communal living; unlike the earlier progenitors, which tended to be rigid and authoritarian, the new communes were more anarchistic in the sense that most required only self-regulation. Most sought equilibrium through self-selection (that is, choosing like-minded individuals with which to live and work) and practical governance; however, like the Summer of Love in the Haight, self-serving outsiders often intruded and spoiled the mix. Because interlopers sometimes abused communal living as a kind of vacation, with do-nothingness supplanting hard work, some communes proved difficult to sustain. Others succumbed to internecine squabbling and petty jealousies. A few, however, not only survived but thrived (the Farm in Summertown, Tennessee, for example, has survived to the present day).

One of the first 1960s communes to form was Morningstar Ranch, which its founder Lou Gottlieb envisioned as a place with no rules and no organization, where individuals could be reborn to live in harmony with the earth. Gottlieb, a folk singer with the pop group the Limelighters, bought a 32-acre apple orchard in Sonoma County, north of San Francisco, which became "a place for people to find the kind of work they'd be doing whether or not they get paid for it—in short, your own thing, the abandonment of materialist values." In the beginning, a few dozen urbanites set up wood-and-canvas shelters among the trees; they planted gardens and picked the fruit. "Inevitably, when you get a good group of people together the

Figure 8.1 Young people working together on a commune in Mendocino, California in July 1967 (Source: © Ted Streshinsky/CORBIS).

vibes go up, and there's a lot of love going around," Gottlieb noted. As word of his commune spread, however, it became a stopover for outlaw bikers and freaks looking to mellow out from amphetamine binges, and the transients threatened to overwhelm the long-termers. Now Gottlieb faced a choice: "Either accept everyone or develop criteria to figure out who's worthy." Clinging to his faith in humanity and his respect for the land, Gottlieb adopted a come-one, come-all attitude.

In communes, some hippies made efforts to break down the barriers between people created by American society: they made an intense push toward *de*-alienation. There was a strong sense of the possible in this segment of the counterculture, as cohabitants attempted to topple entrenched, outmoded assumptions and to resist institutional inertia. One young man, who got rid of "a car, a hi-fi, a million useless things" as he joined a dozen others in a communal living experiment, characterized the process as "retribalizing":

> It was my dream to belong to a tribe, where the energies flow among everyone, where people care for on another, where no one has to work, but everyone wants to do something because we're all mutually dependent for our survival and our happiness. So we got together here, and we've had a lot of problems and real conflicts, but we know the satisfactions of trying to work around them, of growing from them, the way you grow from a good marriage. And we're back to the land here, and I get high just being close to the earth and trying to understand it.

John Sinclair, the founder of the White Panther Party (a political auxiliary created by white leftists to support the Black Panthers, who are described in Chapter 10) and a communalist, explained his commune as: "a conscious community of artists who live together, work together, share all things— smoke dope together, dance and fuck together, and spread the word together every way we can—through our work, our freedom of movement, our music and dance, our economy, our human social forms, through our every breath on this planet." Such places were experiments for the recovery of human potential, attempts to raise new possibilities, formulate alternative societies, and define utopia.

Many hippies, thirsty for spiritual connections in their lives, rediscovered Christianity, while others explored non-Western religions. There were large numbers of hippies among the ranks of the "Jesus Freaks" (young Christians within the counterculture who viewed Jesus Christ as a prototypical hippy), but also a large number of adherents to the peyote religion, a Native American tradition, which used hallucinogens in sacramental ceremonies, and an assortment of Zen-inspired meditational religions. The Beatles, among others, became fascinated with Hinduism.

Communalists often attempted to free sex from its association with monogamous marriage. Some men, excited by the prospects of a variety of sexual partners, inevitably abused the openness and freedom of such practices, and came to communes for the wrong reasons; however, many young men and women strived toward the ideal of unselfish, unpossessive mutual love. While some explored group marriage, the idea that communal life represented some sort of a sexual smorgasbord—a kind of floating orgy—was a myth created and sustained by the media at the time and ever since: despite the counterculture's commitment to liberation and non-repressive sexuality, the sexual practices of many of those who lived in communes were thoroughly conventional, and constituted a familiar form of serial monogamy.

Figure 8.2   A quiet moment on the road to Woodstock, 1969 (Source: © Three Lions/Hulton Archive/Getty Images).

The communes illustrated how reformist activism could give way to a non-politicized form of rebellion. At the beginning of the decade, there had been two readily distinguishable types of nonconformists on college campuses: the beat hipster and the activist. By the late 1960s, lifestyle itself had become an important signifier in the transformation of American culture, and the lines between the two types had blurred. While some young people living on communes sought merely to drop out of society, others saw their experiments in communal living as an attempt to reconcile rejection of the status quo and radical politics through a cultural revolution that transcended politics.

Nowhere was this revolution more palpable than at Woodstock, a multi-day, multiband, outdoor music festival that has come to represent the pinnacle of the counterculture. A definitive moment of the 1960s, it was advertised as the Woodstock Music and Art Fair, "three days of peace and music" which, remarkably, it was. The best rock and folk acts of the decade, including: Joan Baez; the Band; Creedence Clearwater Revival; Crosby, Stills, Nash, and Young; Jimi Hendrix; Jefferson Airplane; Janis Joplin; Santana; and Sly and the Family Stone, blasted a 35-acre farm near the Catskill village of Bethel, New York, almost continuously, day and night. The real show was not onstage but in the crowd, where nearly half a million young people gathered even as a two-day rainstorm turned the pastureland into a sea of mud. The event went on with woefully inadequate food, shelter, and sanitation, none of which seemed to bother the vast audience much. A cloud of pot smoke hung over the field where people huddled together under blankets in the rain (John Fogerty, lead singer and guitarist of Creedence Clearwater Revival, recalled, "it was like a painting of a Dante scene, just bodies from hell, all intertwined and asleep, covered with mud"), but a feeling of camaraderie and the joy of living for the moment prevailed.

The cultural revolution on display at Woodstock, in conjunction with ongoing anti-Vietnam War protests and calls for ethnic empowerment, paralleled whisperings of actual revolution. Young people began to refer simply to "the Movement"—not the civil rights movement or student movement or the anti-war movement, but _the_ movement, an amalgam that incorporated not only militant politics but also militant lifestyle choices, and sometimes militant action, too. In this atmosphere, student groups like SDS radicalized even further, birthing the Weathermen, which splintered away from SDS in 1969 at the University of Michigan. Taking their name from the Bob Dylan song "Subterranean Homesick Blues" ("you don't need a weatherman to know which way the wind blows"), the group (later known as the Weather Underground) bombed a number of government buildings in its efforts to achieve "the destruction of US imperialism and achieve a classless world." While no one was injured in these attacks, three members of the Weathermen did manage to blow up themselves while manufacturing bombs at a Greenwich Village apartment.

While talk of revolution was everywhere, it unfolded erratically, in ways that few could have predicted. On the one hand, activists in groups like SDS, the Weather Underground, and the Black Panthers came to believe in revolution very literally and were prepared to start it. Some procured guns and learned how to use them. In this vein even Regular Joes became revolutionaries: Sam Melville, a family man and draftsman by trade, bombed eight buildings in New York City in 1969 to protest US imperialism and the war in Vietnam. On the other hand, much of the so-called revolution of the 1960s was mainstreamed and normalized as the alternative became increasingly common, and then normal. The business world, for example, co-opted the counterculture and sold it back to anti-establishment consumers as countercultural styles, fashions, clothes—everything. Some were savvy enough to recognize that they were being sold anti-consumerism by advertising men, but many others happily felt they were "stickin' it to the Man" by buying a Volkswagen Beetle or other imported car—and, in some sense, they were. By the 1950s and 1960s, American buyers were long accustomed to Detroit's "Big Three" automakers—Ford, GM, and Chrysler—changing exterior styling every year, even if the hardware underneath the new exterior failed to change much at all, or even improve. Swedish automaker Volvo used this fact to its advantage, satirizing the practice of "planned obsolescence." An advertisement from 1967 bore the headline, "Your car is obsolete. Again." The ad copy read:

> And the irony of it is, a big chunk of the money that you paid for your obsolete car was used to bring out the very cars that made it obsolete. We make a car that hasn't been given a 'big new look' in over nine years... we've been putting the money we save by not changing the way a Volvo looks (a fortune in tail fins alone) into improving the way a Volvo works.

Like Volkswagen ad execs, Volvo copywriters discovered that customers responded to advertising that was self-effacing even as it humorously poked fun at automotive norms. Similar strategies were used to sell other products, from blue jeans to rock albums. Quickly, expressing one's individuality was becoming a commercial endeavor.

To this commercialization of the newly individualized American society of the 1960s responded the Diggers, one of the more radical groups of the entire decade. Self-described "community anarchists," the Diggers were a loosely organized group of activists and improvisational actors who took their name from a 17th-century farming collective that eschewed not only private property but also all forms of buying and selling. The origins of the Diggers can be traced back to the San Francisco Mime Troupe, a theatre repertory founded by Ron Davis in 1959 that began performing in city parks for free three years later. In 1965, Davis wrote a manifesto about what he called "guerrilla theater," which blended the strategies of Cuban revolutionary Che Guevara with theatric performances. For him, both the content and delivery of his productions would be revolutionary: acting out injustices would shed light on "the system," which people would in turn work to correct; and moving performances out of the playhouse and into San Francisco's parks would bring theatre to "the people."

In 1966 one of Davis' writers enacted a revolution of his own: Peter Berg, who had joined the troupe a year earlier, suggested that the stage itself was an artificial construct that separated actors from audience. Even greater transformative power could be had if the players eliminated the artifice of performing on a stage, which encouraged passive consumption rather than active participation in a theatric experience. Berg broke away to form a new group, which he called The Diggers. Serving homemade stew behind a giant yellow picture frame, which they called the Free Frame of Reference, the Diggers provided free meals from donated meat and vegetables to anyone who wanted them in the Panhandle of Golden Gate Park. Stepping through the frame, they posited, symbolized a change in perspective on money and on how people interact socioeconomically. The group also operated a number of Free Stores in the Haight-Ashbury district at which customers could freely leave or take goods. Calling money tempting, unnecessary, and evil, they encouraged citizens to turn in their bills and coins to the nearest Digger—"no questions will be asked." Emphasizing the importance of public space, the Diggers transformed the streets of San Francisco into a stage. One action involved a flatbed truck driving through the Financial District with half-naked belly dancers, beseeching brokers to leave their jobs. If the San Francisco Mime Troupe had tried to educate people about social problems of the day, then the Diggers would perform a new social reality without those problems—dramatizing the counterculture as social fact by involving everyone in the performance, erasing the line between actor and spectator. Like the

Monkees, the Diggers began to create their own reality. Hippies provided volunteer labor for the Diggers, who eventually garnered funding not only from the Grateful Dead but also from dealers of psychedelic drugs in the Haight.

As SDS spawned the Weathermen, so, too, did the Diggers produce the Yippies, who became known for blending prank with protest. When Jerry Rubin moved from Berkeley to New York in 1967, he and his fellow New York Diggers, including Abbie Hoffman, experimented with "media freaking"—absurdist gestures intended to garner media hype—in lieu of life-acting. One of their more evocative "performances" involved dumping money from the visitor's gallery onto the floor of the New York Stock Exchange, where traders scrambled to scoop up the cash. Not only did the traders perform their own greed: the NY Diggers effectively brought trading to a halt. Alerted in advance, the media promptly reported the spectacle. When the San Francisco Diggers protested the act as mere publicity stunt, creating spectators instead of actors, the New York Diggers changed their name to the Yippies. Other performances included an attempt to levitate the Pentagon in 1967 and a six-day "Festival of Life" in Chicago to coincide with the 1968 Democratic National Convention.

The sunny side of revolution promised instant good karma and endless summer—"flower power," some called it—but there was another side to the Sixties, one that emerged after the Summer of Love. Cities—even progressive ones like San Francisco—were no place to go barefoot, figuratively *or* literally. By the end of 1967, speed and heroin had entered the drug mix in the Haight; exploitative carpetbaggers—sexual huntsmen and financial predators—followed the flowerchildren down the rabbit hole. A 1967 leaflet—published by the Communications Company, an underground news outlet that published handbills on everything from poetry readings to where to get free food—painted a bleak picture of life in the once free and easy Haight:

> Pretty little 16-year-old middle-class chick come to the Haight to see what it's all about and gets picked up by a 17-year-old street dealer who spends all day shooting her full of speed again and again, then feeds her 3000 mikes [micrograms of LSD] and raffles her temporarily unemployed body for the biggest Haight Street gang bang since night before last.

> The politics and ethics of ecstasy.
> Rape is as common as bullshit on Haight Street.
> The Love Generation never sleeps.

On the frontlines of the countercultural revolution, the attractiveness of drug use and hippie life were losing their allure. "Haight Street is ugly shitdeath," the handbill warned—and things got worse in 1968 and 1969.

If revolution is defined by violent upheaval and wrenching change, then 1968 was a revolutionary year, twelve months of volatile upheavals across the globe—in Czechoslovakia, in France, in Vietnam, and in the United States. Martin Luther King, Jr., an apostle of nonviolence, was shot and killed by a sniper in Memphis, Tennessee, on April 3; in the aftermath of King's assassination thousands of black Americans took to the streets in violent riots in many cities. On June 5, presidential candidate Robert Kennedy, JFK's brother, was gunned down in Los Angeles by Sirhan Sirhan, a 24-year-old Jordanian immigrant who, dismayed by Kennedy's support of Israel, timed the assassination to coincide with the anniversary of the Arab defeat in the Six-Day War. In Chicago, police gassed and clubbed demonstrators at the Democratic National Convention. During Tet, the Lunar New Year, the North Vietnamese launched a well-coordinated attack across South Vietnam on one hundred cities and military posts, including Da Nang and Saigon itself, where the American embassy and presidential palace came under assault. The so-called Tet Offensive destroyed not only cities such as Hue and Khe Sanh, where US Marines were besieged for 76 days, but also President Johnson's standing with the American public, who increasingly came to disapprove of his handling of the war: it was after Tet that LBJ stunned the nation by announcing he would not run for a second term. And while news of the horrendous massacre of hundreds of civilians by US troops at My Lai in March would remain a secret until the following year, by the end of 1968 some wondered if the Age of Aquarius had already passed. To one young radical, it seemed "as if the world was catching fire."

On August 9, 1969, Charles Manson and four of his devoted cult of followers—"the Family," who lived communally on a deserted ranch in the San Fernando Valley—went on a brutal two-day killing spree in Hollywood and Beverly Hills in which they butchered seven people, including Sharon Tate, the pregnant wife of film director Roman Polanski. The Tate-La Bianca murders confirmed Manson as the most notorious serial killer of the twentieth century and a living embodiment of evil; they also exposed a darker side of the counterculture, one comprised not of harmless, peace-loving flowerchildren and hippies, but of drug-addled slackers and predatory killers whose notions of freedom had devolved into violent anarchy.

"I see a bad moon rising," sang Creedence Clearwater Revival, who performed in 1969 at the Atlanta Pop Festival and at Woodstock, but not at the most notorious concert of that troubled year. On December 6, hundreds of thousands gathered for a music festival at the Altamont Speedway in northern California. The free concert, anticipated by many as the West Coast answer to Woodstock, was marred by violence, including the killing of an 18-year-old concert-goer, stabbed and beaten to death in front of the stage during the Rolling Stones' set by a Hells Angels motorcycle gang member who had been hired along with his fellow bikers as low-cost security by promoters. (The Hells Angels were paid $500 worth of beer for their services.) "It was supposed to be lovely here—not uptight," said Mick Jagger later that evening. "What happened? What's gone wrong?" If Jesus had been there, the distraught Jagger added, he would have been crucified. *Rolling Stone* magazine decried December 6 as "rock and roll's all-time worst day… a day when everything went perfectly wrong." *Esquire* magazine called Altamont "a bummer from the beginning." Woodstock it was not.

The not-so-sunny end of the Sixties fueled a strong backlash on the right. The riots, the assassinations, the drug abuse, the Manson murders, Altamont—in short, the lurid, violent doppelgangers of Sixties liberation— pushed many Americans rightward, where they found political guides who promised to lead them out of the unbridled wildness of the Sixties. The law-and-order prescriptions of Barry Goldwater, Ronald Reagan, and Richard Nixon were less right-wing revolutions than attempts to maintain a pre-1960s status quo, a return to the "good old days" when things made sense. By the end of the 1960s, however, the sum total of the conservative backlash had combined into a kind of revolution of its own, one that arguably proved more lasting, more far-reaching, and more popular than any left-wing revolution in the United States during that time. Indeed, this conservative upswing in American politics, the New Right—which began in the 1960s but accelerated in the 1970s, 1980s, and only recently gave rise to the Tea Party— seemed to eclipse and outlast the New Left.

Nevertheless, the leftist Sixties lingered, leaving a powerful impression in the nation's public consciousness—less because of the raucous revolution- aries and the conservative backlash they spawned and more because of the progressive reforms that peacefully erupted throughout the decade. It was the quiet revolutions of the 1960s that spoke loudest, whispering radical alternatives—revolutions such as the one led by Cesar Chavez, who became not only the voice of voiceless and exploited migrant farmworkers but also the spiritual leader of Mexican Americans and symbol of the Chicano movement. This shy and quiet organizer worked on behalf of migrant field- workers in California and in 1962 founded (along with Dolores Huerta) the first successful union of agricultural workers in the United States. As King had done in Montgomery, Chavez transformed a local struggle in Delano, California, into a national crusade; his campaign to dissuade American consumers from buying non-union-picked produce, until the farm owners agreed to treat the workers who picked them decently, resulted in what historian Marc Carnes has termed "the nation's most celebrated boycott since the Boston Tea Party." The United Farm Workers nonviolently succeeded in winning some of the first labor contracts in agriculture, but Chavez accomplished so much more, as biographers Richard Griswold del Castillo, Richard A. Garcia, Dan La Botz, and others have detailed. Swept up in the new Chicano militancy, Chavez registered Mexican-American citizens to vote; helped to elect legislators who passed laws to aid farm-workers; made bridges between agricultural unions and other labor groups; supported the civil rights movement; stood for nonviolence; championed the poor and downtrodden; and worked diligently to achieve a living wage for working-class Americans. His dictum, *Si, se puede* ("Yes, we can"), encapsulated Chavez's faith in humanity and his belief in action, the twin pillars of participatory democracy. He was, as La Botz has observed, the most important Latino figure in the history of the United States.

Figure 8.3 Cesar Chavez leading a United Farm Workers' strike in Delano, California (Source: © Topfoto/The Image Works).

In 1970, the same year that Chavez ended a grape boycott in Delano and began a lettuce boycott in Salinas, California, a poet explained one truth about revolutions. Gil Scott-Heron's famous spoken-word recording, "The Revolution Will Not Be Televised," was largely misinterpreted as a coda to the Sixties. The centerpiece of his first album, *Small Talk at 125th and Lenox* (1970), the poem has little to do with the medium of TV; rather, it lampoons popular advertisements, national politicians, and mainstream civil rights activists such as Whitney Young and Roy Wilkins (executive directors of the National Urban League and NAACP, respectively). "The revolution will not be brought to you by Xerox in four parts without commercial interruptions," Scott-Heron rapped. "NBC will not be able to predict the winner at 8:32 or report from twenty-nine districts." For him, revolution was an internal phenomenon, not an external one; that is, in order for society to change, people must think and act differently. The final line, "The revolution will be live," meant that the revolution of the 1960s, writ large, would not be mediated or pre-programmed, but would instead require involvement and interpretation. Heron reminded his listeners that, as with civil rights reform, it would not be disaffected white youths who led the way: angry young people of color, questing for a greater presence in American polity, "will be in the street looking for a brighter day."

As Scott-Heron seemed to predict, the armed overthrow of US society by angry militants—the revolution that many Americans expected, that many more feared, and that a few eagerly anticipated—never materialized. Instead, the revolution of the Sixties was a revolution of the mind—a breakdown of old assumptions and attitudes—that relegated the unquestioning acceptance of institutional, authoritarian, top-down truths to the dustbin of US history. American society in the 1960s was upended, leveled not by guns but by ideas.

Revolutionaries were not the only ones fantasizing, hippies not the only ones stargazing. Scientists proved every bit as dreamy and imaginative in the 1960s as hippies in the counterculture—indeed, there was not only crosspollination between the two groups but also considerable agreement. And the public was fascinated by the pursuits of both. In what may have been the only unifying enterprise of a very divisive decade, Americans turned their dreams skyward, and it was here, with scientific breakthroughs and a new environmental awareness that accompanied them, that some of the biggest revolutions took place.

Further Reading

Mark Kurlansky, *1968: The Year that Rocked the World* (New York: Ballantine Books, 2004)

For more on the Merry Pranksters, see *Magic Trip* (2011), dir. by Alison Ellwood and Alex Gibney. On communes, see Keith Melville, *Communes in the Counter Culture: Origins, Theories, Styles of Life* (New York: William Morrow & Co., 1972)

For the definitive account of Altamont, see Ralph J. Gleason, "Aquarius Wept," *Esquire* (August 1970)

Bryan Burroughs, *Days of Rage: America's Radical Underground, the FBI, and the Forgotten Age of Revolutionary Violence* (New York: Penguin, 2015)

9

Small Steps, Giant Leaps,
New Concerns

The year was 1966 and Stewart Brand—army veteran, art student, and soon-to-be publisher—was dropping acid on a rooftop in San Francisco's North Beach. Knowing that both satellites and astronauts had orbited overhead and taken snapshots, Brand wondered why he'd never seen a photograph of the entire planet. Pondering the powerful symbolism of such an image, he claimed to have felt the curvature of the earth that night:

> I imagined going farther and farther into orbit and soon realized that the sight of the entire planet, seen at once, would be quite dramatic and would make a point that Buckminster Fuller was always ranting about: that people act as if the earth is flat, when in reality it is spherical and extremely finite, and until we learn to treat it as a finite thing, we will never get civilization right.

The next morning, Brand began a campaign, making buttons with the question, "Why Haven't We Seen a Photograph of the Whole Earth Yet?" He petitioned NASA. In 1967 a satellite captured such an image, which Brand put on the cover of the first edition of the *Whole Earth Catalog*, providing its readers "access to tools"—do-it-yourself equipment for communal living, everything from garden tools to hi-fi equipment—while promoting sustainable self-sufficiency. The photograph was a powerful symbol, with resonance far beyond even what Brand had imagined, but the story of its inception perfectly illustrates the connection between two seemingly disparate phenomena of the 1960s: the trippy counterculture and the furtive rush of scientific progress. It also demonstrates the tension between the urgency with which government agencies pursued a lunar landing, and the caution

The Long Sixties: America, 1955–1973, First Edition. Christopher B. Strain.
© 2017 Christopher B. Strain. Published 2017 by John Wiley & Sons, Inc.

counseled by a growing group of environmentalists like Brand who felt that "Humanity's habitat looked tiny, fragile and rare" and that humans must tend to it.

In February 1958—one month after *Sputnik* completed its mission, orbiting the Earth over 1400 times—the United States launched its first successful satellite, *Explorer I.* On April 12, 1961, shortly after Kennedy became president, Soviet cosmonaut Yuri Gagarin became the first man in space; Alan Shepard became the first American in space a few weeks later on May 5. This chase—with American astronauts nipping at the heels of Russian cosmonauts—not only defined a new national purpose but also contributed to the accelerated rate at which American science and technology moved ahead during the 1960s. Indeed, the American venture into space touched almost every other scientific and technological endeavor of the decade, from computers, to biotech, to agriculture.

News of *Sputnik* and subsequent Soviet conquests of space jarred the American people. What might the Russians actually do with the capability to send payloads into orbit? Would future rockets carry warheads? Could the Russians establish military outposts on the moon—or ever deeper in space? The implications were depressing. The United States needed to overtake and surpass the Russians: second place in this competition could have dire consequences.

On May 25, 1961, President Kennedy made a special address to a joint session of Congress in which he discussed the new "space race" within the context of Cold War rivalry with the Soviet Union and other communist nations. "Now it is time to take longer strides—time for a great new American enterprise—time for this nation to take a clearly leading role in space achievement which in many ways may hold the key to our future on earth." As with his New Frontier speech, in this one Kennedy promised cost and strife, saying, "No single space project in this period will be more exciting, or more impressive to mankind, or more important for the long-range exploration of space; and none will be so difficult or expensive to accomplish." Recognizing the head start made by the Soviets and acknowledging that the United States needed to catch up, he proffered, "while we cannot guarantee that we shall one day be first, we can guarantee that any failure to make this effort will find us last." He then proposed a shockingly improbable goal, one more ambitious than any before it. "I believe we should go to the moon," he stated simply.

Why go to the moon? The Earth's only satellite had captured people's imaginations for millennia, but the viability of a manned lunar expedition

Figure 9.1 A closeup of astronaut Alan Shepard in his spacesuit seated inside the Mercury capsule (April 29, 1961). He is undergoing a flight simulation test with the capsule mated to the Redstone booster (Source: © NASA. Photo by Bill Taub).

owed much to the vision of one man—and it wasn't Kennedy. Wernher von Braun, the "Father of Rocket Science," was a German aerospace engineer who, under the Nazis in World War II, had perfected the fearsome V-2 rocket. At the end of the war, von Braun was granted security clearance to work for the United States after surrendering to US military personnel. From 1960 to 1970, he served as director of the newly formed Marshall Space Flight Center in Huntsville, Alabama, where his biggest achievement was developing the Saturn V booster rocket which propelled astronauts to the moon; but, even before this time it was he who pushed for the moon as the goal of manned space flight. *Collier's Weekly* magazine published a series of articles and special issues in the early 1950s that popularized the idea of space flight to the moon by human beings; some of von Braun's contributions to *Collier's*, such as "Crossing the Last Frontier" (March 1952) and "Can We Get to Mars?" (April 1954), became influential in setting the national goals of reaching the moon by the end of the 1960s and becoming "the world's leading space-faring nation," which President Kennedy expressed in a speech at Rice University on September 12, 1962.

Von Braun's influence was profound, but so was an even baser drive. When celebrated British mountaineer George Leigh Mallory was asked in a 1923 *New York Times* interview why he wanted to climb Mount Everest, he famously replied, "Because it's there"; for those involved in America's space program, it was likewise enough to know that no human had set foot on Earth's nearest neighbor. To get there, however, it was first necessary to get into space: a frustrating game of catch-up for American engineers chasing the Soviets. NASA conveyed the urgency of this quest by naming its initial project after the Roman god of speed. The twin goals of Project Mercury (1958–1963) were to put a human in space orbit and to do it before the Russians; while the first goal was met, the second was not. After a test run by a chimpanzee named Ham, Shepard reached outer space in May 1961 aboard *Mercury Redstone 3*, 23 days after the cosmonaut, Gagarin. Marine Corps test pilot John Glenn became the first American to orbit the Earth on February of 1962 aboard the *Mercury-Atlas 6* spacecraft, *Friendship 7*. Glenn circled the planet three times, silently rocketing through three sunsets, three sunrises, four Tuesdays, and three Wednesdays in a breathtaking four hours and fifty-four minutes.

While Kennedy was able to marshal a good measure of both congressional and public support for lunar exploration, not everyone was so thrilled. Senator Paul Douglas of Illinois questioned the wisdom of "this man-to-the-moon business" in light of other obligations. "What profits a civilization," he asked, "if it has 20 million people in abject poverty and sends one man to the moon?" Carl Dreher, the science editor of *Nation* magazine, worried not only about misallocated funds but also about the risks to the astronauts and the choice to compete with the Soviets rather than collaborate with them. "Space may be infinite," he opined, "but in the minds of the diplomats and militarists it is compressed into just one more counter in the war game."

Between 1962 and 1966, Project Gemini was tasked with developing "operational capability in space" and investigating "the problems of working and living in space" as NASA continued to assemble the necessary talent and materials to chase a dream. Under the longer-running Apollo Program (1961–1972)—with its thirty-three flights, eleven of which were manned—NASA focused on the task of actually landing on the moon via lunar rendezvous and coupling, in which a smaller lander leaves the main spacecraft in orbit, descends to the moon's surface, then returns to lunar orbit to re-dock with the bigger craft to return to Earth. The work involved was almost unimaginable, constituting the largest scientific and technological undertaking in history. Three hundred thousand engineers and technical staff persons, working for 20,000 contractors, made entirely new inventions—from cordless tools to freeze-dried food—to accomplish the task. The entire science of transistors, integrated circuits, and computer microchips had to be invented and debugged before rocket experts could plan launches and recovery. Working feverishly, NASA scientists and engineers boldly went where none had gone before—and spent tens of billions of dollars in the process. Mistakes were made, lives were lost. Three astronauts, Gus Grissom, Edward White, and Roger Chaffee, died in a pre-launch test when a flash fire engulfed the command module of *Apollo 1* on the launch pad at Cape Kennedy in 1967.

With space travel becoming a reality in the early 1960s, the lines between science and science fiction blurred. As in the 1950s, science and pop culture affected one another. Indeed, many of the technological innovations of the early decade seemed to have been pulled directly from the pages of sci-fi pulp magazines. On May 16, 1960, for example, the American physicist Theodore Maiman operated the first functioning laser at the same time physicists such as R.L. Mössbauer were studying gamma rays (Mössbauer, a German physicist, would win a Nobel Prize in 1961 for his work in the field); with such developments, sci-fi readers marveled that the ray guns of Buck Rogers and Flash Gordon might become reality. Other scientists, fascinated with the possibility of other life forms "out there," pioneered the search for extra-terrestrial intelligence, or SETI. In the March 1955 issue of *Scientific American*, John D. Kraus had described a concept to scan the cosmos for natural radio signals (electromagnetic radiation from celestial objects) using a flat-plane radio telescope equipped with a parabolic reflector; within two years, his concept was approved for construction by Ohio State University. In 1961, as the Ohio State facility neared completion, a group met at the Green Bank Observatory in West Virginia to discuss further the possibility of using radio astronomy to detect evidence of intelligent life beyond the solar system—that is, to track radio wavelengths that might be coming from something *other* than celestial objects. This group included the astronomer Carl Sagan and Dr. John C. Lilly, the physician and neurophysiologist who had developed the first sensory deprivation tank in the 1950s before going on to study marine mammal cognition. Calling themselves the Order of the Dolphin (after Lilly's work with dolphins), they developed something called the Drake Equation to estimate the number of extraterrestrial civilizations in the Milky Way Galaxy. Meanwhile, OSU's

"Big Ear" radio telescope, funded with $71,000 in grants from the National Science Foundation, powered up in 1963; it would become the base for the world's first continuous SETI project.

With scientists scouring the universe for signs of intelligent life, the limits of science seemed as remote as the boundaries of space itself. It was a golden age of science and technology, with Americans leading the way forward. Three factors made it all possible: the imperative of the space race, whose stakes seemed frighteningly high; American ingenuity and know-how, fueled by the dynamo of US postwar economic might; and a seemingly bottomless well of imagination, born, in a sense, of the Sixties themselves.

With each passing year macro-level discoveries went hand in hand with micro-level ones, as scientists explored not only celestial bodies but also cells of the human body. In 1962 (the same year that British scientists were figuring out the molecular structure of DNA), John Glenn became the first American to orbit the earth; Bell Labs and NASA launched the first Telstar satellite, projecting the first television pictures, telephone calls, and fax images through space (as well as providing the first live transatlantic television feed); and the United States launched the unmanned *Mariner 2* to probe Venus in the first successful flyby of another planet. In 1963, scientists plotted the shell structure of atomic nuclei, produced complex molecules from simple carbons, and discovered quasi-stellar radio sources, or quasars, in deep space. In 1964, *Ranger 7* returned close-up photographs of the moon's surface, even as researchers at Texas A&M used the Nimrod Cyclotron to discover a fundamental new particle, omega-minus. In 1965, researchers used gas chromatography to separate rare earth complexes, even as astronaut Edward White "walked" in space—free-floating, tethered to *Gemini 4*, the second manned space flight in NASA's Project Gemini—for 21 minutes. (White, the first American to perform a spacewalk, found it so exhilarating that he was reluctant to reenter the ship and had to be ordered to end his "walk" and return.) For every foray into the solar system there was a new foray into the building blocks of life and matter: using microscopes as well as telescopes, scientists explored both inner and outer space.

From chemicals to plastics to pharmaceuticals, Americans tended to embrace the notion expressed in the Dupont chemical company's decades-old advertising slogan, "Better Living Through Chemistry." In this new "space age," Mother Nature itself could be fine-tuned and improved, modified at a cellular level to better suit human needs. Science was a new religion and scientists its high priests. This attitude had of course been shaped by living in the shadow of the atomic bomb, which stood as the ultimate symbol of humanity's power over nature: splitting the atom showed that nature could be conquered, its energies released and redirected. It was understood that people stood apart from and were superior to the natural world. Science was a public endeavor, underwritten and subsidized by the government, which channeled vast sums of money into universities for research and development. While the average citizen was largely divorced from scientific inquiry, he or she tacitly approved of such spending, believing it was for the greater good. Public understanding of science itself was comparatively low, but public appreciation of the benefits of science was high.

In 1960, computers were still relatively novel, huge machines that might occupy an entire room, operating with vacuum tubes and costing upwards of $1 million. Universities or big companies might rent time on their "mainframes" to smaller organizations for thousands of dollars per month. In 1960 there were only about 2000 computers in use in the United States, but innovations soon brought big changes. That same year in New York, IBM began mass producing transistors: solid-state devices which, along with the integrated circuit, made vacuum tubes obsolete. Not to be outdone, AT&T introduced its Dataphone in 1960. This modem, the first of its kind, enabled a computer to send and receive information over a telephone line by converting digital data into an analog signal, and then converting it back once received on the other end.

The power, size, speed, and ease of operation of computers revolutionized quickly, largely because of the space race. The year 1961 saw the completion of the warehouse-sized Atlas computer, one of the first supercomputers ("like a mad magician's workshop with wires snaking across the floor," according to one programmer). The aim had been to build a computer that could operate at processing speeds approaching one microsecond per instruction, about a million instructions per second. When it was powered up in 1962, the Atlas became the most powerful computer in the world. Project Gemini, however, required more than super-fast number-crunching: NASA demanded from IBM an efficient, foolproof, rocket-control system that could dock vehicles in space—all in a 19" x 15" x 13" package that could fit into the module. Remarkably, just a few years later computers as powerful as the Atlas were indeed slimmed down to television-sized boxes. Finally, unlike Fortran, COBOL, and other early programming languages, BASIC (Beginner's All-Purpose Symbolic Instruction Code), which was designed in 1964, allowed non-programmers greater access to computer science.

Other inventions came fast and furious: the halogen lamp in 1960, nondairy creamer in 1961, the audio cassette in 1962. Permanent-press was invented in 1964, and new fabrics which were hardly fabrics at all, like Astroturf and Kevlar, followed in 1965. The first handheld calculator came in 1967, random access memory (or RAM) in 1968. The automated teller machine was invented in 1969, the same year as the bar-code scanner. Scientists at Dow Corp even found time to invent silicone breast implants.

Some of the biggest innovations came in health care and pharmaceuticals (not just the mind-bending ones). New equipment such as portable electro-cardiographs (EKGs) and cryogenic probes; new procedures, including organ transplants, vascular surgery, and live-virus vaccination; and new drugs such as Valium and blood-pressure-reducing medications enhanced the efficacy of medical care. With new methods of diagnosis and treatment, the healing power of physicians increased exponentially, as did the medical profession itself; between 1950 and 1970 the medical workforce in the United States tripled to 3.9 million people. Medicare and Medicaid, newly created in 1965 as part of LBJ's Great Society reforms, provided comprehensive health care for the elderly and the poor for the first time ever, but they were also expensive: national health-care expenditures increased sixfold to $71.6 billion per year. Nor was medical advancement a steady upward progression. Thalidomide, a drug prescribed to treat morning sickness in pregnant women, was found to cause horrific birth defects in tens of thousands of cases worldwide (banned in the United States after failing to pass FDA safety tests, millions of tablets still found their way to doctors' offices in clinical trials). Cyclamates—sugar substitutes such as saccharine—sweetened numerous low-calorie foods and drinks as additives for diet-conscious Americans, but were later found to cause cancer and, like thalidomide, were banned because they did not meet FDA standards. The most amazing medical advancement may have been the first heart transplant in 1964, when surgeons used a chimpanzee heart to replace a human one temporarily while awaiting another heart from a human donor. Science fiction was fast becoming science fact.

Sci-fi and hard science continued to blur at mid-decade and beyond. TV shows such as *Lost in Space* (1965) and *Star Trek* (1966), along with Stanley Kubrick's film *2001: A Space Odyssey* (1968), paralleled the interest in space exploration and helped to inspire it. Science fiction even touched on the decade's interracial tension. Rod Serling's experience with writing scripts for the hugely popular television series *The Twilight Zone* (which premiered in 1959 and ran for five seasons, until 1964) had taught him that "it was possible to have Martians say things that Democrats and Republicans can't say." When Serling adapted Pierre Boule's 1963 novel for film, it was the apes doing the talking, and the racialized subtext of *Planet of the Apes* (1968) invited viewers to imagine a world in which primates dominate humans. A choice bit of dialogue by one primate inverted an old stereotype: "To apes, all men look alike." Sammy Davis, Jr., a highly popular black entertainer of the day, deemed *Planet of the Apes* the best allegory on race relations he'd ever seen. During screenings, black audiences drowned out much of the dialogue by cheering "Right on!" In reply, placards reading "NAACP: Planet of the Apes" became common sights at white supremacist rallies.

As sci-fi reflected racial worries, atomic jitters continued to percolate into public concern. As nations rushed to test bigger and better hydrogen bombs (the United States conducted 122 atomic bomb tests in the 1950s, the Soviet Union at least 50, and Great Britain 21), researchers collected more and more evidence to indicate that radioactivity could travel from these test sites thousands of miles through the Earth's atmosphere before "falling out" somewhere else, where it could endanger life; strontium-90 and other radioactive isotopes caused leukemia, cancer, birth defects, and genetic mutations in humans and animals. In short order, radioactive substances were found in the soil, water, milk, rice, wheat, and other foods all over the world. Atomic anxieties peaked at flashpoints such as the Cuban Missile Crisis, but across the nation there was a steadily growing unease as people began to consider if humans had been tinkering with Mother Nature too much.

As cities, and the population in general, continued to grow, city and state governments had little time to devise plans for necessary urban development and the expansion of city services. Litter started to accumulate as people carelessly dumped their garbage wherever they liked. Each year five million automobile husks were dragged into junkyards. Industries produced an immense array of boxes, cans, bottles, and paper products: the detritus of a throwaway society. Litter threatened to become a permanent part of the landscape as the nature of litter itself changed from largely bio-degradable trash (the leftovers of food and wood products) to new, synthetic materials such as plastic and nylon that did not decompose like natural products and could take hundreds of years to breakdown.

Though few noticed, the excesses of the 1960s took their greatest toll on the natural environment. The production and use of chemicals such as DDT, which reduces insect damage to crops, had increased after World

War II: the chemist who discovered the insecticidal properties of DDT was awarded the Nobel Prize in 1948. The use of such chemicals spread rapidly. In 1947, the United States had produced 124 million pounds of chemical pesticides; by 1960, the country was producing 638 million pounds annually, which farmers applied liberally to maximize crop yields, and which homeowners applied on their neatly manicured lawns to reduce insect pests. As more houses were built in the suburbs, more chemicals followed, percolating into the soil and groundwater.

Lands in the public domain, most notably those in the cherished National Park system, came under threat from overuse and mismanagement; water and air pollution became acute. Motivated by greed, real estate developers and businessmen justified short-term gain by soft-pedaling long-term damage. Growth, after all, was a sign of success, and Americans assumed that problems would dissipate in a future governed by the march of progress and neatly managed by scientific know-how. With the twin assumptions that science could fix almost anything, and that science was only getting better and better, it became easy to bequeath potential problems to future generations.

A major wake-up call came from an unlikely source: a book about robins' eggs. Most Americans were unaware of how manmade chemicals poisoned the environment, until the publication of Rachel Carson's *Silent Spring* (1962), which discussed the haphazard use of DDT and its spread through the food chain. "Over increasingly large areas of the United States," she wrote, "spring now comes unheralded by the return of birds, and the early mornings are strangely silent where once they were filled with the beauty of bird song." Robins and other songbirds were dying from the chemical, as were ospreys and bald eagles, and Carson explained why: DDT was making the egg shells of birds so thin that they broke apart before the hatchlings had a chance to develop. In plain terms, the author used scientific evidence to show how with every application of insecticide the toughest insects survived, passing immunities to the next generation of insects and, in turn, making the development and use of increasingly stronger pesticides necessary. She also explained to readers how chemicals such as DDT— though diluted in large bodies of water—became concentrated as it worked its way up the food chain from plankton to fish to birds, and, eventually, back to people, many of whom were horrified by Carson's revelations.

Silent Spring was a pioneering work in twentieth-century ecology—the scientific study of how living *systems*, not simply individual organisms, interact—something that most people were just beginning to understand

Figure 9.2 Rachel Carson warned Americans about the dangers of progress (Source: © CBS Photo Archive/Getty Images).

and appreciate. It was Carson, in fact, who introduced the idea of ecosystems to the American public. When making observations such as: "It is not possible to add pesticides to water anywhere without threatening the purity of water everywhere," she was popularizing ecological thinking. "Seldom if ever does Nature operate in closed and separate compartments," she warned.

Carson cautioned not only against the spread of pesticides but also against the rapidity of technological innovation and the speed of societal change itself. Chemical companies as well as industrial factories of all kinds were ceaselessly pumping new synthetic compounds into the air and soil. Plants and animals and people were being asked to adapt to 500 new chemicals every year at a pace that outstripped the glacier-like evolution of nature; not surprisingly, they could not. By entering environments incapable of breaking them down into base ingredients, those chemicals that so efficiently killed insects were also killing other organisms in the form of cancer and other diseases about which scientists understood relatively little. In declaring war on bugs people had, in fact, inadvertently declared war on themselves.

To a people conditioned to accept unquestioningly the notion of better living through chemistry, Carson's message gained traction slowly. The realization that the indiscriminate use of synthetically-manufactured substances in agriculture and industry had unforeseen and often disastrous consequences began to capture the attention of the American public, which increasingly supported controls over pollution in all its forms, especially that of the air and water. Individual states gradually banned the use of DDT, and the federal government followed suit in 1972. Yet, Carson's message also met staunch resistance, especially from colleagues in the scientific community and the chemical companies themselves. Industry representatives went so far as to charge that *Silent Spring* was part of a communist plot to ruin US agriculture. The president of one company that manufactured DDT called Carson a "fanatic defender of the cult of the balance of nature." John Maddox, a theoretical physicist, charged that Carson had played a "literary trick" on her readers. "The most seriously misleading part of the narrative is the use of horror stories about the misuse of DDT to create an impression that there are no safe uses worth consideration," he charged. "Miss Carson's sin was the use of 'calculated overdramatization.'" As *New York Times* reporter Philip Shabecoff has noted, some male colleagues in the scientific community seemed particularly hostile, sexualizing their contempt and couching their disagreement in gendered terms. To them, the alarmist "Miss" Carson seemed overly emotional, even hysterical. A Federal Pest Control Review Board member said she must be "a spinster, [so] what's she worried about genetics for?"

After testifying before Congress in 1963 and warning the world about the hidden toxins around us, Carson died of cancer in 1964. Her message was echoed and amplified in contemporary books such as Murray Bookchin's *Our Synthetic Environment*, also published in 1962. Bookchin called for a "sound, ecologically oriented social movement," one that scaled economies to human needs rather than industrial appetites. Due in part to these seminal works, the relationship between people and nature was becoming a public issue, the environment a focal point of social and political concern. The wellbeing of particular species ushered in this burgeoning environmental movement, and the first catalyst of ecology and the conservation movement came, like robins' eggs, in a rather surprising form.

With its seafaring tradition, New England had secured the United States' place in the early nineteenth century as the preeminent whaling nation in the world, though whaling ships plied Pacific waters, too. Whalers targeted not only right whales and humpbacks but also sperm whales, prized for the globs of spermaceti in their heads which Americans and Europeans used as lamp oil. At the turn of the twentieth century, new harpoon guns and faster chaser boats made hunting even the most elusive of whale species easier. Vast fortunes were made in hunting the massive marine mammals, whose oils were now rendered into a wider variety of products, including industrial lubricants, cosmetics, and margarine. By this time American fleets faced fierce competition from foreign factory ships, which trolled international waters and processed whale carcasses with astonishing speed. The US whaling industry declined sharply in the 1920s, as foreign whalers captured more whales and as American capitalists channeled their cash into railroads, oil, and steel, but the hunting continued with gusto worldwide.

In 1960, competing interests in the Antarctic whaling trade met to decide how to "distribute" the remaining population of the largest animal ever known to have existed: blue whales, which had been heavily reduced over the first half of the century when 350,000 were killed by whaling fleets in the southern hemisphere. Increased awareness about marine mammals came from both popular and academic sources. *Flipper* (1963), a heart-warming story about a boy and his pet dolphin, increased awareness about the plight of marine animals and helped to bring the whaling industry under closer scrutiny, as did the work of John C. Lilly, who studied the communication and behavior of whales and dolphins and concluded that these "minds in the water," with much bigger brains than humans, had the capability for complex language transference.

Public concern soon translated into a concerted effort by activists to protect these gentle giants. "Save the Whales," a simple phrase reprinted on buttons and stickers, become the slogan of the early environmental movement. Whaling in British Columbia actually ceased in 1967 after public outcry and protest.

Other environmental issues, unlike pesticide use or even whaling, were too immediate and dramatic to overlook, even for a moment longer. When the Cuyahoga River—choked with old tires, refuse, and other debris—actually caught fire near a steel mill in Cleveland, Ohio, in June of 1969, the problems of unrestricted consumption and abuse of the environment could no longer be ignored. For over a century, industrial cities such as Cleveland had treated their waterways as an open sewer, a means to an end and nothing more. The spectacle of a river literally burning, however, prompted a national reevaluation of industrial success: perhaps this was progress gone wrong? *Time* magazine described the Cuyahoga as "the river that oozes rather than flows," in which a person "does not drown but decays." Thoroughly embarrassed, the city of Cleveland worked to clean up its main thoroughfare, which many had come to accept as a regular eyesore.

Less than a month later, on July 20, 1969, Kennedy's vision of sending a person to the moon became a reality when *Apollo 11* deposited Edwin "Buzz" Aldrin, Jr., and Neil Armstrong in the lunar Sea of Tranquility 9 (staying aboard the Columbia command and service module, Michael Collins, the third astronaut sent to the moon, had to "stay in the car" orbiting 60 miles above). When Armstrong stepped down, becoming the first person to set foot on the moon, he famously quipped, "That's one small step for a man, one giant leap for mankind." It was a jaw-dropping moment for people everywhere. Aldrin would follow Armstrong onto the moon's powdery surface. "Beautiful view," he remarked. "Ain't that somethin'?" Armstrong marveled.

Reaching the moon made earthlings reconsider their terrestrial habitat in a new light and helped to extend the back-to-earth movement beyond communes; indeed, going to space created new ecological concerns largely unrelated to space travel itself. People were accustomed to moon-gazing, but looking back from the vantage point of astronauts created something of a paradigm shift. Photographs of Earth from its moon offered a new perspective on this planet: a beautiful, small, fragile-looking sphere of blue, alone against the black backdrop of space. In light of these photos, Earth no longer seemed quite so big or inexhaustible. Fresh understandings of the cosmos, our home planet, and our own relationship to them were now possible. A new dawning of environmental consciousness, one that began in the 1960s and reached fruition in the 1970s, was at hand.

If the centuries-old American notion of progress was coming into question amidst the rapid-fire scientific developments and technological advancements of the 1960s, then one group still labored to enjoy a taste of the fruits of that progress. In the face of terrible odds, against violent opposition, African Americans marched ahead, pressing onward in their struggle for equality. For some activists, this struggle would morph from a battle *for* civil rights into a war *against* white supremacy itself, and this new quest involved not only African Americans but also people of color from a multitude of racial and ethnic backgrounds. The civil rights movement, long simmering and heating up, was about to boil over.

Further Reading

Walter A. McDougall, *The Heavens and the Earth: A Political History of the Space Age* (Baltimore: Johns Hopkins University Press, 1997)

Rachel Carson, *Silent Spring*, anniversary ed. (New York: Houghton Mifflin, 2002)

Fred Turner, *From Counterculture to Cyberculture: Stewart Brand, the Whole Earth Network, and the Rise of Digital Utopianism* (Chicago: University of Chicago Press, 2006)

Gene Kranz, *Failure is Not an Option: Mission Control from Mercury to Apollo 13 and Beyond* (New York: Simon & Schuster, 2000)

John M. Logsdon, *John F. Kennedy and the Race to the Moon* (New York: Palgrave, 2013)

10

Minority Empowerment:
From Margin to Mainstream

In the mid-1960s, activists continued the struggle for black equality, but that fight would soon balloon beyond desegregation and voter registration—indeed, beyond civil rights. In the latter part of the decade, the major reforms gained left many Negroes—especially young ones who began to experiment with calling themselves "black"—hungry for more; having garnered what Elaine Brown would call "a taste of power," they now broadened the civil rights movement into a wider movement based on political autonomy, economic parity, and social clout. Inspired by black militants, other peoples of color initiated their own movements toward liberation and equality. Following on the heels of landmark national legislation, a more militant push toward empowerment came not only from black Americans but also other racial groups tired of living on the margins of the mainstream. Ramrodding his predecessor's civil rights bill through the legislative process, President Johnson told a joint session of Congress on November 27, 1963: "No memorial oration or eulogy could more eloquently honor President Kennedy's memory than the earliest possible passage of the civil rights bill for which he fought so long." Filibustering the measure, Senators James Eastland (D-Miss.), Richard Russell (D-Ga.), and Strom Thurmond (D-S.C.), among others, viewed the bill as a top-down, federally intrusive trampling of white Southern rights, comparable in scope to Radical Reconstruction, when Republicans in Congress placed the former Confederacy under military control and ruled the region with an iron hand. But LBJ had the votes, the bill passed the House and Senate, and on July 2, 1964, Johnson signed into law the Civil Rights Act of 1964, the most comprehensive civil rights

The Long Sixties: America, 1955–1973, First Edition. Christopher B. Strain.
© 2017 Christopher B. Strain. Published 2017 by John Wiley & Sons, Inc.

bill of the twentieth century. The law banned racial discrimination in employment, eliminated segregation in all publicly owned facilities, and authorized the US attorney general to file lawsuits on behalf of any American citizen denied rights guaranteed her or him by the US Constitution.

That same summer, civil rights activists targeted the least reconstructed of the former Confederate states, Mississippi. The concept behind "Freedom Summer" was simple: enlist white college students in voter registration and other efforts begun by local leaders (many affiliated with the NAACP) and organizers (mostly from SNCC but also from CORE and SCLC), all cooperating together as COFO, the Council of Federated Organizations. Approximately 600 volunteers flocked to orientation and training in Ohio from places like Cambridge, Massachusetts; Ann Arbor, Michigan; and Berkeley, California. The result was a strange union of impoverished, embattled, black Southerners—many of whom had no formal education— and privileged, young, white Northerners, hoping (naively perhaps) to change the world by changing Mississippi. The volunteers went door to door encouraging local sharecroppers to vote, showing them how to fill out registration forms, and inviting them to meetings. They set up "freedom schools" with alternative curriculums centered on civics and black history. But such efforts did not go unnoticed or unchallenged: strides were made only at great cost in terms of effort and even personal safety, and a backlash of terrorist attacks by local white racists surprised the whole nation by their brazenness and ferocity. According to one figuring, white violence resulted in 35 shootings; 30 homes and businesses bombed; 35 churches bombed or burned; and at least 80 beatings of civil rights activists and black residents they were trying to assist.

There were six murders in connection with Freedom Summer, the most infamous of which involved three young civil rights workers reported missing in Neshoba County on June 21, 1964. They were James Cheney, a 21-year-old black CORE worker from Meridian; Michael Schwerner, a 24-year-old white social worker from New York City and veteran member of the CORE staff whose very presence, as a Northern Jew with a goatee, threatened many nativist Mississippians; and Andrew Goodman, a 21-year-old New Yorker enjoying his first day in Mississippi as a COFO summer project volunteer. The three had driven to Neshoba County to investigate the burning of Mount Zion Methodist Church, which they had hoped to use for a freedom school. On their way into Philadelphia, Mississippi, the county seat, they were stopped and arrested by a sheriff's deputy on charges of speeding and arson. The three were jailed, then released later that night. Shortly thereafter they disappeared.

As public outcry over the disappearance of the three young men increased, President Johnson ordered the involvement of J. Edgar Hoover and the FBI in the case. Before long, hundreds of FBI agents were scouring the Mississippi countryside, looking for the young men. Horrifyingly, while dredging local rivers for evidence, searchers found the bodies of *other* young black males, including two students expelled from Alcorn Agricultural and Mechanical College for their participation in civil rights protests; a boy wearing a CORE T-shirt; and several unidentified corpses. After spreading around informant money, it soon came to light what had happened: after being released from jail, Cheney, Schwerner, and Goodman were stopped again, this time by the sheriff's deputy and a number of KKK members. The Klansmen took the men to a rural area and shot them to death after beating Cheney, then buried their bodies in an earthen dam. On August 4, the FBI took a bulldozer to the dam and exhumed the bodies.

The murderers undoubtedly considered their deeds a justified response to the "invasion" of Mississippi by "outside agitators," but the rest of the nation and the world thought otherwise. Although it was widely known who had probably done the killings, it was also understood that in that part of the South those individuals would likely never be convicted of murder by a jury of their peers; therefore, after much goading by civil rights activists, the Justice Department charged 19 men with "conspiracy to deprive civil rights," a federal violation under the new Civil Rights Act. In 1967, seven of the men, including the sheriff's deputy, were convicted and sentenced to prison terms of three to ten years; three others were acquitted, and three were freed by a hung jury. The conviction, even in federal court and even on a conspiracy charge, was a first for the state of Mississippi. The martyrdom of Cheney, Schwerner, and Goodman had horrified the nation, and for the first time since the civil rights movement began, activists in grave danger knew that the federal government might offer them a measure of protection, however slim and oblique.

Malcolm X, the outspoken minister in the Nation of Islam who offered a compelling counterpoint to the dominant civil rights narrative of integration and nonviolent direct action, would enjoy no such reassurance. Continuing to emphasize self-determination, self-protection, and Pan-African unity, he had become increasingly politicized, which met with disapproval from some of his brethren in the Nation of Islam, including leader Elijah Muhammad. In February 1965, just after he had begun to address an Organization of Afro-American Unity (OAAU) rally at the Audubon Ballroom in Harlem, Malcolm X was shot several times at the podium; three Black Muslims, including Talmadge X Hayer (a.k.a. Thomas Hagan, the only one of the three who confessed to the crime) were arrested. The fallen minister was taken to Columbia Presbyterian Hospital where he was pronounced dead on arrival. In death Malcolm X would become even bigger than he had been in life, as the posthumously published and widely read *Autobiography of Malcolm X* (1965) told his story to millions of readers, inspired by his uncompromising views, commanding intellect, and personal transformation from two-bit hustler to charismatic leader.

Back down South, civil rights activists labored in the face of brutal enmity in Alabama against the twin evils of segregation and disfranchisement. In Selma—where half of the city's residents were black but less than 2 percent of eligible black voters had been allowed to register to vote—local African Americans united with SCLC and SNCC in 1965 to initiate the Voting Rights Campaign: like their counterparts in Mississippi, white racists responded savagely. An Alabama state trooper shot and killed Jimmie Lee Jackson, a 26-year-old deacon attempting to save his mother and grandfather from a vicious beating during a nonviolent protest in nearby Perry County. Black activists and white sympathizers organized a march in Selma to protest Jackson's death; the violent attack by state troopers and deputies on the nonviolent protestors as they attempted to march across the Edmund Pettus Bridge on their way out of town toward Montgomery became known as "Bloody Sunday." Two days later, white thugs attacked and killed James Reeb, a Unitarian Universalist minister from Boston, in downtown Selma shortly after an aborted second march to Montgomery. A third attempt to trek to the state capitol—this time successful—ended with the death of Viola Liuzzo, a 39-year-old mother of five from Detroit shot to death in her car by Klansmen on US Route 80 while shuttling marchers back to Selma from Montgomery.

These sacrifices reverberated in the halls of Congress. Ten days after Bloody Sunday, a voting reform bill was introduced in the US Senate. Later that summer, on August 6, President Johnson signed into law the Voting Rights Act of 1965, lauded as "the most successful piece of civil rights legislation ever enacted" and "one of the most important legislative enactments of all time" by a former attorney general and former chairman of the US Civil Rights Commission, respectively. The landmark bill regularized voting across the South by prohibiting the disqualification or intimidation of qualified minority voters, and by establishing extensive federal oversight of local electoral procedures.

In light of such reforms, certain practices and policies became increasingly anachronistic. As African Americans (re-)entered the body politick, the national origins quota system that had defined US immigration policy for 40 years began to seem particularly antiquated, reminiscent of bygone prejudices. Ever since the 1920s, official policy had excluded Asians and Africans while favoring western and northern Europeans over eastern and southern Europeans. That system, now embarrassing to most forward-thinking Americans, was replaced under the Immigration and Nationality Act of 1965 (or Hart-Cellar Act) with one based on immigrant skills and family ties. President Johnson signed that bill into law on October 3, 1965, at the foot of the Statue of Liberty.

The Voting Rights Act and the Hart-Cellar Act signaled major changes at the federal level regarding the place of racial and ethnic minorities in American life. Once marginalized, African Americans were moving closer to the center, and the victories of black Southerners in dismantling Jim Crow and gaining real access to the ballot inspired other minorities to lobby for fuller inclusion in American life. Taking their cues from a new frontline of black militants, other minority activists soon followed suit in petitioning for greater involvement in civic and political affairs.

What black activists and their white allies had achieved thus far was impressive, but having successfully challenged desegregation and disen-franchisement, they now increasingly focused on other issues, including economic disparity, lack of opportunity, and the perniciousness of white supremacy. This widening involved a broader conceptualization of civil rights (that is, rights belonging to an individual by virtue of being a citizen), alloyed with cries for empowerment, that gave rise to what historian Jeffrey Ogbar has termed "radical ethnic nationalism" and "new constructions of ethnic identity" in the mid- to late-1960s. In some localities, activists had consistently pushed for more than civil rights (historian Hasan Jeffries has described the struggle in Lowndes County, Alabama, as a quest for "freedom rights," an amalgam of civil rights, civil liberties, property rights, human rights, and assurances of safety and security); now that impetus was transforming the civil rights movement into something greater than a movement for civil rights.

Widespread civil unrest outside the South reified the idea that civil rights reform by itself would not satisfy the discontent unleashed by the civil rights movement. Rioting in Harlem in 1964 spread not only to neighboring cities in New Jersey but also to Rochester, Philadelphia, and Chicago later that summer. The Los Angeles neighborhood of Watts, which exploded in fiery chaos in 1965, came to symbolize the seething discontent and frustration of urban blacks outside the South, away from the main battlegrounds of the civil rights movement. Viewing the riots apolitically—less as urban uprisings than as lawless episodes of looting— whites tended to be baffled by the violence. Should the Civil Rights Act of 1964 and Voting Rights Act of 1965 not have placated black Americans? And why were black folks in Northern inner cities so angry? Many whites failed to grasp that the civil rights bills, while enormously important, were not enough. Legislation alone would not suffice to address the despair and alienation experienced by a majority of impoverished African Americans, Southern or not, increasingly discouraged by the halting progress of the civil rights movement and the impunity with which those in power violently protected white privilege. Rioting would continue during the "long hot summers" of the mid- to late-1960s in places like Detroit, Newark, even Washington, DC. Some of this formless rage found its way into new cries for black nationalism, cultural pride, and economic liberation.

Some activists described this seemingly new form of militancy as "Black Power," a phrase educed by Stokely Carmichael and Willie Ricks at a civil rights march in Greenwood, Mississippi, in 1966. "What do you want?" the two SNCC activists asked a crowd of marchers, angered at rough treatment by local law enforcement personnel. "Black Power!" the crowd roared in reply. Ominous to most whites, the phrase was at base level an expression of political and social empowerment. It was Black Power that would eventually turn "Bloody" Lowndes County—a bastion of white supremacy in Alabama—into a stronghold of black militancy and empowerment. Black activists in Lowndes (with SNCC help) ran a slate of black candidates in the county's general election. While none in the slate was initially elected, persistent electoral efforts eventually shifted the balance of power there. To distinguish these candidates, the Lowndes County Freedom Organization chose a new ballot symbol: a snarling black panther.

The symbol of the black panther became even better known in Oakland, California, where two street-wise community activists not only initiated armed patrols to curtail police brutality but also created an organization with that name. While taking classes at Oakland City College (now Merritt College), Huey P. Newton befriended Bobby Seale, with whom he worked in the North Oakland Neighborhood Anti-Poverty Center and the local chapter of the Revolutionary Action Movement (RAM). In October 1966, Newton and Seale wrote a Ten-Point Program—not only a list of demands on behalf of "black and oppressed people" but also an unequivocal call for self-determination—and joined with Reggie Forte, Sherman Forte, Elbert "Big Man" Howard, and "Lil" Bobby Hutton to form the Black Panther Party for Self-Defense; Seale became its chairman, Newton its "minister of defense." Exercising their constitutional right to bear arms, the Black Panthers postured aggressively as they spoke out against the abuse of authority by law enforcement officers. Armed with a gun and a law book, Newton would shadow and confront white police officers who attempted arrests in the ghetto. By brandishing firearms in public and speaking out against violence by the Oakland Police Department, the Panthers politicized the issue of self-defense by and for African Americans and spotlighted the problem of white police brutality against black residents of inner cities.

Panther leaders recruited "brothers off the block"—tough guys like themselves with a proclivity for violence, many of whom were gang

Figure 10.1 Black Panthers outside the New York City Courthouse in April 1969 (Source: © David Fenton/Getty Images).

members and ex-cons—to protect Oakland's ghetto from "the pigs": the white police officers who, in their view, aggressively policed their community from the outside in, as marauding invaders. For their part, some police officers viewed Newton and his comrades as "crazy niggers" (as Seale claimed in his 1968 autobiography *Seize the Time*) itching for a fight—an image Newton did little to dispel. Dressed in powder-blue shirts, black leather jackets, and berets, the Panthers were angry, earnest, disciplined, and—with their array of weapons—very, very frightening to most white folks.

Mixing anti-colonial rhetoric with bellicose defiance, Newton drew a combination of radical intellectuals and gangsters into his orbit: Stokely Carmichael, H. Rap Brown, Eldridge Cleaver, Kathleen Cleaver, Elaine Brown, Ericka Huggins, David Hilliard, and other future Panthers gravitated toward Newton, his ideas, his charisma, and his bold posturing. In 1967, Oakland police officer John Frey was shot to death during an altercation with Newton at a traffic stop, and Newton went to jail for Frey's murder. What might have destroyed the organization instead invigorated it, as Seale and the Cleavers mobilized a "Free Huey" campaign in which thousands protested at the Oakland Coliseum and at the Alameda County Courthouse in downtown Oakland. The campaign helped turn the organization into a national phenomenon as the Panthers expanded to other American cities. In 1968, the group shortened its name to the Black Panther Party, focusing directly on social activism and political action. Peak membership was 10,000 in 1969, the same year the Panthers initiated a Free Breakfast Program for kids in Oakland; the group's newspaper, *The Black Panther*, had a circulation of 250,000. What had begun as a self-defense advocacy group had evolved into an organization with Marxist and socialist predilections: the new revolutionary vanguard of the Sixties.

Other groups were soon patterning themselves after the Panthers. In East Los Angeles in December 1967, teenager David Sanchez formed the first unit of the Brown Berets who, like the Panthers, demonstrated against police brutality; they also protested the general oppression of Mexican Americans, including farmworkers who had begun to organize a couple of years earlier under Cesar Chavez. Like African Americans in the South, Mexican Americans in California had long been exploited as cheap agricultural labor. The second largest ethnic group in the state, they suffered from underrepresentation in the state legislature and widespread discrimination in housing, education, and employment. Many now sought to cultivate a new dignity and pride in their ethnic heritage, in *La Raza* (The Race), and in Aztlán, their spiritual homeland. In Denver, Rodolfo

"Corky" Gonzales popularized a new term to describe this militant radicalism: *Chicano* replaced Mexican American in much the same way that "black" replaced "Negro."

In 1968, black students at San Francisco State College petitioned for the creation of a new academic program in "Black Studies," a curricular initiative devoted to the black experience in the United States and in the African diaspora. Other students of color joined forces with African Americans to form the Third World Liberation Front (TWLF), a coalition of black, Chicano, and Asian American students whose efforts soon arced across San Francisco Bay to that hotbed of student activism, the University of California at Berkeley. Students on campuses around the Bay Area demanded a more diversified curriculum and the hiring of more people of color for faculty and staff positions. The TWLF-led student strike at SFSU succeeded, resulting in the first ethnic studies department in the nation, as did the one at Berkeley—after beatings, mass arrests, and the intervention of hundreds of police officers and National Guardsmen.

It was also at Berkeley where students formed the Asian American Political Alliance (AAPA) in 1968. This coalition represented the first time that students with heritages from among the different ethnic groups in Asia presented a united front. The AAPA had close ties with the Black Panther Party as well as the Red Guard, an Asian-American organization modeled after the Panthers. In fact, the exchange between all three of these groups was often quite fluid, as evidenced by the actions of individuals such as Richard Aoki, a Japanese American from West Oakland and classmate of Huey Newton and Bobby Seale at Merritt College. Aoki joined the Black Panther Party while at Merritt and became a field marshal for the Panthers; he later joined the AAPA after transferring to Berkeley and became a prominent spokesperson for the group (a 1968 photograph shows him wearing Panther garb, raising a fist, and holding a sign that reads, "Yellow Peril Supports Black Power"). Like their black and Chicano counterparts, Asian student activists demanded an end to US involvement in the Vietnam War and to police brutality. They also demanded an end to the exploitation of Asian farmworkers on the West Coast, and they lobbied for the admission of more faculty and students of color at Berkeley.

Named after Chairman Mao Tse-Tung's cadre of young revolutionaries during the Chinese Cultural Revolution, the Red Guard was founded in 1969 in San Francisco. Like the Brown Berets, they styled themselves after the Panthers and openly carried guns. Declaring themselves a Communist organization, the Red Guard fought to prevent the closing of a neighborhood tuberculosis ward and modified the local Breakfast for Children program to accommodate poor senior citizens in Chinatown. Such efforts were met with both appreciation and apprehension by older Chinese Americans, alarmed by leftist political activity and clinging tenuously to recent advances such as the 1965 lift on immigration restrictions from China.

In New York, college-educated, middle-class youth founded the I Wor Kuen (IWK), named after a secret society of rebels who attempted to expunge Westerners from China and depose the Qing dynasty in the nineteenth century. Known as Boxers in the West, the original I Wor Kuen (literally "Righteous and Harmonious Fists") were peasants in northern China who banded together in the late 1890s to train in a form of martial arts that they believed would make them impervious to bullets; they specifically targeted and massacred Christian missionaries as symbols of foreign imperialism. In 1969, the modern IWK read anti-colonial theorist Frantz Fanon, Mao Tse-Tung, Vladimir Lenin, and Karl Marx for inspiration and instruction in forming their own class-based revolution against oppression.

That same year in Los Angeles, working-class radicals—including not only former street gang members and ex-cons but also many Nisei and Sansei, second- and third-generation Japanese Americans—came together as the Yellow Brotherhood (YB). Together, these groups and others not only inverted stereotypes of Chinese and Japanese Americans as apolitical and meek but also promoted "Yellow Power." Adopting a new kind of pan-Asian unity, they rejected the term "Oriental" in preference of a new term: *Asian-American.*

"Red Power" also made an impact, paralleling that of Black, Brown, and Yellow Power. The poorest of the poor, and the smallest ethnic group numerically, Native Americans had for centuries suffered the cruelties of racism and white supremacy, which had, among other things, disposed them of their ancestral lands. By the end of the 1960s, they had the lowest standard of living of any ethnic group in the United States, with the highest rates of alcoholism, unemployment, and high school dropouts, among other societal ills: the suicide rate of Indian teenagers was one hundred times greater than that of white teenagers. Despair on reservations was more commonplace than diplomas. Like the youth of other minority groups at the time, young Native American activists took their cues from black activists in trying to find ways in which to address problems in their own lives and experiences.

In 1961 a Cherokee college student named Clyde Warrior helped to form the National Indian Youth Council (NIYC), modeled after SNCC. Beginning in 1963, its newspaper, *ABC: Americans Before Columbus*, became a leading voice in the burgeoning Red Power movement. NIYC activists were joined in 1964 by celebrities such as comedian Dick Gregory and actor Marlon Brando (both deeply involved in the struggle for black equality) at a "fish-in" in Washington State's Nisqually River, where fishing rights had been guaranteed to the Nisqually Indians by an 1853 treaty (wardens and state officials claimed that tribal privileges were now superseded by new fish and game laws). When Indian activists took over and occupied Alcatraz—the deserted island prison in San Francisco Bay—later that same year (see below), they claimed ownership by citing another old treaty that had once relinquished unused surplus land to the Sioux. Such actions emboldened Indian activists to protest insensitive museum exhibits that exhibited sacred regalia and desecrated ancestral bones; to boycott Thanksgiving and Columbus Day holidays; to close public beaches and bridges on old lands; to demand Indian Studies programs in schools; to demand rehab centers in cities and on reservations for those suffering from alcoholism; and to picket insensitive portrayals of Native Americans in books and movies.

In 1968, Dennis Banks and George Mitchell founded the American Indian Movement (AIM), self-consciously styled after the Black Panthers. In fact, like the Panthers, AIM sought to end police brutality in Minneapolis where the group first organized; like the Brown Berets and others, those who joined AIM also created a statement of beliefs and goals redolent of the Panthers Ten-Point Platform. In November 1969, a group of Indian activists landed again on Alcatraz Island, which they claimed "by right of discovery." They offered to buy the island for $24 in glass beads and cloth: a reference to the 1626 purchase of Manhattan from the Manhate Indians by the director of the Dutch West India Company.

In these ways cries of Black Power echoed loudly, affecting not only other people of color but also the "moderate" activists who had catalyzed the early success of the civil rights movement. Always radical, Martin Luther King, Jr., himself evolved from reformer to revolutionary in the mid- to late-1960s. It was a much less conciliatory—perhaps even dangerous—King who discussed the social mission of the church to combat poverty and speak out against violence. Referring to himself as a "Christian Socialist," he increasingly embraced the social gospel: championing the poor, allying with labor unions, speaking out against the war in Vietnam, and

Figure 10.2   Native American activists change a property sign on Alcatraz Island from "US" to "Indian" on November 21, 1969 (Source: © Vince Maggiora/San Francisco Chronicle/CORBIS).

exploring theories of not only economic parity but also economic redistribution. As a Baptist minister who found guidance in scripture, redemption in service, and salvation in God's grace, King was called on to move and to act. For him, social justice was a Christian tradition, not a liberal agenda. His commitment to social ethics was born out of his understanding of the gospel: Know Jesus. Love thy neighbor. Help the poor. Feed the hungry. Care for the sick. Do justice. Love kindness. King's wholehearted embrace of these messages—so simple, taken straight from scripture—somehow alienated him from many churchgoers who found it easier to lie low, be quiet, and fit in.

While troubled by the violent rhetoric of Black Power, King saw value in its stridency and self-determinism and refused to condemn it outright. He intuited that the violence inherent in Black Power's righteous anger might undercut his own nonviolent efforts. "Violence has been the inseparable twin of materialism, the hallmark of its grandeur and misery," he wrote in 1967. "This is one thing about modern civilization that I do not care to imitate." Paradoxically, he was attracted to the energy and promise of Black Power, which arrived on the scene just at the time when his own focus was shifting, his energies were flagging, and his reputation suffering.

In 1966 King went to Chicago to try to alleviate the problems of urban poverty and dispel the illusion that poverty and racism were peculiar to the South. He said that he had three objectives in Chicago: 1) to educate people about slum conditions, 2) to organize renters into a union to force landlords to meet their obligations, and 3) to mobilize tenants into an army of nonviolent demonstrators. Soon after, King's condemnation of American policy in Vietnam marginalized him from mainstream America. When President Johnson had sent ground troops to Southeast Asia in 1965, King had begun to speak out against the growing war there and he continued to do so in 1966 and 1967, *before* a sense of moral urgency regarding Vietnam spread throughout the American public. Rattled by King's more militant style and new stand against the war, the national headquarters of the NAACP and the Urban League both went on record as opposing the union of civil rights and anti-Vietnam War protest. Other civil rights leaders encouraged King to give up one role or the other—either to remain a civil rights leader or become an international peacemaker, but not both. King, however, saw no distinction; in fact, he saw the two issues as inherently linked. "We are committing atrocities equal to any perpetrated by the Vietcong," he noted. "The bombs in Vietnam explode at home—they destroy the dream and possibility for a decent America." He talked about the disproportionate number of poor people and people of color who were drafted and shipped overseas to Southeast Asia to fight. The attorney of the SCLC told King that his outspokenness on the war would bankrupt the organization, to which King replied, "I don't care if we don't get five cents in the mail. I'm going to keep preaching my message."

Clearly Black Power reverberated across the diaspora and affected a range of individuals, from young militants to the older generation of civil rights leaders—and beyond. The 1968 Olympics provided one of the most iconic if unlikely stages for the Black Power movement. On the winner's podium for the men's 200-meter final at Olympic Stadium in Mexico City,

American medalists Tommie Smith and John Carlos donned black gloves and raised their fists in the air in a Black Power salute. Smith, not only the first person to run 200 meters in under 20 seconds but also a Reserve Officer Training Corps (ROTC) cadet at San Jose State College, and Carlos, seeking to show solidarity with people fighting around the globe for human rights, acted out of concern for ongoing racial segregation in the United States as well as apartheid in South Africa. The silent protest was met with murmurs of surprise, then boos and catcalls; Avery Brundage, the president of the International Olympic Committee and a known racist who had opposed Jesse Owens in 1936, forced the athletes out of the Games (silver medalist Peter Norman, the white athlete who shared the podium with Smith and Carlos and wore an Olympic Project for Human Rights button to show support, was ostracized when he returned to Australia and blacklisted from future Olympics). The silent protest sent shock waves beyond the sports world. While some viewed the demonstration as heroically brave, others argued that the Olympics should be apolitical—even as they thrilled to see the United States win more gold medals and more total medals than the Soviet Union that year.

New coalitions created a formidable alliance of young leftists in some cities. Influenced by the new momentum in the civil rights movement and Black Power, Puerto Rican gang leader José "Cha Cha" Jimenez began to politicize the Young Lords in Chicago in 1968. Fred Hampton, a magnetic speaker, effective organizer, and deputy chairman of the Black Panthers in Chicago, worked with Jimenez to transform these gangsters into revolutionaries. From Hampton's perspective, the poor, marginalized, angry young men who joined gangs were the perfect candidates for political recruitment: the *lumpenproletariat* that Marx had described in his writings. The Latin Kings, the city's largest Latino gang, also radicalized, joining with the Panthers and the Young Lords. This "Rainbow Coalition" even included poor whites from the Deep South, now living in Chicago's Uptown neighborhood, a gang known as the Young Patriots. Working side by side with the Young Patriots, the Panthers, the Kings, and the Young Lords valued these incongruous "hillbilly nationalists" as stalwart comrades. Whenever the Patriots, clad in jean jackets and Confederate-flag shoulder patches, provided security for Fred Hampton and the Black Panthers in 1969, the effect was jarring to outside observers but not atypical. Chicago's radical activists stood together—an alliance of poor and working-class rainbow militants, united against the triple evils of capitalism, racism, and imperialism.

White student radicals fought to stay on top of the tide of revolutionary unrest that they had helped to unleash. The SDS of the late 1960s hardly resembled the SDS of the early decade, as the Weathermen made head-lines for the "Days of Rage" demonstrations in October 1969. The group threatened to "bring the war home" with rioting through the affluent Gold Coast neighborhood of Chicago: vandalizing homes, smashing cars, and assaulting police officers. With time the group became even more violent, manufacturing and planting bombs.

These violent acts did not go unchallenged or unanswered, but even talk of violence proved dangerous for would-be revolutionaries. Across the nation young radicals were vilified, attacked, imprisoned, and sometimes killed. Local law enforcement often did their part to bully "longhairs" and "lefties" and to make their lives unpleasant, as did the federal government. Through its COINTELPRO initiative, the FBI targeted a host of organizations on the New Left (including all of the ones mentioned here). In the name of national security, COINTELPRO used overt and covert tactics to disrupt organizations that FBI head J. Edgar Hoover deemed dangerous; agents infiltrated organizations as moles and provocateurs, eavesdropped to gather incriminating information, smeared and blackmailed individuals using forged documents, planted false reports in the media, heightened tension and hostility between groups, and harassed and intimidated everyone from mainstream civil rights activists to white college students who merely spoke of revolution. At times it seemed as if New Left activists were being singled out simply because they were nonconformist, but the more violent the rhetoric, the more violent the response from law enforcement. The Black Panther Party drew special attention and concentrated fire: when the Panthers declared war on the police, the police wasted no time in declaring war on the Panthers. In April 1968, Eldridge Cleaver was wounded in a shootout he had deliberately provoked with Oakland police, an incident in which Bobby Hutton lost his life. In another incident shortly before dawn on December 4, 1969, 14 police officers fired 99 shots into Fred Hampton's apartment on Chicago's West Side: several Panthers were wounded; Mark Clark was killed, as was Hampton, shot to death in his bed. Systematic repression became normalized and many of those Panthers who were not imprisoned or killed went underground or fled the country.

Black militants and nonviolent warriors alike fell in the quest for minority empowerment. When Dr. King was murdered by a white supremacist while standing on a motel balcony in Memphis, Tennessee, on April 4, 1968, the res-idents of many of the nation's urban centers exploded in grief and rage: more than a hundred cities experienced violent civil unrest in the wake of King's death. His assassin, James Earl Ray, was arrested at Heathrow Airport in London and extradited back to the United States; he pled guilty to the crime, for which he was sentenced to 99 years in prison. Some within the civil rights movement interpreted King's assassination as a death knell for peaceful social change and braced for more violence; others doubled down in their commitment to nonviolence. Misunderstanding King's role, many outside the movement saw his death as the end of the civil rights movement itself.

It was not. King's assassination only served to anger militants further. His death reinvigorated activists of all kinds and all races, reiterating the need for minority empowerment and intensifying efforts to achieve radical change. The civil rights movement did not die with King: rather, it dispersed into a diverse array of reform efforts, initiated not only by African Americans but also by other minorities moved to make the United States a better place for their peoples and their communities.

Like the civil rights movement, which eventually folded back into the larger struggle for black equality, the decade did not suddenly cease. Wrung out from what had been more than a decade of change in all facets of American society and culture, many Americans eagerly eyed their calendars and welcomed a new decade—but the Sixties, it seemed, were in no hurry to end. The hope for a return to normalcy quickly faded as the Sixties seemingly failed to stop in the final days of 1969. In time the 1970s would look different, taking on its own textures and grains, but initially those years were all but indistinguishable from the Sixties, which marched right through the first years of the 1970s as if they were their own.

Further Reading

Jeffrey O.G. Ogbar, *Black Power: Radical Politics and African-American Identity* (Baltimore: Johns Hopkins University Press, 2004)

Christopher Strain, *Pure Fire: Self-Defense as Activism in the Civil Rights Era* (Athens: University of Georgia Press, 2005)

Hasan Kwame Jeffries, *Bloody Lowndes: Civil Rights and Black Power in Alabama's Black Belt* (New York: New York University Press, 2009)

Joshua Bloom and Waldo E. Martin, Jr., *Black Against Empire: The History and Politics of the Black Panther Party* (Berkeley: University of California Press, 2013)

11

Sucking in the Seventies (or, That 70s Chapter)

Some contend that the 1970s were a transitional nothing period, a bridge between the liberal Sixties and the conservative Eighties. In the wake of the turbulent 1960s came a decade of comparative torpor, what President Jimmy Carter would identify as a "malaise" concurrent with an economic nadir of stagflation, the concurrence of high rates of employment and inflation. To many who had just lived through the 1960s, the 1970s by contrast seemed almost blasé. "The 60s were clutter," explained Andy Warhol. "The 70s are very empty." One early history of the 1970s was accordingly entitled *It Seemed As If Nothing Happened* (1982).

Such a characterization, however, ignores the importance of the Seventies in the shaping of modern American life, a time when all of the recognizable signposts of contemporary culture—from personal computers and credit cards to foreign cars and cable television—came into being. Indeed, historians have begun to recognize the 1970s as enormously important period, one that defined the next 30 years at least, maybe more—hence the appearance of a revisionist history, *Something Happened* (2006). In this view the Seventies were hardly blasé—in fact a better descriptor would be crucial.

One can make a case for both representations—the Seventies as inconsequential, the Seventies as momentous—though neither view is entirely satisfactory, as each fails to gauge the pace of change as it occurred. In fact what may be most notable about the 1970s (about the first few years of the decade, in any case) is how remarkably similar they were to the 1960s. Indeed, a few key events that many Americans tend to associate with the 1960s (such as the Kent State shootings) actually occurred in the early part of the next decade. As writer Jenny Diski has put it, the early Seventies were

The Long Sixties: America, 1955–1973, First Edition. Christopher B. Strain.

"a seminal period… for discovering that not so much had changed." In this sense, the early 1970s can best be understood as an extension of the 1960s. To paraphrase an iconic 1968 cartoon by Robert Crumb, the Sixties just kept on truckin'.

The social movements of the 1960s, for example, marched into the following decade, during which three in particular—the environmental movement, the women's rights movement, and the gay rights movement—came to full fruition. The new environmental consciousness—first articulated by Rachel Carson in *Silent Spring* and later manifested in the Save-the-Whales campaign—led to the first Earth Day on April 22, 1970: a national celebration organized, in which concerned citizens (many of them college students) came together not only to celebrate the natural environment but also to express apprehension over pollution, including oil spills, toxic dumps, and indiscriminate pesticide use, among other worries. Indeed, by the turn of the decade the environmental movement was afoot and would soon yield concrete results: spurred largely by popular interest, Congress amended the Clean Air Act (1970), which required industrial regulatory controls for smokestack emissions from factories to try to curtail air pollution; passed the Clean Water Act (1972), similarly aimed to reduce the amount of toxic substances released into rivers and lakes by industrial concerns; and passed the Endangered Species Act (1973), designed to protect a list of threatened animals and plants native to the United States from extinction.

While having begun in the 1960s, the women's movement belonged to the 1970s. By politicizing reproductive rights, sexual harassment, domestic violence, divorce, and rape, the members of the women's movement focused the public's attention on formerly private issues and compelled officials not only to acknowledge but also to act on them. It also marshaled forces, primarily comprising men but also including women, who opposed the women's movement and what it stood for; as historian Susan Hartmann has observed, linking anti-feminist issues to larger, longstanding, conservative concerns is what made the New Right "new" as it developed its so-called "pro-family" focus in the 1970s.

On the one hand, women's rights activists succeeded in putting their concerns front and center before the American public. Feminists labeled the age-old problems of on-the-job discrimination and unwanted attention from male co-workers and bosses as "sexual harassment." In the expectation that women and men were fundamentally equal, and that women should not suffer merely for being women, feminism was

becoming mainstream. On the other hand, to complain too loudly in
the early 1970s about women's rights or men's patronizing attitudes
towards women was to invite accusations of being a bra-burning, hairy-
legged "women's libber." In part due to their strong challenges to deeply
entrenched gender roles, which many people interpreted as part of the
natural order of biological differences between men and women, and in
part due to their inability to reconcile the tension between militancy
and femininity within the movement, feminists managed to alienate
not only many men but also many women. Facing male chauvinism
and outright sexism, the women's movement suffered one prominent
defeat—ratifying the Equal Rights Amendment—and one landmark
victory—the 1973 Supreme Court decision in *Roe v. Wade* to legalize
abortion, a prerogative which would come under attack almost as soon
as the judgment was rendered.

Title VII of the Civil Rights Act of 1964 prohibited discrimination on
the basis of race, color, religion, national origin, or sex. It did not, however,
have a provision for sexual orientation, and gay men and lesbian women
continued to face an uphill battle toward acceptance in American society.
It would be another nine years, in fact, before the American Psychiatric
Association (APA) would remove homosexuality from its list of mental
disorders. While the 1973 APA reclassification was a milestone victory,
it was an incomplete one because, in taking homosexuality off its list of
pathologies, the APA instead labeled it a "sexual orientation disturbance."
Clearly, even though the issue no longer went unspoken, gays and lesbians
still had a long way to go in the struggle for equality.

The high tide of harassment and repression of homosexuals that
accompanied the anticommunist hysteria of the early 1950s—when state
officials viewed homosexual behavior as sexual deviance, and any sort
of deviance as a risk to national security—had not receded much by the
early 1970s. Prior to 1962, sodomy was a felony in every state, punishable
by a lengthy term of imprisonment and/or hard labor. That year, Illinois
became the first state to eliminate its criminal code for sodomy; however,
gay sex was still widely criminalized, and lawmakers and police still used
"morals charges" to target and harass an underground, closeted gay
community. The Illinois law was part of a few quiet efforts in the early
and mid-1960s to shift public understanding of homosexuality toward
something other than a sin, crime, or mental disorder; but gay rights
activism was still largely impossible until the revolutionary fervor of the
latter Sixties empowered gay activists—people who were tired of suffering

Figure 11.1   Philadelphia's first gay pride parade, 1972 (Source: © Photo by Kay Tobin, Manuscripts and Archives Division, The New York Public Library).

under the weight of having to appear as something they were not—to challenge publicly the deeply held prejudices about sexual orientation.

Most historians agree that the gay rights movement began in 1969, when patrons of the Stonewall Inn, a gay bar in New York's Greenwich Village, resisted a raid by police, who routinely arrested male customers for "lewd conduct," which often consisted of little more than dancing together. Two days of rioting during what became known as the "Stonewall Rebellion" marked a new, bolder emphasis on direct action. Twelve months later, gay pride parades were held in New York, Chicago, and Los Angeles to commemorate the one-year anniversary of the Stonewall riots. Both attitudes and laws changed in the early 1970s as the gay rights movement broadened and intensified. In short order came enormous achievements, as when Elaine Noble became the first openly gay person elected to office in the United States in 1975 (she served in the Massachusetts house of representatives until 1979), and Harvey Milk's election to the San Francisco board of supervisors in 1977, which proved that the gay community could be organized into an effective electoral block. There were also enormous setbacks, as when Milk was assassinated at San Francisco City Hall in 1978 and his shooter was acquitted of first-degree murder. An article entitled

"The Least of These" in *the Ladder*, a pro-lesbian bimonthly, had pointed out in 1968 that homosexuals were the last totally persecuted minority group in the United States, and that lesbians were "even lower in the sand hole" than gay men. "[W]e are women (itself a majority/minority status)," the article continued, "and we are Lesbians: the last half of the least noticed, most disadvantaged minority." By the middle of the 1970s, the picture had changed considerably, but there was still a long way to go toward full inclusion and acceptance.

As with social movements, so, too, did the technological innovations born in the vibrant US industrial economy continue in the early 1970s, when big and small inventions alike continued to transform American life. The first floppy disks appeared in 1970, making data transference from computer to computer easier and more convenient; the first daisy-wheel printers appeared that same year, followed in 1971 by dot-matrix printers. The first video game—Pong, in which two dashes lob a dot—debuted in 1972 (for those less technically inclined there was the Hacky Sack that same year). The videocassette recorder (VCR) was invented in 1971, the same year as the liquid-crystal display (LCD). Gene splicing came in 1973, the same year that Bic invented the disposable lighter. Major new ingenuities and minor gewgaws both vied for consumer attention and all held the promise of making life a little easier, a little more convenient, a little better— sometimes, as in the 1960s, with hidden costs.

Indeed, the new technologies of the so-called "Jet Age" simultaneously enabled new wonders and brought new terrors. With bigger and faster passenger jet aircraft, air travel once reserved only for the wealthiest Americans became more commonplace in the early 1970s, even as a number of horrific crashes of commercial airliners dramatically underscored the perils of flying. In fact, the new technologies not only brought new risks but also exposed new dangers, some of which coincided with the radical politics of the day. The previously unheard of crime of hijacking, for instance, became a terrifying new tool of revolutionary groups seeking a high-profile way to draw attention to their respective causes. Beginning in 1968, the number of attempted hijackings rose dramatically; in 1969, there was a record high of 82 attempts. By the end of 1972, 159 US aircraft had been successfully hijacked, the majority to Cuba ("skyjackings" to Cuba became so routine that US pilots began to carry approach plans for the Havana airport).

The violence of the 1960s—the police brutality, the revolutionary stirrings of radical militants, the forceful clampdown on anti-war protestors and

Figure 11.2   Firing tear gas canisters, National Guardsmen advance toward Kent State University students at Taylor Hall on May 4, 1970 (Source: © May 4 Collection. Kent State University Libraries. Special Collections and Archives).

other New Left activists—did not stop at decade's end, as bloodshed at home continued to parallel bloodshed overseas. There were the killings of four anti-war demonstrators on May 4, 1970, at Kent State University by members of the Ohio National Guard. The actions of the soldiers, who fired indiscriminately into a crowd of student protestors after being taunted and pelted with rocks, were found in an official investigation to be "unnecessary, unwarranted, and inexcusable." A Pulitzer-Prize-winning photograph of a young woman crying in anguish over one of the fallen victims became one of the enduring images of the anti-war movement; students at NYU unfurled a banner reading "They Can't Kill Us All" from a dorm window. There were two students killed and twelve wounded ten days later in a similar incident at Jackson State, a historically black college in Mississippi where, as at Kent State, none of the shooters were arrested, tried, or convicted. There were the riots at Attica state prison in western New York in 1971 when, in the wake of unanswered complaints about mistreatment and abuse, prisoners overtook the prison on September 9. After four days of negotiation, Governor Nelson Rockefeller authorized one thousand New York State troopers, sheriff's deputies, and correctional officers to retake the prison with tear gas and short-barreled shotguns. Twenty-nine inmates (including the NYC bomber Sam Melville, transferred to Attica after a 1970 escape attempt) and ten hostages were shot to death in what CBS news anchor Walter Cronkite called "the bloodiest prison incident the country has seen in four decades"; as the shooting stopped, officers on the scene clapped and triumphantly cheered "White Power!" There were the 1972 Olympics in Munich, where the spirit of competition and international goodwill was eclipsed by the kidnapping and killing of eleven Israeli athletes and coaches by Palestinian terrorists. And there was the war.

Over everything else Vietnam cast a long shadow. In the early 1970s, the war became increasingly unsustainable and, to many, increasingly unbearable. Some devoted themselves fulltime to ending it, as the popular young film actress Jane Fonda did after returning from a visit to Hanoi in 1972. While in Vietnam, Fonda had investigated some particularly disturbing reports of the war's toll, those of tens of thousands of civilians killed since the previous spring, of the United States' methodic bombing of earthen dikes to flood rice paddies in North Vietnam in order to try to starve the population en masse. She helped to publicize American missteps abroad across the United States, but her own missteps—namely, photos of her in peasant garb atop a North Vietnamese anti-aircraft gun, and messages asking US servicemen to search their hearts about injustices being done (which were misrepresented by the North Vietnamese as implorations to defect)—confirmed her status for many Americans as a traitor and an enemy of the state. New battle-lines were being drawn, oversimplified ones that belied many of the complexities involved: lines between pushy activists and those content with the status quo; between assertive women like Fonda and the men (and women) who wished they would just shut up; and between those who blindly supported the American war effort and those who actively and passionately worked to end it.

In the wake of LBJ's war-weary refusal to seek reelection in 1968, the national political landscape soured, though the full extent of the spoilage would take time to become apparent, rotting steadily under the administration of Johnson's successor, President Richard M. Nixon. While others have done it since, Nixon may have been the first presidential candidate to exploit the politics of fear in order to get elected, offering (ironically) lawfulness and stability in a world gone mad. When the predominately Negro Watts neighborhood of South-Central Los Angeles had exploded in violent riots in 1965, a stunned President Johnson had asked, "How is it possible after all we've accomplished? How could it be? Is the world topsy-turvy?" Three years later, voters confirmed that the world, or at least US society, *was* topsy-turvy and that the Democrats did not know how to quell the chaos. Black people were burning their own neighborhoods; white kids were openly rebelling (against what it was not always clear); and hippies were taking over. Old-fashioned values were AWOL; public decency was in arrears; and drugs were everywhere. Violence was escalating—"Five Serious Crimes Every Minute Now… A murder every hour… a rape every 23 minutes… a burglary every 27 seconds… a car stolen every minute…" shrieked the August 8, 1966 issue of *US News and World Report*—and politicians seemed lax on those creating the mayhem. Overseas an unpopular war dragged on; at home, a race war seemed imminent. In 1968—an election year marked by the assassination of Martin Luther King, Jr., and subsequent riots across the nation, the assassination of Democratic presidential candidate Robert F. Kennedy, widespread protests against the Vietnam War across university campuses, and bloody confrontations between police and anti-war protesters at the Democratic National Convention in Chicago—the Democratic party split. "Who is responsible for the breakdown of law and order in this country?" candidate Nixon asked. Certainly not the Republicans, he implied, and not Nixon himself, who rode public apprehension into the White House past the aspirations of incumbent vice president Hubert Humphrey (and third-party challenger George Wallace, the once and future governor of Alabama) with 43.4% of the popular vote and 301 electoral votes.

Promising peace at home and abroad, Nixon threw himself into the job. On the domestic front, he pursued reforms in welfare, health care, civil rights, energy, and environmental policy and racked up an impressive list of successes. He created the Office of Management and Budget to implement new policies and programs and the Office of Energy Policy for advice on oil policy. He imposed wage and price controls to bolster the flagging economy. He supported the Clean Air Act of 1970 and established the Environmental Protection Agency to safeguard human health and the natural environment. He also proposed the Family Assistance Plan, a welfare reform that would have guaranteed an income to all Americans had Congress supported it. He insisted that Congress broaden the mandate of the US Civil Rights Commission to include sex discrimination, and he signed all civil rights legislation passed by Congress, including Title IX of the Education Amendments of 1972, which banned sexual discrimination in educational benefits. He expanded enforcement of affirmative action. As he had promised, he supported new anticrime laws and appointed

Justices with conservative outlooks to the Supreme Court. Finally he also supported the Constitutional amendment lowering the minimum voting age from 21 to 18.

Nixon enjoyed successes in his foreign policy, too. Forging new bonds with old foes, he eased Cold War tensions by initiating strategic arms limitation talks with the Soviet Union in 1969. His visits to Beijing and Moscow in 1972 were historic: he was the first US president to visit Communist China, and his summit with Soviet leader Leonid Brezhnev led to the Strategic Arms Limitation Treaty (SALT), the first programmatic nuclear weapons limitation pact between the United States and the Soviet Union. He also began to wind down the war in Vietnam. In 1969 he announced his plan of "Vietnamization," or reducing American troop levels in Vietnam while transferring the burden of fighting to the forces of South Vietnam; accordingly, US troop strength in Vietnam shrank between April 1969 and March 1973. In 1971 he signed legislation abolishing the draft. Even as Nixon wound down the war effort in Vietnam, however, he stepped up bombing raids against Communist strongholds in neighboring Cambodia towards the end of his first term. Southeast Asia was a thorn in Nixon's side, as it had been for other presidents before him; but, like Johnson, he was politically savvy and effective, and like Johnson, in his first few years as president Nixon was well on his way to becoming a memorably admirable and effective presence in the Oval Office.

Also like Johnson, however, Nixon worried incessantly about the surety of his own political power. Having lost his bid for the presidency in 1960 and for the governorship of California in 1962, he fretted about his security in office. Whereas Johnson stepped down in 1968, Nixon doubled down in 1972 in his efforts to secure his reelection to a second term, something over which the president obsessed. And it was in this obsession that his character flaws manifested. When this inner storm of paranoia and ambition finally broke, the American people would see Richard M. Nixon—as well as the US presidency—in a new light.

If he came to power by using "the angers, anxieties, and resentments produced by the cultural chaos of the 1960s," as journalist Rick Perlstein has noted, then Nixon *stayed* in power by scheming, stealing, conspiring, and lying. He made an "enemies list" of liberal journalists and congressional critics. In 1970 he approved the so-called Huston Plan, a 43-page document drafted by an aide (Tom Charles Huston) that proposed the use of burglary, electronic surveillance, and mail fraud to harass and intimidate left-wing campus radicals; the plan would employ the CIA and FBI in a variety of illegal missions. When FBI chief J. Edgar Hoover refused to back the plan (not because of any moral qualms but because he felt that it compromised the FBI's independence), the president created his own team to discredit his opponents, consolidate power, and promote executive secrecy. Nicknamed "the Plumbers" by White House insiders because of their assignment to stop leaks to the press, the team was headed by a former CIA operative, E. Howard Hunt, and an ex-FBI agent, G. Gordon Liddy.

In mid-1971 Daniel Ellsberg, an analyst for the Department of Defense, turned over to the press the secret Pentagon Papers, a documentary history of US involvement in Vietnam prepared during the Johnson administration. While the Pentagon Papers revealed nothing damning about the Nixon administration, they did reveal a long history of government lies—to foreign leaders, to Congress, and to the American people—and the president obtained a court injunction barring further publication of the documents by the *New York Times*, which protested to the Supreme Court. Lifting the injunction, the Supreme Court ruled that the First Amendment forbade such censorship. Livid, Nixon not only directed the Department of Justice to indict Ellsberg for theft and espionage but also ordered the Plumbers to smear his credibility. In August 1971, Hunt and Liddy broke into the office of Ellsberg's psychiatrist to search for information that might be used to discredit him. Using campaign contributions, Nixon's reelection team (led by John Mitchell, who resigned his position as US Attorney General to head the team), financed a series of "dirty tricks" in 1972 to spread dissension among Democrats, including a scheme by a special internal espionage unit, led by Liddy and Hunt, to spy on the opposition party.

One of the schemes approved by Mitchell was a plan to wiretap telephones at the Democratic National Committee headquarters at the Watergate office complex in Washington, DC. However, when several burglars associated with Liddy and Hunt—along with James McCord, the security coordinator of the Committee to Reelect the President (CRP, or CREEP to those who enjoyed a sardonic acronym)—broke in early in the morning of June 17, 1972, to install the bugs, a security guard caught them red-handed. A White House cover-up of the operation began immediately, as Nixon reassured the public that "no one in this administration, presently employed, was involved in this bizarre incident." Secretly, Nixon ordered staff members to purge Hunt's name from the White House directory; spread around $400,000 in hush money (along with hints of presidential pardon) to buy the silence of those arrested; and, on the pretext that the inquiry would damage national security, ordered the CIA to halt the FBI's investigation of the Watergate break-in.

With no knowledge of Nixon's enemies list, the Huston plan, the dirty tricks, the Plumbers, or the attempted cover-up, and with Democratic nominee George McGovern's campaign foundering (in part due to revelations that his running mate, Thomas Eagleton, suffered from severe clinical depression and took powerful anti-psychotic drugs), the electorate overwhelmingly voted for Nixon's reelection a few months later. At the subsequent trial of the accused Watergate burglars, however, federal judge "Maximum John" Sirica, known for his toughness on criminals, refused to believe that the burglars acted alone and pressured James McCord to reveal that White House aides had known in advance of the break-in into the offices of the DNC in the Watergate building. McCord also confessed that the White House had pressured him and his co-defendants to "plead guilty and remain silent." Meanwhile, Carl Bernstein and Bob Woodward, two reporters for the *Washington Post*, ferreted out clues from an unnamed informant in the Nixon administration (codenamed "Deep Throat") and published a series of front-page stories linking the break-in to the illegal use of campaign contributions and the dirty tricks against the Democrats paid for by CRP.

The extent of the web of lies and deception perpetuated by the president and certain members of his administration slowly unraveled, and the details of what became known as the Watergate Scandal would eventually bring the Nixon administration down, as well as put a stain on the US presidency from which the office has never fully recovered. In February 1973, the Senate established the Special Committee on Presidential Campaign Activities, led by North Carolina senator Sam Ervin, to investigate the alleged election misdeeds. As allegations led closer to the Oval Office, the president fired special counsel John Dean, who refused to become a scapegoat; on April 30, two of the president's top assistants, H.R. Haldemann and John Ehrlichman, both resigned as the president pledged to get to the bottom of the scandal; and in May, the Ervin committee began a televised investigation, which revealed a sordid tale of political corruption but no concrete evidence of criminal behavior by the president himself. When another aide, however, revealed the existence of a secret taping system in the White House which recorded all conversations in the Oval Office (along with telephone calls), the Ervin committee insisted in July that Nixon turn over those tapes to them so that they might hear all the conversations Nixon had secretly taped while working in the Oval Office. The president refused, claiming executive privilege and national security considerations; but, the special Watergate prosecutor, Archibald Cox, sought a court order to obtain the tapes in October. In response, Nixon ordered his new attorney general, Elliott Richardson, to fire Cox; instead, Richardson resigned in protest, as did the deputy attorney general. It was then left to the third-ranking official in the Department of Justice, Solicitor General Robert Bork, to fire Cox in what the press termed "the Saturday Night Massacre," which sent Nixon's public-approval rating rapidly downward in October. It was a tough time for the president—and for all Americans, for that matter.

Indeed, 1973 was an auspicious year, a kind of bookend for the raucous Sixties, a year that began momentously. In the course of nine days in January, American history seemed to move in fast gear. On January 22, the Supreme Court had handed down its momentous *Roe v. Wade* decision, which legalized abortion; just six days later, on January 28, the United States along with North and South Vietnam signed the Paris Peace Accords, signifying an end to the fighting in Vietnam and the withdrawal of US troops from South Vietnam; three days later, on January 31, G. Gordon Liddy and James McCord were convicted, found guilty of burglary and spying on the Democrats at Watergate. It was a historic nine days.

On February 27, approximately 200 Oglala/Lakota Sioux Indians and members of AIM seized and occupied the town of Wounded Knee, South Dakota, on the Pine Ridge Indian Reservation in symbolic protest against not only a poorly managed tribal government but also the treatment of the tribe by the US federal government. A 71-day siege by US Marshals and FBI agents ensued, with tense standoffs and wild shootouts in which both sides liberally exchanged gunfire. By the time the siege ended, two activists had lost their lives and one agent had been shot and left paralyzed. There was widespread public sympathy for the goals of the occupation, which ended on May 8. AIM leaders Russell Means and Dennis Banks were indicted but later acquitted (over the next three years, conflict between factions at Pine Ridge continued and scores of others died).

J.R.R. Tolkien died on September 2 and with him died a part of the counterculture. At first glance, few persons would have seemed as different from the hippies and the world they made. A conservative Catholic born in 1892, the British author was classically educated at Oxford, from whence he headed off to fight in World War I after graduating in 1915. He went on to become a linguist and a professor, a scholar of dead and forgotten languages like Old English, Middle English, and Medieval Welsh (as well as archaic Scandinavian tongues such as Old Norse). Eighty-one years old when he died, he was firmly ensconced in the older generation, yet Tolkien had created *The Hobbit* and *The Lord of the Rings* trilogy and created his own world, one of magic and fantasy and make-believe whose archetypes and epic battles between good and evil reverberated through Sixties counterculture. First published in 1954, *The Fellowship of the Rings'* first clothbound printing with Houghton Mifflin was as diminutive as the halflings it celebrated; however, an unlicensed bootleg printing in the United States by paperback publisher Ace Books sent college students scrambling for copies. The relaxed priorities of happy, hedonistic, beauty-loving hobbits— with their second breakfasts, pipeweed, and smoke rings—appealed to many longhairs. "The hobbit habit seems to be almost as catching as LSD," reported a July 1966 *Time* magazine article. "On many US campuses, buttons declaring FRODO LIVES and GO GO GANDALF—frequently written in Elvish script—are almost as common as football letters." A March 1967 *Ramparts* magazine article called *The Lord of the Rings* "absolutely the favorite book of every hippie." By the end of 1968 more than three million copies of the newly authorized Ballantine Books version of *The Lord of the Rings* had been sold; Tolkien and his world, Middle Earth, had inspired the counterculture; bands such as Led Zeppelin were including Tolkein references in songs such as "The Battle of Evermore," "Misty Mountain Hop," and "Over the Hills and Far Away"; and *The Lord of the Rings* had embarked on a quest toward becoming one of the bestselling books of all time.

Less than three weeks later, on September 20, Billie Jean King defeated Bobby Riggs in their famous, nationally televised tennis match. In October, Arab members of the Organization of Petroleum Exporting Countries (OPEC) announced an oil embargo to punish the United States and other allies of Israel in the Yom Kippur War; the embargo in turn prompted an energy crisis in the United States, by this time dependent on the importation of foreign oil. Distributors began to ration gasoline; at gas stations across the nation, long lines of frustrated motorists formed, wrapping around pumps and stretching for city blocks. It was the 1973 oil embargo that not only started Americans on their search for renewable, alternative energy sources such as solar and wind power, but also began a long, downward, economic spiral in the United States. The long run of national prosperity had ended.

On November 6 the Berkeley-based Symbionese Liberation Army (SLA), a self-styled leftist revolutionary group, murdered Marcus Foster, an African-American school superintendent in Oakland who had introduced a plan for school ID cards, which the SLA deemed "fascist." A few months later, in February 1974, the now fugitive and wanted members of the SLA would kidnap Patty Hearst, a UC Berkeley undergraduate and granddaughter of publishing magnate William Randolph Hearst. After being brainwashed and indoctrinated into the group's anti-racist, anti-colonialist ideology, Patty Hearst participated along with other SLA members in a spree of violent crimes for which she was convicted (although her sentence was commuted in 1979 by President Jimmy Carter and she was later granted a pardon by President Bill Clinton in 2001). The year 1973 wound down with Nixon staunchly maintaining his innocence, defending his record and, in an hour-long televised question-and-answer session on November 17, adamantly shaking his head and insisting "I am not a crook," his flapping jowls doing most of the talking.

One by one, Sixties icons fell or faded from view. By 1973, Huey Newton was lying low, writing a memoir; former SNCC chairman and Black Panther leader H. Rap Brown was convicted for armed robbery; Timothy Leary was arrested in Afghanistan and extradited to the United States; and Abbie Hoffman had disappeared, going underground. None fitted easily into the zeitgeist of the new decade.

Much more would happen in the latter part of the Seventies: economic doldrums, an inward turn toward self-improvement and self-involvement, the election of a high-minded but hapless president from Georgia whose notable achievements (including negotiating peace accords between Israel and Egypt, the bitterest of enemies) were offset by the public's perception of him as inept (and who emerged phoenix-like as arguably the best ex-president in US history). But for most Americans the Sixties were already squarely in the rearview mirror—a distracting roadside attraction, a colorful stop on the way to someplace else.

The Sixties were history. Or were they?

Further Reading

Howard Brick, *Age of Contradiction: American Thought and Culture in the 1960s* (Ithaca: Cornell University Press, 2000)

Peter N. Carroll, *It Seemed Like Nothing Happened: America in the 1970s* (New Brunswick: Rutgers University Press, 1990)

Edward D. Berkowitz, *Something Happened: A Political and Cultural Overview of the Seventies* (New York: Columbia University Press, 2007)

Thomas Borstelmann, *The 1970s: A New Global History from Civil Rights to Economic Inequality* (Princeton: Princeton University Press, 2011)

Rick Perlstein, *Nixonland: The Rise of a President and the Fracturing of America* (New York: Simon & Schuster, 2014)

Andreas Killen, *1973 Nervous Breakdown: Watergate, Warhol, and the Birth of Post-Sixties America* (New York: Bloomsbury, 2006)

12

Legacies

In March 1974 the House Judiciary Committee subpoenaed President Nixon for the tape recordings of the Oval Office meetings following the Watergate break-in. Still trying to cover up the conspiracy, Nixon released redacted transcripts of the tapes, heavily edited and gappy. In May, the House Judiciary Committee began impeachment proceedings, which culminated in July in three articles of impeachment against Nixon: 1) obstruction of justice, 2) abuse of power, particularly his partisan use of the FBI and IRS, and 3) contempt of Congress in refusing to obey a congressional subpoena to release the unedited tapes—which, on August 5, Nixon finally relinquished, providing the smoking gun that investigators had sought. The unedited tapes revealed that Nixon had indeed ordered the cover-up of the Watergate break-in and then lied about his role in it for more than two years. On August 7, as Nixon wavered, still refusing to surrender, Republican leaders in Congress informed him of the certainty of his impeachment and conviction. Two days later, he became the first US president to resign from office. In the bitter aftermath, a disgusted electorate lost faith in national politics and recoiled from all things Washington. Gonzo journalist Hunter S. Thompson credited Nixon with "the death of the American Dream."

In 1975, the remaining Americans in Saigon, the capital of the besieged South Vietnam, evacuated, abandoning the US embassy there. In short order, South Vietnam then fell to the Communists. It was an ugly, chaotic scene, as helicopters touched down on the roof of the embassy building, shuttling terrified American diplomats and some of their South Vietnamese co-workers to aircraft carriers off the coast. With their American allies gone, the South Vietnamese were left to face the invading army on their own.

The Long Sixties: America, 1955–1973, First Edition. Christopher B. Strain.
© 2017 Christopher B. Strain. Published 2017 by John Wiley & Sons, Inc.

Figure 12.1 Nixon leaving the White House on August 9, 1974 (Source: © Bettmann/ CORBIS).

President Gerald Ford, who would enrage the American public further by pardoning ex-President Nixon of his high crimes in office and proclaiming an end to "our long national nightmare," and Democratic president Jimmy Carter, who won office in the election of 1974 by pledging to be honest and forthright—in an obvious contrast to the Nixon administration— shepherded the nation through the languor of the 1970s. Clear of Vietnam and Watergate, the nation seemed to exhale in the mid-1970s, even as Americans began the long process of trying to figure out what the hell had happened.

In the year 1980 the Republican candidate Ronald Reagan, the former B-movie actor and governor of California took the White House, by which time he and his many supporters in the New Right had written its own script to explain what had happened. Ignoring his own wanton spending on defense, for example, Reagan blamed LBJ's Great Society programs of the 1960s for the ballooning national deficit. Indeed, President Reagan and the New Right believed that the chaos of the 1960s continued to cause significant damage. As Bernard von Bothmer has observed, throughout his eight-year presidency, Reagan blamed "the Sixties" for various problems, especially the nation's educational, economic, and moral decline, and the concurrent rise in crime and drug abuse. His wife, first lady Nancy Reagan, made the "war on drugs" the focus of her "Just Say No" campaign, which one speechwriter described as her own personal attempt to "roll back the Sixties."

This attempt made sense in light of the fact that the Sixties seemed to hang about—loitering, for example, around the 1988 presidential campaign. When in a vice-presidential debate Dan Quayle, the running mate of Republican presidential hopeful George H.W. Bush, repeatedly drew parallels between himself and JFK as a candidate (noting their similarities in age and experience), Texas senator Lloyd Bentsen, running on the Democratic ticket with Michael Dukakis, laid him low with a now famous retort: "Senator, I served with Jack Kennedy; I knew Jack Kennedy; Jack Kennedy was a friend of mine. Senator, you are no Jack Kennedy." The Republicans counterpunched, using the term "liberal," which Kennedy had used to describe himself as an inheritor of the New Deal tradition, to insult Dukakis, who come November lost the election spectacularly.

The Sixties still seemed to be hanging around the 1990s, too. "By God, we've kicked the Vietnam syndrome once and for all!" President George H.W. Bush crowed at the end of the brief and decisive US victory of the Gulf War in 1991, in which US and allied forces drove the forces of Iraqi dictator Saddam Hussein out of neighboring Kuwait. Since the mid-1970s, conservatives had told themselves that the US loss in Vietnam had created an aversion among the American public for any kind of foreign intervention, a hesitancy to apply force abroad or commit military power anywhere in the world unless absolutely necessary to protect national interests; this avoidance was termed "the Vietnam syndrome." In a 1980 speech at the Veterans of Foreign Wars Convention in Chicago, Ronald Reagan—then a Republican presidential hopeful—identified this phenomenon as a creation of the North Vietnamese, who sought to "win in the field of propaganda here in America what they could not win on the field of battle in Vietnam." Ours was a "noble cause," he told the veterans, and the lesson of Vietnam was simple. "If we are forced to fight," he said, "we must have the means and the determination to prevail or we will not have what it takes to secure the peace." For Reagan, this determination meant meeting the Soviets with force, if necessary, in an invigorated Cold War. This bellicose sense of mission led President Reagan in 1983 to invade the tiny Caribbean island of Grenada to restore constitutional government after a coup there. After Reagan's vice president and successor in the White House, President George H.W. Bush, attacked Iraq, he interpreted that victory as a reestablishment of pre-Vietnam US hegemony. With the collapse of the Soviet Union later that same year—in the wake of progressive reforms (namely "glasnost," or political openness, and "perestroika," or economic restructuring) by Soviet president Mikhail Gorbachev, the falling of the Berlin Wall in November 1989, and a series of peaceful revolutions and independence movements across Eastern Europe—it seemed as if the Sixties were indeed finally interred. As the rock band Jesus Jones put it in their 1990 hit "Right Here, Right Now" about the sudden end of the Cold War, "Bob Dylan didn't have this to sing about..."

And yet the Sixties would not be "kicked" like a bad habit, as the first President Bush prematurely intoned: they would instead linger, informing politics around the world. France had its *soixante-huitards*—the "sixty-eighters" who participated in the student and worker protests of May 1968—and, in Russia, Mikhail Gorbachev defined himself in the 1980s and 1990s as one of the *shestidesyatniki*, the "people of the 1960s." Never exorcised, the ghosts of the Sixties continued to haunt American electoral politics. From William H. Clinton to George W. Bush to John Kerry, American politicians and their supporters in the 1990s and 2000s figuratively refought the literal battles of the 1960s. Throughout his political career, for example, Bill Clinton—the first baby-boomer president—dodged charges of failing to serve in Vietnam; when accused in 1992 of smoking marijuana in the 1960s, Clinton confessed, noting (a bit too cleverly) that he tried it but "did not inhale." Similarly, Americans wondered what kind of political favoritism allowed George W. Bush to spend his six-year military service obligation (1968–1974, with an early honorable discharge in 1973) in the Texas Air National Guard rather than flying sorties in Vietnam. When John Kerry—a naval officer who pulled dangerous assignments captaining swift boats in the Mekong Delta and who, upon returning from the war, testified before the Senate Foreign Relations Committee in 1971 that the war should be ended immediately—ran for the presidency himself in 2004 (after serving as a US Senator since 1985), his tour in Vietnam became the focal point of the campaign, with right-wing critics (the "Swift Boat Veterans for Truth") actually questioning his service record. This particular

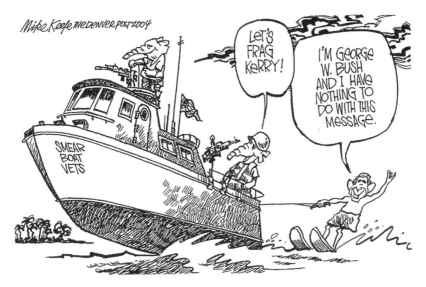

Figure 12.2 Ghosts of the 1960s haunted American electoral politics in the 2004 presidential campaign, as depicted in this Denver Post cartoon by Mike Keefe (Source: © Mike Keefe, InToon.com).

campaign against Kerry's presidential bid received widespread publicity but was later discredited, with the neologism "swiftboating" coming to mean an untrue or unfair political attack.

Perhaps it was the end of American exceptionalism (the notion that the United States is inherently better than other nations), or a post-Soviet realignment of former Cold-War priorities, or a post-Afghanistan/Iraq war-weariness, or just plain commonsense (or most likely some combination thereof); but, interestingly, the Vietnam syndrome had returned by 2013, according to a report by the Brookings Institute. With Kerry and Chuck Hagel—two distinguished Vietnam veterans—serving as President Barack Obama's Secretary of State and Secretary of Defense, respectively, the United States was learning to "keep its powder dry," according to Brookings fellow, Marvin Kalb. The messy situations in Afghanistan and Iraq reminded the nation that tiptoeing into questionable military engagements without crystal-clear objectives is a formula for long, costly, bloody wars. Said William Wohlforth, a government professor at Dartmouth College, "There does seem to be an Iraq syndrome, at least in the foreign policy establishment, in showing virtually no commitment for something that might morph into an Iraq or an Afghanistan."

Figure 12.3 Twenty-first-century US engagements in Afghanistan and Iraq have drawn comparisons to Vietnam, as in this 2009 cartoon by John Darkow for the *Columbia* [Missouri] *Daily Tribune* (Source: © Photo courtesy of *Columbia Daily Tribune*).

The Sixties, it seemed, were stubbornly clinging to the present—and not just in regard to electoral politics and foreign policy. Interest in the decade's unsolved hate crimes, for example, resurged in 1994 when Byron De La Beckwith, whose two previous trials in 1964 had ended in hung juries, was successfully convicted for the murder of NAACP field secretary, Medgar Evers. Authorities began to revisit other civil-rights-era murder cases in the early 2000s, which resulted in the solving of three other heinous crimes. In 2001 (the same year De La Beckwith died in prison at the age of 80), Thomas Blanton, Jr., and Bobby Frank Cherry were convicted for the 1963 bombing of the Sixteenth Street Baptist Church in Birmingham, Alabama. Ernest Avants was sentenced to life in prison in 2003 for the murder of Ben White, an elderly black farmworker, in 1966. In 2004 the case of Emmett Till was reopened after the airing of a PBS documentary, "The Murder of Emmett Till" (prosecutors considered but ultimately declined to indict Carolyn Bryant, the wife of one of the alleged killers who was in the truck that took young Till away from his relatives' house and to his brutal murder). Finally, in 2005 Edgar Ray Killen was convicted of manslaughter and sentenced to three twenty-year sentences for his role in the deaths of civil rights activists Cheney, Goodman, and Schwerner in Mississippi in 1964.

Intent on hunting the white vigilantes who had killed black Southerners, the FBI in 2007 began its Cold Cases Initiative, reopening racially motivated murder cases from the 1950s and 1960s. Agents pursued leads, tracked down witnesses, pored over documents, and found relatives. It was a monumental task: after nearly 50 years or more, evidence had been lost, suspects and witnesses had died, and memories had faded. The initiative wound down after six years. Despite hopes for justice, almost all of the investigations ended similarly, with agents writing letters to victims' families to notify them that their cases were now closed. With two notable exceptions—the prosecution of a former Klansman in the death of two young black men in Mississippi in 1964, and the prosecution of a former Alabama state trooper in the shooting death of Jimmie Lee Jackson in 1965—the vast majority of the reopened cold cases ended with no prosecutorial action taken. Of the 20 cases still open in 2013, there had been no breakthroughs. Justice remained elusive.

This elusiveness may help to explain why the Sixties have never really ended, replaying in recurrent loops, echoing and reverberating across American life in myriad ways. We prefer to imagine history as over and done—*terra firma* existing safely in the past—but this particular decade has managed to ripple through subsequent decades in ways that cannot be ignored, destabilizing truths and assumptions we wish to be immutable, challenging us to answer lingering questions. Perhaps it is this ongoing resonance that makes it difficult to distinguish between the decade itself and our ongoing collective memory of it, between the 1960s and the Sixties. It's the decade that never ends.

Liberals look back on the 1960s as nirvana, a time of innocence and freedom—a golden moment for communal experimentation and freethinking, when people worked to actualize love in interpersonal relations and in society at large. For them the decade remains a touchstone of hope, possibility, and human potential. For conservatives, on the other hand, the 1960s represents a whipping boy for everything that has gone wrong in American society ever since. What, they ask, caused the racial animosity of the 1970s, the divisive identity politics of the 1980s, not to mention rampant drug use, violence, and street crime? Their answer is to blame the 1960s. What lay behind sexual promiscuity and rising divorce rates? The social fragmentation and loss of community, the disillusionment and loss of patriotism? The Sixties!

It's as if the decade itself had loosed a host of social ills on the world: if Americans could simply put the genie back in the bottle, then they might recapture something of the idyllic 1950s, a time when everything was—at least as many conservatives choose to remember it—hunky-dory.

Such reasoning is problematic, not because it is wishful thinking but because it romanticizes life in the Fifties to the point of a reckless form of revisionism. In the 1970s the allure of the 1950s heightened, with a longing for what now seemed to be a calm, tranquil decade; one 1970s TV sitcom, *Happy Days* idolized that retrospectively simpler time (just as another sitcom, *That '70s Show*, which aired in the late Nineties and early 2000s, would later idolize the 1970s). But to pine for the America of the Fifties is also to pine for a place and time when people of color had yet to enter public life, when women functioned as glorified house servants, and when gays and lesbians languished in the shadows, not to mention a time in which the nation went seemingly mad during its second Red Scare and folks everywhere lived with the very real threat of nuclear annihilation. Who today would deliberately resurrect the daily anxieties of the Atomic Age, the injustices of Jim Crow segregation, or the horrors of the war in Korea? Yet the Fifties would be incomplete without them.

A deeply felt nostalgia is often associated with remembrances of the 1950s—blissed-out, *Leave-It-To-Beaver* fantasies of suburban backyard barbecues and cul-de-sac treehouses—but many memories of the 1960s are no less saccharine. From Gen X to the Millennials (who, at 80 million strong, are the biggest age grouping in US history, much bigger than the highly vaunted baby-boomers), each generation has tried to recapture the magic of Woodstock, usually without success. From mud pits to mosh pits—from Crosby, Stills, Nash, & Young to Godsmack, Kid Rock, and Korn—the vibe at Woodstock '99 (held in Rome, New York, two hundred miles from the first Woodstock) was totally different from its namesake: angry crowds rioted and set fire to vendor booths and a dozen tractor trailers packed with camping gear and memorabilia for sale. In May 2014, Mysteryland concertgoers flocked to the site of the original Woodstock; a time traveler from 1969 would have found the music (electronic, including house, bass, trap, and dubstep), the fashion, the decor, and the feel almost totally foreign, though the two events shared an earnest attempt at peace through music.

This wistful, if unrealizable, desire to return to Woodstock speaks not only to a temporal impossibility but also to a spatial one: one cannot turn back the clock any more than one can "be near" the Sixties. If there were a way to dust off the decade and separate the salvageable from the ruined—to comb Johnson's Great Society from the anguish of Vietnam, to cull the biracial unity of civil rights reform from the bombings and burnings and beatings and deaths, to divide the heady trips from the terror-stricken hallucinations—then the Sixties might be much less contentious today. Setting aside our preferences for the Beatles or the Rolling Stones in common appreciation of the Beach Boys, we could all sit back and California-dream of VW microbuses and Flower Power and endless summers… Wouldn't it be nice?

Unfortunately, the Sixties come to us a total package: a big, messy grab-bag of people, places, happenings, and ideas, many of which still hold allure. Looking at the whole of history without nostalgia does not mean that the entire thing is spoiled, nor does it mean that we can overlook the dark places and ugly moments. We might only agree that it was a long, strange trip—but even that level of consensus might be out of the question, seeing as how this time still evokes strong feelings born of deep divisions.

The United States split and re-split along familiar fault lines in the 1960s: black and white, rich and poor, liberal and conservative. While perhaps less noticeable, other significant lines in American history, such as North-South or urban-rural, were cracking too, most noticeably in the riots of the "long hot summers." Some have remained and worsened. It was a decade of dichotomies: JFK and LBJ, MLK and Malcolm X, war and peace, love and hate, the 1960s and the Sixties, the Beatles and the Stones, Woodstock and Altamont. If such pairings are diametrical opposites, then which halves represent the true Sixties? Eric Danton, a reporter for the *Hartford Courant*, finds Altamont to be a more accurate representation of the decade than Woodstock, the iconic happening that has come to symbolize the peace-and-love vibe of the Sixties. "In too many ways, Altamont was a condensed version of the preceding decade," he writes, "with queasy race relations, well-intentioned non-conformism turned reckless, and a bid for peaceful harmonious co-existence—among the most valued ideals of the 60s—shattered by senseless violence." And perhaps he is correct. Perhaps it took the Hells Angels to annihilate the myth of the Sixties, to silence the siren song.

Mistakes were undoubtedly made. Such was the potential energy and undirected power of change that it sometimes spilled over, flooding its banks and sweeping in unfortunate directions. Directing their ire at returning Vietnam veterans, for example, rather than at the politicians who sent them overseas, seems in retrospect to have been an egregious error by anti-war protestors, sanctimoniously critical of those who bravely served their country (many of whom had been drafted, too poor to get deferments). Even the greatest triumph of this generation was also its greatest error: making the older-World-War-II generation who had worked so hard to provide for their children the enemy in the culture wars. Families were tested, riven, sometimes irrevocably broken by the Sixties.

It is difficult, too, to look at drug use in modern American society as anything other than negative and destructive: the meth labs and crack houses of rural and urban America speak more of anguish and desperation than they do spiritual enlightenment. Only slightly less depressing is the massive abuse of prescription drugs by middle-class suburbanites and the medicine-cabinet raids by their children, who combine them with designer street drugs to escape their intolerably "boring" lives. If these features of American life are a legacy of the Sixties, then it is a dark legacy indeed. If it is possible to disaggregate the abuse of drugs from the alternatives to which they once pointed—without, of course, romanticizing the brief window during which they suggested new possibilities—then perhaps it is possible to understand the former without damning the former. Regardless, drugs have left a trail of broken bodies and fried minds, then and now. Some people got very ill or lost their minds. Many lost their lives.

Heavily vaunted by the babyboomers, sexual freedom also proved to be something of a mixed bag. Viewing themselves as liberated from the complexities of possessive responses engrained by the rigidly repressive mores of the 1950s, when many (women, at least) suffered frustration, the Sixties generation assumed that freer sex, and more of it, was a good thing. But along with the sexual revolution of the 1960s came other unforeseeable problems, as rates of divorce and sexually transmitted diseases (STDs) went up and many couples and families broke up. And the sexual merry-go-round ended rather abruptly in the 1980s with the advent of a new and lethal STD: Acquired Immune Deficiency Syndrome, or AIDS.

Before effective and reliable birth control, even happily married couples feared that too many births could mean the difference between a comfortable middle class life and a life of poverty. The Pill nullified some fears from the 1950s, when the percentage of women who had sex before the age of 21 rose from 40 to 70%, the percentage of brides giving birth within eight and half months of marriage climbed to 30% (the highest percentage since 1800), and the average age of marriage for women fell to 20, the lowest in a century. Since FDA approval of the Pill in 1960, the average age of marriage for women has risen steadily to almost 26 today, the highest age ever recorded in the United States. Overall fertility has dropped to near replacement levels, while shotgun marriages and adoptions have plummeted. Recognizing its benefits, college-educated women adopted the Pill quickly; but, if it introduced a revolution, then not everyone has shared in its benefits.

Inroads made by the new feminism were, even at the time, constricted and winding. For the men who continued to call the shots, the roles of their female counterparts were often ancillary, even as they gave a patronizing nod to feminism. Straight males, whether CEOs or fraternity brothers, were not exactly known for their embrace of gender equality—but, then again, neither were those men involved in the New Left or the counterculture. When asked about the position of women in his organization in 1966, SNCC leader Stokely Carmichael (who was far better on gender equality than most of his male comrades) jokingly replied, "Prone"—a glib answer that nonetheless revealed something about how even progressive men might marginalize the women upon whom they depended. Like other women who lived through the 1960s, many female activists recall that their value seemed to be mostly sexual, domestic, secretarial, or even ornamental to the men who set about changing their world.

Like racial equality, women's liberation continues to be honored more in private attitudes than in public policies, more in theory than in practice, despite a general sense that gender imbalances have calibrated. Asked in a 2013 Huffington Post survey if they believed that "men and women should be social, political, and economic equals," 82 percent of respondents said they did (with equal percentages of men and women saying they agreed); only 9 percent said they did not. About half of working-age American adults think traditional gender roles no longer apply in today's world, and many young women consider feminism as having nothing to do with them: just 20 percent of Americans—including 23 percent of women and 16 percent of men—consider themselves feminists.

However, the difficulties and expense of childcare means that women often participate in a zero-sum game, going to work to pay for childcare in order to be able to work. Work roles were still heavily gendered in the 1970s and early 1980s—to the point that the prospect of a "house husband" in the popular comedy flick *Mr. Mom* still brought laughs in 1983—though it has subsequently become more common to see husbands and fathers helping out with housework and childcare. Few Americans, in fact, believe women should be barefoot and pregnant in the kitchen but, interestingly, *men* may have had a harder time shedding the stereotype of primary breadwinner: while only one in four working-age people in 2014 say a woman's primary duty is to be a full-time caretaker for her family, new research finds that nearly one in two still believe a man's primary duty is to provide financially for their families.

At any rate, the sexual revolution of the 1960s was still decidedly one-sided: sexual liberation, while part of a larger feminist project, worked to the advantage of men who exploited the lofty ideals of free(r) love. Male hetero-sexuality changed little in the 1960s. Men continued to adhere to a cluster of gender roles centered on strength, stoicism, and hardened emotion, and John Wayne remained the ideal man for many. While these attitudes and expectations would soften a bit in the 1970s, real change came with more open expression of same-sex relationships in subsequent decades.

The only part of the triad, then, that survived the era unscathed was popular music: if sex and drugs come with tarnished legacies, then rock and roll still shines on. Few people would argue that one of the best things to come out of the 1960s was the music that helped to define the genre. Meaningful and accessible, it still resonates, now ruling the FM dial as over-played "classic rock."

If the music still appeals, then there is little nostalgia in the post-1960s trajectories of various Sixties personalities, many of which are surprising, sometimes unsettling. Jane Fonda, for example, opened a fitness studio in Beverly Hills in 1979 and went on to star in a series of workout videos. Guitarist and singer Barry Melton, who co-founded the band Country Joe and the Fish, passed the bar in California in 1982, after which he became Public Defender in Yolo County. Tom Hayden, whose name was synony-mous with SDS, was tried as one of the Chicago Seven, charged with inciting riots at the Democratic National Convention in Chicago in 1968. In 1976, he entered mainstream politics and lost to the incumbent. He subsequently held a number of elected offices in California. Abbie Hoffman, another of the Chicago Seven, gained acclaim in the early 1970s as a journalist and author. "It's embarrassing," he said of his success with his new book, *Steal This Book*, "when you try to overthrow the government and you wind up on the bestsellers list." Charged with cocaine possession in 1974, he avoided trial by undergoing plastic surgery and changing his name to Barry Freed. After surrendering to authorities in 1980, he was released in 1982 (the same year that LSD guru Timothy Leary and Watergate conspirator G. Gordon Liddy, after the former's release from prison, went on a joint speaking tour). Seven years later, Hoffman was found dead of an apparent suicide in his apartment.

Abbie Hoffman notwithstanding, the white radicals of the 1960s tended to fare better than their black counterparts. Life after the Party was often unkind to those Black Panthers who survived government persecution, incarceration, and exile in the 1960s and early 1970s, and the cadre of Oakland's BPP leaders went on to pedestrian, sometimes ignominious ends in the 1980s. Elaine Brown—who had been appointed chairman of the party in 1974, when Huey Newton again faced murder charges, this time fleeing the United States—left the country herself and entered psychotherapy to end her addiction to Thorazine. While his wife Kathleen became a law professor, Eldridge Cleaver became a Mormon and a Republican who battled drugs; in 1994 he again made headlines in Berkeley after a drug arrest, a mysterious head injury, and nearly five hours of brain surgery. Newton returned to the United States in 1977 to face charges of killing a 17-year-old prostitute and pistol-whipping his tailor; both trials ended in hung juries. In 1988, Newton was shot to death by a drug dealer, a gang member who once benefitted from the Party's "Free Breakfast" program. His corpse was found near a crack house, lying in a pool of blood in the street, in the same West Oakland neighborhood where he first organized two decades earlier.

Memories of the Sixties are brighter without these where-are-they-now updates, in part because of a natural tendency to freeze celebrities in the moment of their fame, and in part because it is difficult to see an insurrectionist trade his or her convictions for profit or expedience: better to remember Bobby Seale as the co-founder of the Black Panther Party than as the author of *Barbeque'n with Bobby*, a cookbook published in 1987. But those same memories, even if fond ones, are also false and incomplete without them. It would have been decidedly strange if 1960s icons had *not* changed after the Sixties, a decade famous for expending and consuming those idealists who believed the most in the transformative power of the era. For every optimist who clung to the peace-and-love ethos, there was an apostate, burnout, or sellout; for every survivor a casualty. For every Pete Seeger, determinedly singing "We Shall Overcome" until his death at age 94 in 2014, there was a William C. Gearing, Jr. (killed in action in Vietnam and immortalized on the June 27, 1969 cover of *Life*), a Janis Joplin, or Fred Hampton, martyred by war, an overdose of drugs, and a barrage of police bullets, respectively.

Platitudes about desperate times and desperate measures only partially explain these denouements. Huey Newton's personal decline paralleled some bigger trends in America's cities. The Huey Newton who exorcised his demons long enough to lead the Black Panther Party, pen his thoughts on

Marxist revolution, and earn a Ph.D. in 1980 from UC Santa Cruz, later succumbed to the quick, cheap, and highly addictive rush of crack cocaine, which wreaked havoc on his brain, just as it wreaked havoc on urban ghettos in the 1980s. There was truth in the Kerner Report—the report by the National Advisory Commission on Civil Disorders, created by President Johnson in July 1967 to explain the riots that had plagued cities each summer since 1964—which summarized, "Our nation is moving toward two societies, one black, one white—separate and unequal."

It may be that the 1960s were not nearly as revolutionary or as transformative as our collective memory would tell us. Racism and sexism are alive and well, as are hunger and suffering. Economic inequality is still heavily racialized. Peace was fleeting in the 1960s and has yet to make an appearance since, as wars proliferate and interpersonal conflicts persist. Stephen Holden was correct in noting in a 1999 review for the *New York Times* that "the lessons taught by the 60s are not the ones that those who lived through them imagined they would be." Collectively, the American people did not learn that war is awful and drugs expand consciousness and sex is liberating. If anything we forgot how terrible Vietnam was as we stumbled into other military conflicts, found drugs to be fairly addictive and destructive (if ubiquitous), and learned that love is complicated, no matter how or when or under what circumstances it is consummated.

Part of the problem may relate to differing interpretations of freedom; that is, a possible mistake of the Sixties generation may have been in assuming that freedom meant the same thing to everyone. As author Jenny Diski has observed, liberation could not equate with libertarianism; "doing one's own thing" became problematic when it clashed with others' right of ability to do *their* own things. Having believed wholeheartedly in the Movement as a young person in the 1960s, Diski now finds herself disillusioned on the other end. "For a decade so notorious for its politically radical youth," she writes, "it's quite remarkable how little effect we had." Her writing lacks the wry glee of P.J. O'Rourke, whose essay, "The Awful Power of Make-Believe," describes how he once believed in "the usual hippie blather, yea drugs and revolution, boo war and corporate profits." In his mind he did not sell out so much as wise up, donning a suit and tie to join the establishment he once railed against. For him, the 1960s became a "learning experience" in what *not* to want. While one writer mourns the loss of the Sixties, the other revels in their demise.

Diski and O'Rourke replay the familiar split between liberals and conservatives, the either-or choice between accepting or rejecting the Sixties.

But what if there were a third option? Perhaps the key to understanding this crazy decade lies in the liminal spaces between its dichotomies—in the paradoxes themselves. Perhaps the pairings we use to understand this decade are not as diametrically opposed as they might initially seem. As political descriptors, for example, the terms "conservative" and "liberal" were largely a product of the 1960s, but the two camps were not so terribly different at the time. The former mistrusted government and abhorred governmental spending, while the latter favored a welfare state, but both hated communism and despised socialism. In the 1960s, radicals drove a wedge between conservative and liberals, creating a crack in American politics that remains unfilled—and has in fact only been widening over time. Forcing people out of their comfort zones, the 1960s radicals forced liberals to choose sides and take a harder stance, with some (like O'Rourke) falling into the conservative camp and others (like Diski) aligning themselves against the forces of reaction.

The decade forced stark choices in other facets of American life too. Far from abstract geopolitical affairs, the Cold War touched the lives of ordinary Americans: it was an ever-present influence in everyday life. Events overseas, whether in Cuba or Vietnam or elsewhere, resonated at home in profound ways, and the constantly looming prospect of nuclear annihilation birthed a kind of sunshine millennialism that governed life in the 1960s. Many of those who lived through the decade anticipated the end of the world—in fact, they expected it. The extant possibility of what American and Soviet military officials held out as "mutually assured destruction" (MAD) meant a less probable future, which in turn helps to explain much of the immediacy (some would say recklessness) of individual behaviors in the 1960s: the willingness or unwillingness to go to Vietnam, for example, or the inclination to experiment with hard drugs, or even the casual sexual liaison. Now was the important time, perhaps the only time, and it was important to seize the day, enjoy the moment, and proclaim one's allegiances. From Barry McGuire's "Eve of Destruction" ("even the Jordan River has bodies floatin'") in 1965 to Country Joe McDonald's "Fixin' to Die Rag" ("Whoopee! We're all gonna die") in 1967, pop music endorsed a happy resignation to the prospect of an abruptly abbreviated mortality.

Similarly, fifty-plus years later John F. Kennedy still holds national attention, much of it morbidly focused on his sudden and premature death. Webs of blood, gore, and speculation, conspiracy theories continue to abound for two main reasons. First, it is difficult to accept the fact that a lone lunatic could topple the President of the United States. It is somehow easier to spin a grand web of conspiracy involving many plotters and accomplices; to admit the truth is to acknowledge something very fragile about American strength and power. Second, during the turbulent Sixties and even beyond, the counterfactual history of JFK's survival comforted a nation collapsing in on itself. Caught in a spin-cycle of wishful conjectures and what-ifs, the members of the babyboom generation in particular had difficulty in laying Kennedy to rest. (If Kennedy not been killed that day in Dallas and gone on to serve out his administration, likely for two full terms, would US involvement in Vietnam have deepened when it did? Would race relations have progressed beyond the brief period of black and white activists working in unity to achieve civil rights reform? Would optimism, the American Camelot, have endured?) His promise and potential shone brightly even beyond his death.

At the beginning of the decade, only 15 years after the United States had prevailed in the most horrific war in world history and emerged from its Great Depression as one of only two Superpowers in the world, Americans had the sense that they were in control—of their nation, their lives, their world. But by the end of that same decade much of that vision and confidence had been tested—perhaps, they realized, they were not in control after all. "We thought we could engineer the future and discovered that the future wouldn't cooperate," writes *Washington Post* journalist Robert J. Samuelson. "Our continuing seduction by the Kennedy narrative presumes that had he lived, the future would have been better." Kennedy would have grasped the folly of Vietnam, embraced the new youth culture, and advanced civil rights, it is presumed (or hoped). It is this subtext that sustains what Samuelson calls "the JFK fascination."

There is likewise no consensus over LBJ's legacy after more than 50 years. George Will has found a nation in slow decline since Johnson launched the Great Society. E.J. Dionne, Jr., on the other hand, has noted a "Johnson comeback," a "revival" in which historians and politicians have reevaluated not only LBJ's legacy but also the Sixties as "a consensual period when a large and confident majority believed that national action could expand opportunities and alleviate needless suffering." Johnson proved that these dreams were not empty political rhetoric and that Americans could find realistic ways of creating a better world. "The earthily practical Johnson showed that these were not empty dreams," writes Dionne, "and that finding realistic ways of creating a better world is what Americans are supposed to do."

Were the Sixties unique in this regard? Yes and no. The babyboomers liked to reflect back on their rebellion as brave and novel—the first serious attempt to embrace alternative politics—but were they any different in this regard from earlier generations of Americans? The Old Left predated the New Left, and while the Sixties generation perfected the art of embracing the irresponsibility of youth, so, too, had the flappers and gin-swillers of the 1920s, the "beautiful and damned" of the Lost Generation. The film *Bonnie & Clyde* (1967) banked on the connection between the 1930s and the 1960s; this film about young, Depression-era rebels bucking the system struck a chord with the Sixties generation. Indeed, the babyboomers did not invent rebellion. What made their generation unique was the self-assured (and rather naive) conviction that they *were* unique, bravely shaking their world to its foundations. That conviction, combined with their sheer size and numbers, made them powerful, whether as agents of change or as buyers and consumers.

According to popular lore, many young people in the mid-1970s put the counterculture behind them, donned suits, and went off to work, assuming the normal lives that their parents had always hoped for them. By the early 1980s they had become the acronymic "Yuppies": young, urban professionals, upwardly mobile in their aspirations to own an Audi or BMW and the best house or apartment on the best block in town. Perhaps it was just as the older generation had assured themselves (and their children): the Sixties were just a phase, the most recent variant of the follies of youth. But to what degree did countercultural attitudes trail along into the boardrooms and clinics and offices and courtrooms? From casual Fridays in the 1990s to deconstructed work environments in the twenty-first century that hardly seem like offices at all, the corporate culture shifted dramatically in subsequent decades. At the Internet giant Google, employees wheel around their self-designed workspaces on Razor scooters, climb ladders between floors, jog on treadmills, futz about with Legos and Tinker Toys for inspiration, and jot ideas on the walls; if any of those pursuits prove too taxing, the free massages, yoga classes, and TGIF parties provide relief. With the rise of social entrepreneurship that blends for-profit and non-profit business practices, the difference between "straights" and hippies has also shifted, even blended. How, for example, does one characterize the late Apple Inc. founder Steve Jobs, or Whole Foods CEO John Mackey? Businessmen or dreamers? Regarding corporate norms, it seems more a case of the counterculture becoming mainstream than slinking away to die in a corner.

Even if the New Left did fail to remake the world, revolutions did occur, and Gil Scott-Heron happened to be proved wrong: the revolution *was* televised. Post-1960s TV looked much different from earlier television programming, with sitcoms such as *Sanford & Son* (NBC, 1972–77) and *Good Times* (CBS, 1974–79) showing African Americans in nonsubservient roles; *The Jeffersons* (on CBS, 1975–85) and later *The Cosby Show* (on NBC, 1984–92) depicting comfortable black middle-class existences; and a host of shows from *The Mary Tyler Moore Show* (on CBS, 1970–77) to *Murphy Brown* (on CBS, 1988–98) representing strong women in lead roles.

What else had changed? Fifty years after Jim Crow segregation was practiced with impunity across the South, a black president and his family now occupied the White House. The war on drugs had diminished. As of 2014, the possession and use of marijuana, medical as well as recreational, was completely legal in two states—Colorado and Washington—with other states loosening their statutes on the medical use of marijuana. If racism outlived the 1960s, then racial inequality before the law was a thing of the past; if chauvinism remained, too, then "the problem with no name" was long since identified. Much really had changed.

But much had not, and the more things changed, the more they circled back to reprise the 1960s yet again. In the twenty-first century, for example, the civil rights movement—the heart and soul of the Sixties—again became the center of social change. In 2013, two Supreme Court rulings bolstered gay marriage crusaders who argued that an American should be free to marry the person he or she loves. As of March 2014, 17 states and the District of Columbia allowed same-sex marriage, with 58% of the American people, according to one poll, favoring it. Transgender people—those whose gender identity does not conform to their biological sex—were moving in from the margins to fight for equality. Immigrant rights advocates fought on behalf of undocumented workers to move them out of the shadows of American life and include them in the body politick. Testing long-held beliefs and cultural norms, a new civil rights movement was reemerging not only to challenge American notions of who is equal and what is normal but also to revisit issues that had supposedly been settled, issues such as police brutality. A social media blitz after the deaths of Michael Brown, Eric Garner, Freddie Gray and other African Americans during the period 2013–2015 and a simple Twitter hashtag—#blacklivesmatter—resulted in a renewed campaign to force authorities to acknowledge the victims of fatal violence at the hands of law enforcement officers.

Likewise, some of the greatest achievements of the Great Society came under attack in the early twenty-first century. In June 2013 the US Supreme

Court in a 5–4 vote struck down a key provision of the Voting Rights Act of 1965, thereby freeing nine states (mostly in the South) to change their election laws without advance federal approval. In question was whether racial minorities in states with a history of discrimination continued to face impediments at the poll, and in 2014 there was continued talk in Washington, DC, about "fixing" a Voting Rights Act that many Americans saw as unbroken. There were similar debates in 2010 over the Affordable Care Act, which helped to put quality health care within reach for more Americans. Enacted with the goals of increasing the quality and afford-ability of health insurance, lowering the uninsured rate by expanding public and private insurance coverage, and reducing the costs of health care for individuals, the most sweeping health care change in the United States since the creation of Medicare and Medicaid in 1965 also required insurance companies to accept patients with pre-existing conditions; but, right-wing congressional critics derided "Obamacare" as a government takeover of the health care system. In such ways, twenty-first-century politics reprised those of the 1960s, still divisive after all these years. In the wake of these debates and others, civil discourse and the ability to work together "across the aisle" are largely absent in the nation's capital: routine politics in Washington ground to a halt in 2013 with a bitterly partisan congressional budget fight, a failure of Democrats and Republicans to work together, a 16-day government shutdown, and near financial default with potentially worldwide economic repercussions. The disgust registered by the American public failed to rival that following Watergate, but a student of history could not help but recall the title of Dr. King's 1967 book, *Where Do We Go From Here: Chaos or Community?*

Peter Hitchens discussed the legacy of the Sixties with his older brother Christopher in 1998, when the two authors, both of whom saw the stir-rings and outcomes of the decade flawed to varying degrees, debated in an article for *Prospect* magazine. Citing a host of problems, including the destruction of traditional institutions, the erosion of language and manners, the leveling of culture, the elevation of "musical, artistic, and literary garbage" instead of high art, rampant drug use, unrestricted abortion, easy divorce, lax educational standards, and poor child rearing, Peter admits that "we wanted everything designed for our convenience and gratification, chose causes because they made us feel superior to our parents rather than because we were truly concerned about them, and then called our selfish wails a revolution." The elder Hitchens replies that many of these troubles were "hardly the outcome of a flower-child ethic" and points out that many people in the 1960s (he cites Dr. King) acted out of neither self-interest nor self-involvement. The question is not, "Were things bad then?" counters Peter, but rather, "Are they worse now?" Motion is not necessarily progress, he cautions, noting that we may not have the "proper moral equipment" needed to handle liberty. "I quite understand that there's no going back," Christopher retorts. "But there are ways forward, even through the inevitable thicket of unintended consequences."

Such lamentations are shared by those on both the left and the right. Pessimists might further claim that the greatest legacy of the 1960s was an ironic one: an upswing in conservatism and the rise of the New Right. Ostensibly about rights and freedoms, the 1960s were really, as the post-60s era has demonstrated, about power and privilege.

While a profound conservative backlash might be a lasting vestige of the Sixties, the radical alternatives suggested by the counterculture have lingered in the public consciousness: fifty years later, one would be hard-pressed to argue that the 1960s were anything but a liberal decade. There is also a compelling argument to be made—as historians Van Gosse and Richard Moser have done—that the Sixties moment has not only endured but triumphed, that "manipulation by the Right, resentment among sections of the public (especially white men), and weariness on the Left cannot obscure the fact that we live in a world the Sixties made." Consider what has changed. Political equality exists, even if social equality does not. White supremacy is no longer acceptable. Gays and lesbians are uncloseted. Women have entered the public sphere. And every day all across the United States, individual men and women work at the local level to better their communities by initiating grassroots campaigns for change. In relation to these outcomes, the Sixties "failed" only insofar as the new revolutionary order that some Sixties-era radicals wanted—a socialist onslaught on the seats of private and corporate power in the capitalist system—never came to pass.

Today the Sixties sometimes resemble a cliché, a funny gag for younger generations who don tie-dyes, wag peace signs, and pretend on Halloween to be what they imagine a hippy to have been. Marches and demonstrations do not carry the same resonance they once did. Direct actions, while still effective in some ways, have become rote and commonplace, almost anachronistically quaint. It is not that dissent has disappeared: it has merely blended in. Protests have moved out of the street and into cyberspace; social

"THAT'S MY GRANDFATHER ... I TOLD YOU HE WAS VERY OLD-FASHIONED."

Figure 12.4 There's no shortage of parodies of hippies and their ideals (Source: © www.CartoonStock.com, artist: Carroll Zahn).

media has largely replaced posters and placards; the counterculture has become mainstream. In this sense the Sixties as parody are everywhere—and nowhere at all.

Perhaps it was all an illusory dream, a bad trip; if so, the flashbacks may one day lose their vibrancy. But in the words of singer-songwriter Elvis Costello (himself a look-alike of 60s icon Buddy Holly), "What's so funny about peace, love, and understanding?" Highlighting what happened *after* the 1960s or reducing the decade to a cliché both deny the decade its historical moment as a triumph of participatory democracy and leftist politics. It pays to remember that by the decade's end a cross-section of American citizens—many of them young, from different racial and ethnic backgrounds—had torn down the scaffolding of Jim Crow in the South; ended an unjust and unpopular war in Southeast Asia; and ousted a corrupt president. They gave peace a chance. They thought openly, ultimately preferring freedom to the orthodoxies of repression and prohibition. If they gravitated toward extremes and excesses, then it may have been a case of learning to handle the newfound liberties that decade brought—a lesson still being learned by all of us, the inheritors of the Sixties.

Further Reading

Robert J. Samuelson, "The JFK Fascination," *Washington Post* (Nov. 10, 2013)

Hank Stuever, "JFK anniversary on TV: An onslaught of stale shows, and a nation stuck in a freeze frame," *Washington Post* (Nov. 7, 2013)

Christopher Hitchens, "The legacy of the sixties," *Prospect* (March 20, 1998)

E.J. Dionne, "On the 50th anniversary of the Civil Rights Act, politicians should follow LBJ's way," *Washington Post* (April 9, 2014)

Jenny Diski, *The Sixties* (New York: Picador, 2009)

P.J. O'Rourke, "The Awful Power of Make Believe" in Peter Stine, ed., *The Sixties* (Detroit: Wayne State University Press, 1995)

Van Gosse and Richard Moser, eds, *The World the Sixties Made: Politics and Culture in Recent America* (Philadelphia: Temple University Press, 2003)

Index

The Long Sixties: America, 1955–1973, First Edition. Christopher B. Strain.
© 2017 Christopher B. Strain. Published 2017 by John Wiley & Sons, Inc.

New Right, 127, 163, 178–181, 183–184, 196; *see also* conservatism
Newton, Huey, 151–153, 175, 189–190; *see also* Black Panther Party
Nixon, E.D., 45
Nixon, Richard M., 9, 19, 24, 25, 89, 110, 127, 169–173, 175, 177–178; *see also* Watergate scandal
nonviolence, *see* civil rights movement
NSC-68, 8, 36

Old Left, 13, 65, 69, 193
O'Rourke, P.J., 190–191

Parker, Charlie "Bird", 14, 15
Parks, Rosa, 16, 45–46, 51
participatory democracy, 65–66; *see also* Port Huron Statement
Peace Corps, 29, 35
peace movement
   in collective memory, 179–186
   in the 1950s, 1, 12–13, 110
   in the 1960s, 13, 83, 87–88, 116, 185–186
   in the 1970s, 166–167, 168
Pentagon Papers, 171
Planet of the Apes, 139
Pollock, Jackson, 14–15
Port Huron Statement, 64–66, 110; *see also* Students for a Democratic Society (SDS)
poverty, *see* economy, and poverty
Powers, Gary Francis, 30
President's Commission on the Status of Women, 27, 96–97
Pritchett, Laurie, 57

Randolph, A. Phillip, 60
Reagan, Ronald, 110, 127, 178–180
Red Guard, 154–155
Red Power, 155
riots, 150–151, 161, 167–168, 168–169, 190
Robinson, Jo Ann, 45
Roe v. Wade, 95–96, 104, 164, 173
Rolling Stone (magazine), 110, 111, 127
Rolling Stones, viii, 74, 127, 185, ix
Roosevelt, Eleanor, 27, 96
Roosevelt, Franklin Delano, 18, 80
Rosenberg, Julius and Ethel, 10–11
Rubin, Jerry, 73, 125
Rusk, Dean, 36, 81
Rustin, Bayard, 46, 48–49, 54

San Francisco, 13, 72; *see also* communes; hippies; Summer of Love
   Bay Area activism, 70, 72, 114, 151–155
   Haight-Ashbury district, 117–118, 124–126
Savio, Mario, 68, 70–71
Schwerner, Michael, *see* Cheney, James, Andrew Goodman, and Michael Schwerner, murders of
science and technology, 1, 11–12, 19–20, 130, 131–145
   computers, 19, 137, 138, 166
   and counterculture, 131
   faith in, 11, 12, 19–20
   and health care, 138, 195
   inventions, new, 1–2, 10, 19, 134–138, 166
   and progress, 19, 20
   and science fiction, 135, 138–139
Scott-Heron, Gil, 129, 193–194
Seale, Bobby, 109, 151–153, 189; *see also* Black Panther Party
Shepard, Alan, 132, 133
Shuttlesworth, Fred, 49, 58
sit-ins, 51–54, 56, 58
The Sixties; *see also* the 1960s
   the "bad Sixties", 118, 125–127, 183–184
   in collective memory, 177–178
   and conservatism, 110, 127, 177–184, 190–191, 196
   and contemporary U.S. politics, 179–180, 181, 182
   definition of, vi, 51, 75, 161
   as different from 1960s, vi, 51
   and freedom, 190, 197
   the "good Sixties", viii, 18, 183
   the "long Sixties", vi–ix
   as mix of fantasy and reality, 116–117, 190
   as ongoing, viii, ix, 162–175, 179–184
   in popular imagination, vi–vii, viii–ix, x, 115–116, 183–197
   as revolutionary, 108, 109–129, 196–197
   and spiritual enlightenment, 114–115, 120–121
skyjackings, 166
Southern Christian Leadership Conference (SCLC), 49–50, 58, 60, 64, 149
Soviet Union, diplomatic relations with, 7–10, 19, 30–44, 64–65, 80–81, 132–134, 170, 180, 191; *see also* Cold War